IMAGES
of America

SACRAMENTO'S NEWTON BOOTH AND POVERTY RIDGE

I0806186

On the Cover: This c. 1895 photograph shows the Herman H. Grau family posing in front of their stunning Queen Anne–style Poverty Ridge home. From the tower of the residence, Herman Grau could keep watch over his brewing operations just four blocks away at the Buffalo Brewery. (Courtesy of Center for Sacramento History.)

IMAGES
of America

SACRAMENTO'S NEWTON BOOTH AND POVERTY RIDGE

Sean Manwaring

ARCADIA
PUBLISHING

ISBN 978-1-4671-0529-3

Published by Arcadia Publishing
Charleston, South Carolina

Printed in the United States of America

Library of Congress Control Number: 2020930293

For all general information, please contact Arcadia Publishing:
Telephone 843-853-2070
Fax 843-853-0044
E-mail sales@arcadiapublishing.com
For customer service and orders:
Toll-Free 1-888-313-2665

Visit us on the Internet at www.arcadiapublishing.com

To the E.K. McClatchy Friends and the Newton Booth Neighborhoods Association, which continue to promote quality of life and historic continuity in our neighborhoods.

Contents

ACKNOWLEDGMENTS

The Center for Sacramento History (CSH) is a repository of historical documents, photograph collections, relics, and ephemera from Sacramento County's past. Except where indicated otherwise, photographs in this book are sourced from the collections of the CSH. The research staff and archivists at the CSH have been invaluable to this project. I am very appreciative of the time, patience, and expertise they have offered to my research. In particular, I would like to thank Rebecca Crowther, Kim Hayden, and William Villano for their resourcefulness and guidance.

The archivist and reference librarian for the Sacramento Room at the Central Branch of the Sacramento Public Library, James Scott, was also a tremendous help in identifying and compiling historic photographs relevant to this work.

I am especially grateful to the staff at the California State Library's (CSL) California History Section for their help in identifying and locating pertinent research material for this book. For any lover of early California state history, a visit to this very special place is certainly in order.

I would also like to give special thanks to Allan Fisher from the Western Railway Museum (WRM), the volunteers at the Sacramento Portuguese Historical and Cultural Society (SPHCS), and Chris Boyles David and Kay Sprinkel Grace for the time, knowledge, and material they provided.

Additionally, I would like to thank my editor at Arcadia, Caitrin Cunningham, for helping to keep me on track and for providing guidance and feedback along the way.

I am also appreciative of the support provided by the Newton Booth Neighborhoods Association and the Friends of the Ella K. McClatchy Library, to whom the author's proceeds for this work will be donated. Many longtime neighborhood residents who shared their personal recollections of relevant neighborhood historical figures were invaluable in helping to capture the spirit of 20th-century Newton Booth and Poverty Ridge.

Lastly, my husband, Jacob, provided great encouragement and enthusiasm. Without him, this book wouldn't have happened.

INTRODUCTION

The Poverty Ridge and Newton Booth neighborhoods comprise the southeastern corner of Sacramento's original central city grid of 1849. For practical purposes, the modern boundaries of Poverty Ridge are Nineteenth Street to the west, Twenty-Third Street to the east, R Street to the north, and W Street to the south. Newton Booth shares the same northern and southern boundaries of R and W Streets. Its western flank bounds Poverty Ridge at Twenty-Fourth Street, and it stretches east to Twenty-Eighth Street.

In 1850 Sacramento, the area that became known as Poverty Ridge stretched from P Street to W Street and from Twenty-First to Twenty-Fourth Streets. The city blocks that comprised the peak area of the ridge remain as the 22nd blocks of S, T, U, and V Streets today. Between the 1860s and 1870s, much of the land extending to P Street was excavated and used to construct area levees. This section of the city was the last to be developed, in part due to its proximity to the Sacramento Valley Railroad on the R Street levee as well as the presence of the Sacramento Drainage Canal, which emptied the city's raw sewage into a nearby open ditch at Thirty-First and Y Streets. Until the late 19th century, "the Ridge," and the area to be known as Newton Booth farther east, remained sparsely populated by small farms. Most of the patriarchs of these small outfits maintained fulltime employment in the industrial sector along the adjacent R Street corridor or in the railyards downtown, while the small farm plots were managed by other family members.

In 1891, the arrival of the Central Electric streetcar brought growth to the southeastern portion of the grid. The four-mile line carried passengers between downtown and the new suburb of Oak Park. The streetcars were routed through Twenty-First and Twenty-Eighth Streets, bringing with them speculative land investments and opportunities for development. By 1896, a wood-frame schoolhouse was constructed to serve the educational needs of children living in the southeastern portion of the city. Soon after, the school was named in honor of California's 11th governor, Gold Rush–era merchant, and US senator Newton Booth.

In Poverty Ridge, the 21st and 22nd blocks of T through V Streets, which for decades had been occupied by farmers and dairymen, were also undergoing change. The convenience of the Twenty-First Street electric car line brought with it politicians, entrepreneurs, capitalists, lawyers, and other white-collar professionals. From the 1880s onward, new stately homes began to rise along the high point of the Ridge. Many of Sacramento's wealthy pioneer families opted to build homes in the fashionable district, a sector which developers sought to rebrand as Sutter Terrace. In re-naming the hill after Capt. John Augustus Sutter, residents hoped that their wealth, affluence, and social permanence would be easily recognizable.

Newton Booth and Poverty Ridge appear to have developed in tandem. In many regards, the history of one neighborhood is a reflection of the other. As industry continued to develop along the R Street corridor to take advantage of prime access to shipping, blue-collar workers steadily streamed into Newton Booth to take jobs at businesses such as the California Winery and, later, the Buffalo Brewery. Meanwhile, the owners of these R Street enterprises built large homes in

Poverty Ridge, in part to shorten their commute and more easily maintain a close eye on business. Residents of Newton Booth, which was very much a middle- to working-class neighborhood, found additional employment helping to build, cook, clean, and tend to the wealthy households of Poverty Ridge.

The intent of this pictorial history is to illustrate how these southeastern central-city neighborhoods evolved over the 170 years that followed the Gold Rush. The timeline begins in 1850, focusing on the first 49ers to settle in the area, followed by the arrival of the Sacramento Valley Railway, the R Street corridor, and subsequent development of the electric streetcar. It covers the construction booms that followed both world wars, as well as the population decline that preceded urban decay, which stemmed from an increased emphasis on freeways, suburbs, and redevelopment. The book concludes with the preservation and community activism movements that preceded the most recent urban revival of the central city.

One

High Ground in a Land of Rivers

In 1839, Capt. John Augustus Sutter erected his fort along what would become the 27th block of L Street. His intent was to maintain close proximity to the American River for easy access to natural resources and trade. When gold was discovered at his Coloma-based sawmill nine years later, he probably could not have imagined that the area surrounding his fort would become a new, modern city. After all, Sutter's Fort, as it was called, was located in a floodplain halfway between the banks of the Sacramento and American Rivers.

In January 1850, just months after Sacramento was established as California's first chartered city, disaster struck. Turbulent winter floods enveloped Sacramento in torrents of muddy river water. Most of the fledgling city was submerged, with the exception of a small hill located along the undeveloped city blocks between what are now Twenty-First, Twenty-Third, R, and W Streets. Early on, this solitary hill was known as Oak Hill or Oak Ridge. However, in the years following the flood of 1850, it began to be known as Poverty Hill and Poverty Ridge, as well as Zabriskie's Ridge after an early resident. Early Sacramentans were said to have sought refuge from floodwaters upon the hilltop.

There is at least one record that disputes this story. According to an 1886 article in the *San Francisco Examiner* that referred to Poverty Ridge as "Sacramento's Nob Hill," a handful of early Sacramento lawyers and future state politicians built their homes upon the top of what was originally called Oak Hill (not to be confused with the Oak Hill located along the Brighton-Coloma Road), referring to it as "a most pleasant spot" in Sacramento. According to the article, the name Poverty Ridge is attributed to the jealousies of other city residents who did not have the good fortune to live on the elevated land. Whatever the origin, Poverty Ridge was the name that stuck. Today, the district is often referred to colloquially as the Ridge.

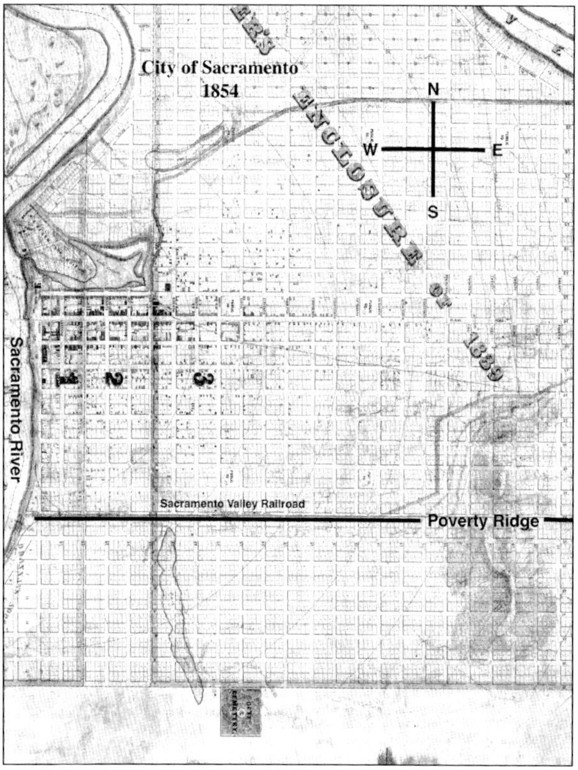

This 1854 map of Sacramento shows a hill to the southeast of downtown. As early as 1850, it was known as Oak Hill or Oak Ridge, presumably for the oak trees that once dotted the areas of modern Richmond Grove and Poverty Ridge.

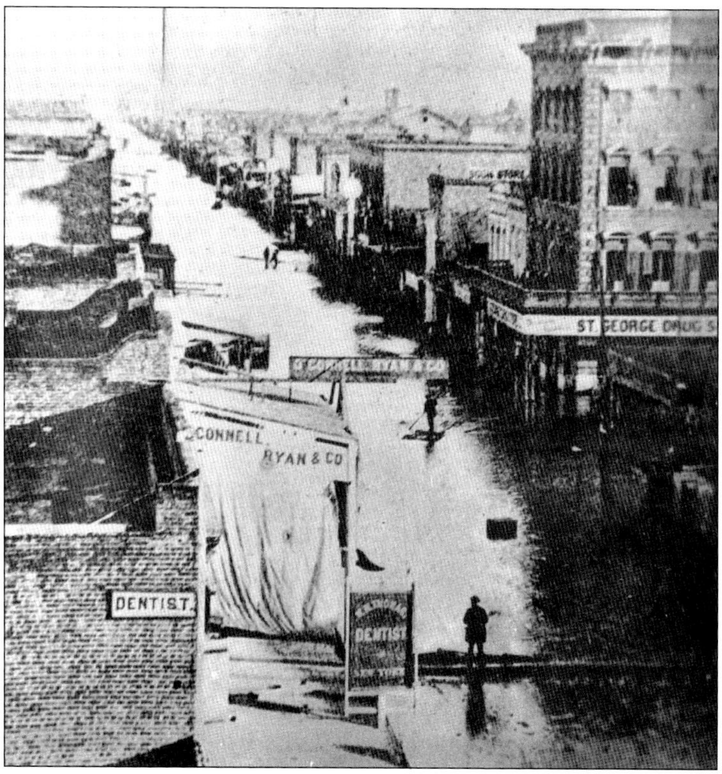

Early Sacramento was prone to flooding from the Sacramento and American Rivers. During the floods of 1850 and 1862 (right), citizens sought refuge atop Poverty Ridge. Some reports indicate that those fleeing the floodwaters looked poor and down-and-out, which likely contributed to the colorful moniker. (Courtesy of CSL.)

Col. J.C. Zabriskie arrived in Sacramento in 1849 and served as second magistrate to the original city government. Zabriskie was a well-respected lawyer who purchased the north half of the block of T Street bounded by Twenty-First and Twenty-Second Streets, where he lived with his family until roughly 1860. In the years following the flood of 1850, Zabriskie advocated for the removal of earth from the high point of the ridge to fortify and build levees around the city, which led to the ridge also being referred to as Zabriskie's Ridge. (Courtesy of CSL.)

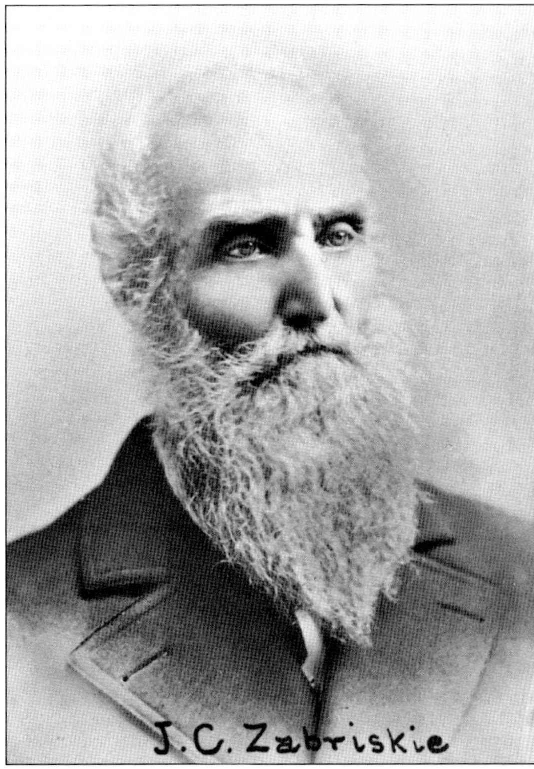

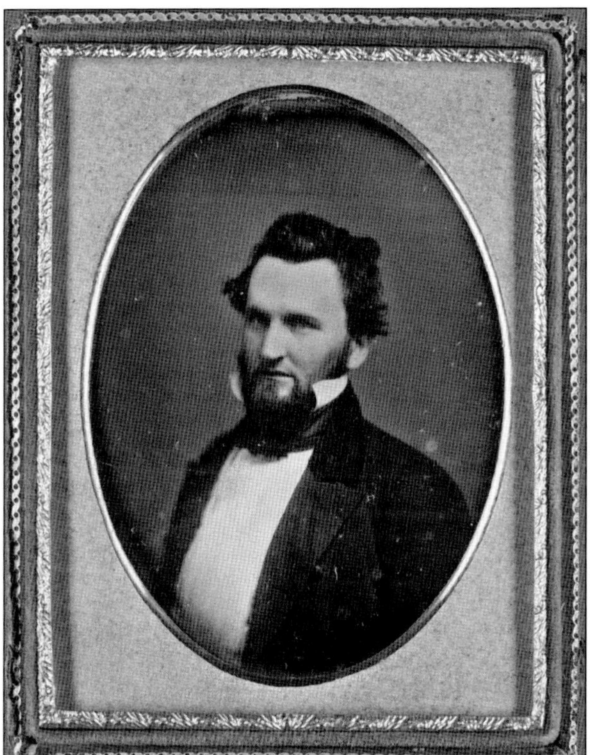

In 1851, a young and aspiring attorney by the name of J. Neely Johnson was wed to Colonel Zabriskie's daughter Mary. The wedding took place at the Zabriskie property, and the newlyweds also lived on what was then called Oak Hill with Mary's parents. Five years later, J. Neely Johnson was elected California's fourth governor. (Courtesy of CSL.)

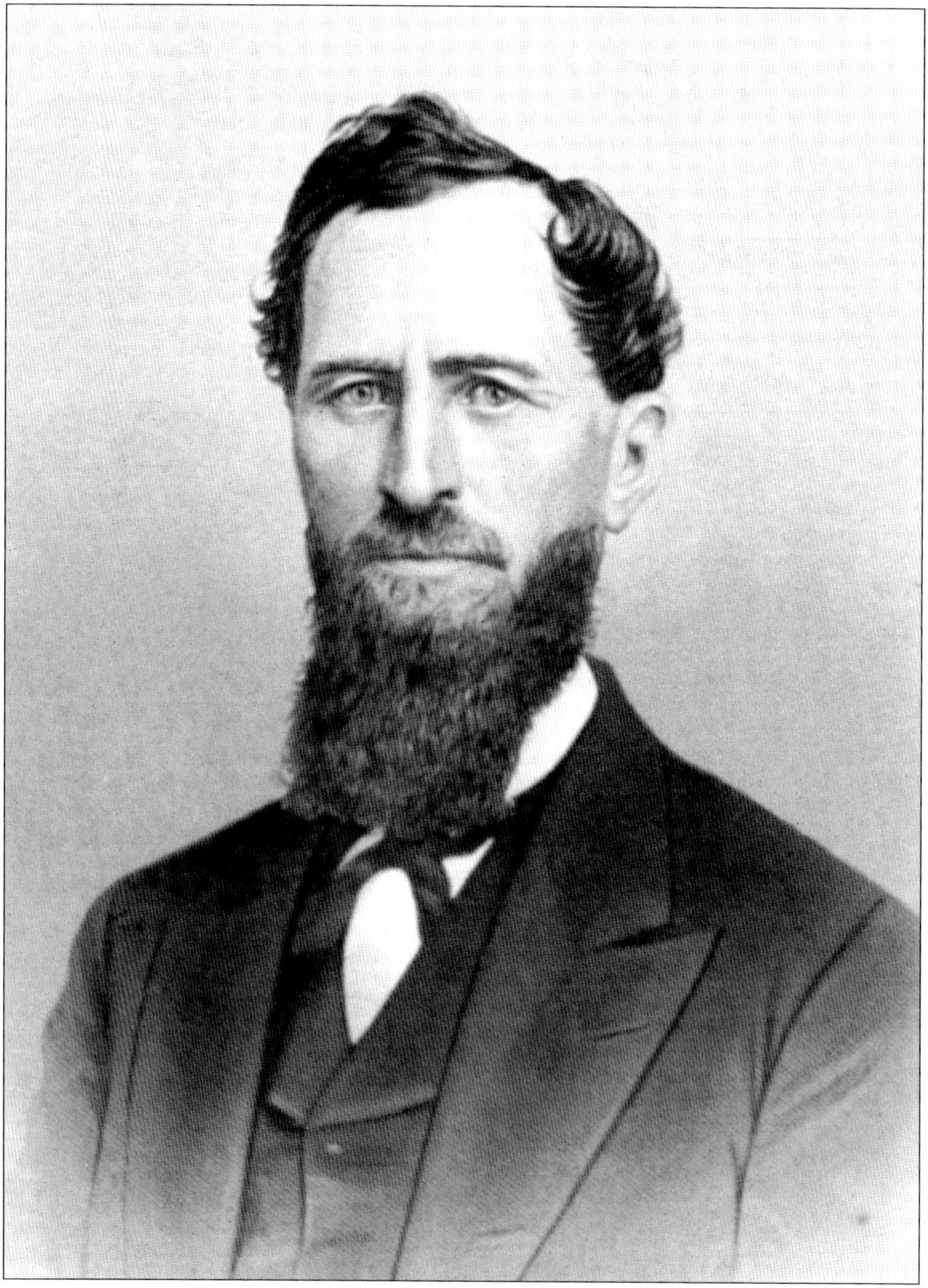

In December 1849, Col. Edward J.C. Kewen arrived in Sacramento after crossing the central Great Plains with the Dr. Thomas White family. Shortly after their arrival, Colonel Kewen married Dr. White's eldest daughter, Fannie, and settled with the White family on land they had acquired atop Poverty Ridge. The wedding was heralded as one of the first marriages—if not the first—to be officiated in the new city. Colonel Kewen was employed as an attorney in Sacramento, and at the age of 24, became California's first attorney general. (Courtesy of CSL.)

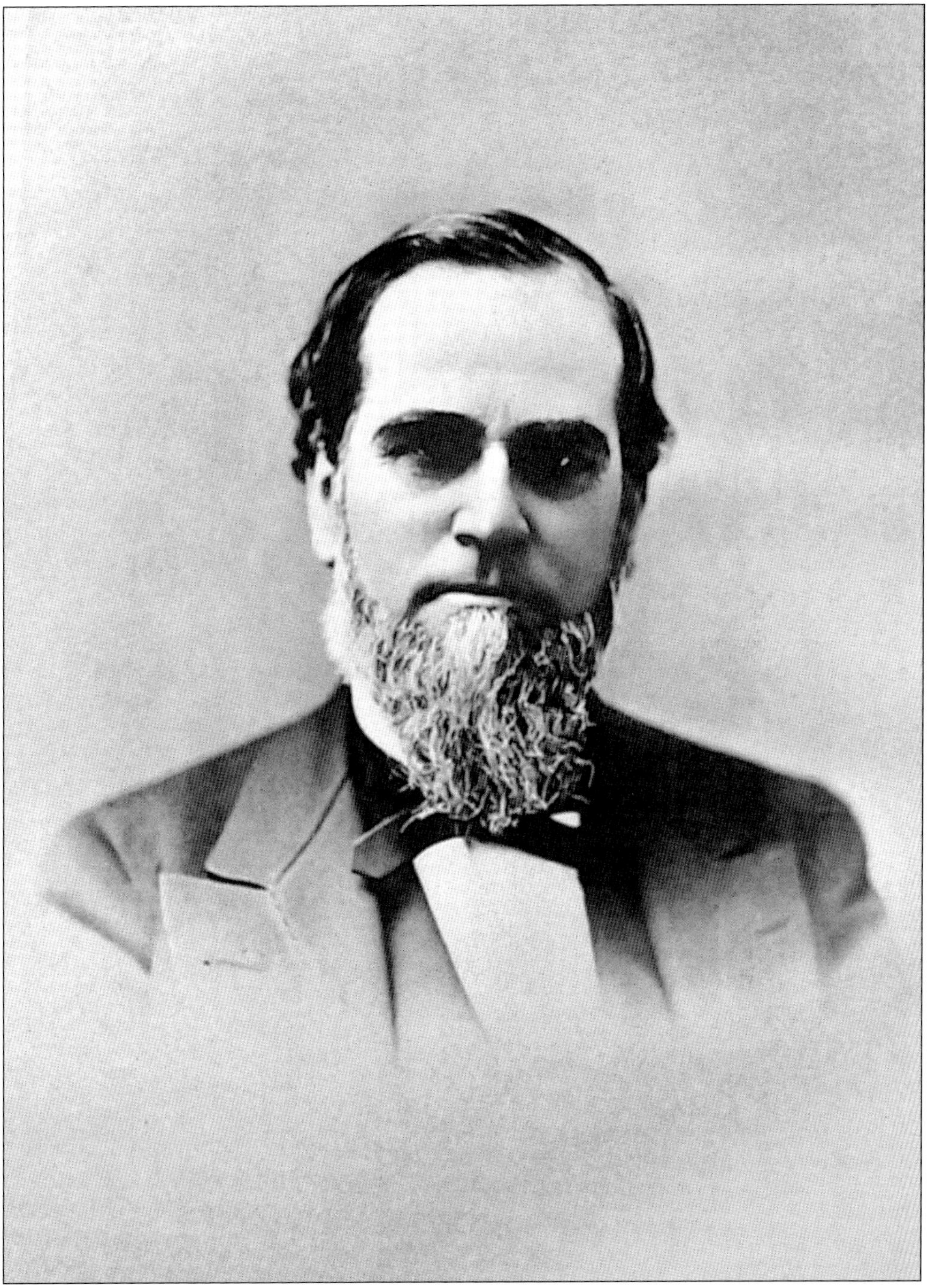

Robert Morrison arrived in Sacramento in 1850 and settled with his brother Murray on Poverty Ridge. The two brothers opened a law practice with fellow Poverty Ridge resident J. Neely Johnson. Robert Morrison also served as the district attorney for the City of Sacramento. Decades later, he would become the 13th chief justice of California. (Courtesy of CSL.)

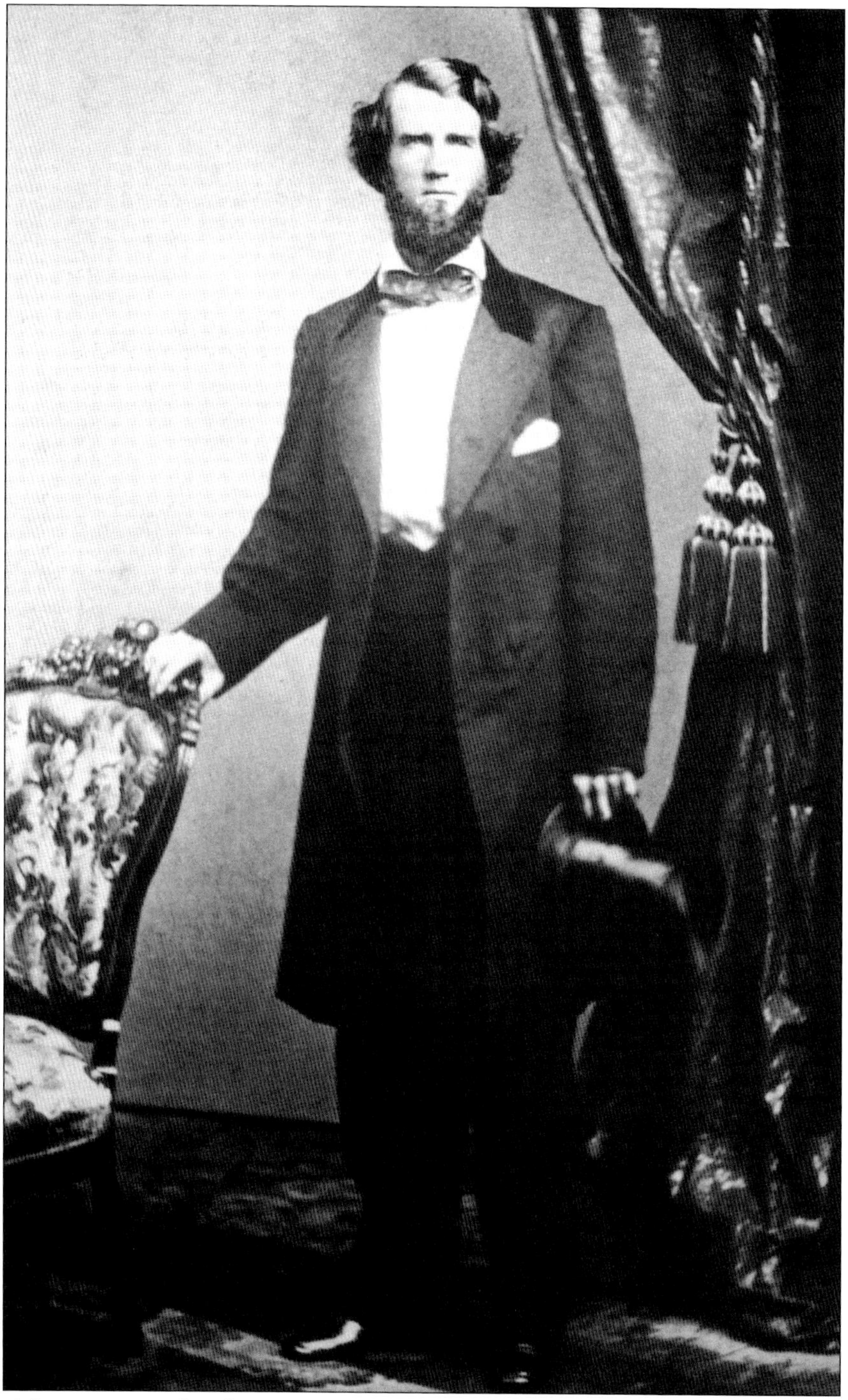

Murray Morrison arrived in Sacramento in 1849 and established a law practice with his brother Robert. The Morrisons purchased the land bounded by Twenty-First and Twenty-Second Streets from modern Uptown Alley south to V Street. Murray married one of the daughters of Poverty Ridge neighbor Dr. Thomas J. White, who served as speaker of the assembly in California's first legislature. (Courtesy of CSL.)

Two

Of Industry, Railroads, and Ranches

In 1855, construction began on the Sacramento Valley Railroad, California's first incorporated transit rail project. The line operated from Front and L Streets east along R Street, then continued for nearly 23 miles to the city of Folsom, northeast of Sacramento. To ensure the tracks remained above the flood line, a levee was built down the length of R Street and crowned with fresh railroad tracks.

In the decades that followed, the railroad expanded, and commercial industry began to steadily develop along the R Street corridor. Notable examples of development include the c. 1882 erection of a hospital at Twenty-Second and R Streets, which was acquired by Dr. G.L. Simmons and named the Ridge Home Sanitarium. By 1896, Dr. Simmons had successfully convinced the Sisters of Mercy to take over the Ridge Home and to expand operations with the construction of a new, larger hospital on the adjacent lot. In 1897, the sisters opened a 30-bed facility known as Mater Misericordiae Hospital, the predecessor to modern day Mercy Hospital.

Soon after, in 1889, Herman Grau, one of Sacramento's premier brewers, broke ground on the Buffalo Brewery at Twenty-First Street between Q and R Streets, followed in 1890 by Manuel Nevis's California Winery nearby at Twenty-Second Street between R and S Streets.

As the R Street industrial corridor continued to develop, the owners and entrepreneurs of these and other enterprises began to build their homes along Poverty Ridge to shorten their commutes and keep a close eye on their growing businesses.

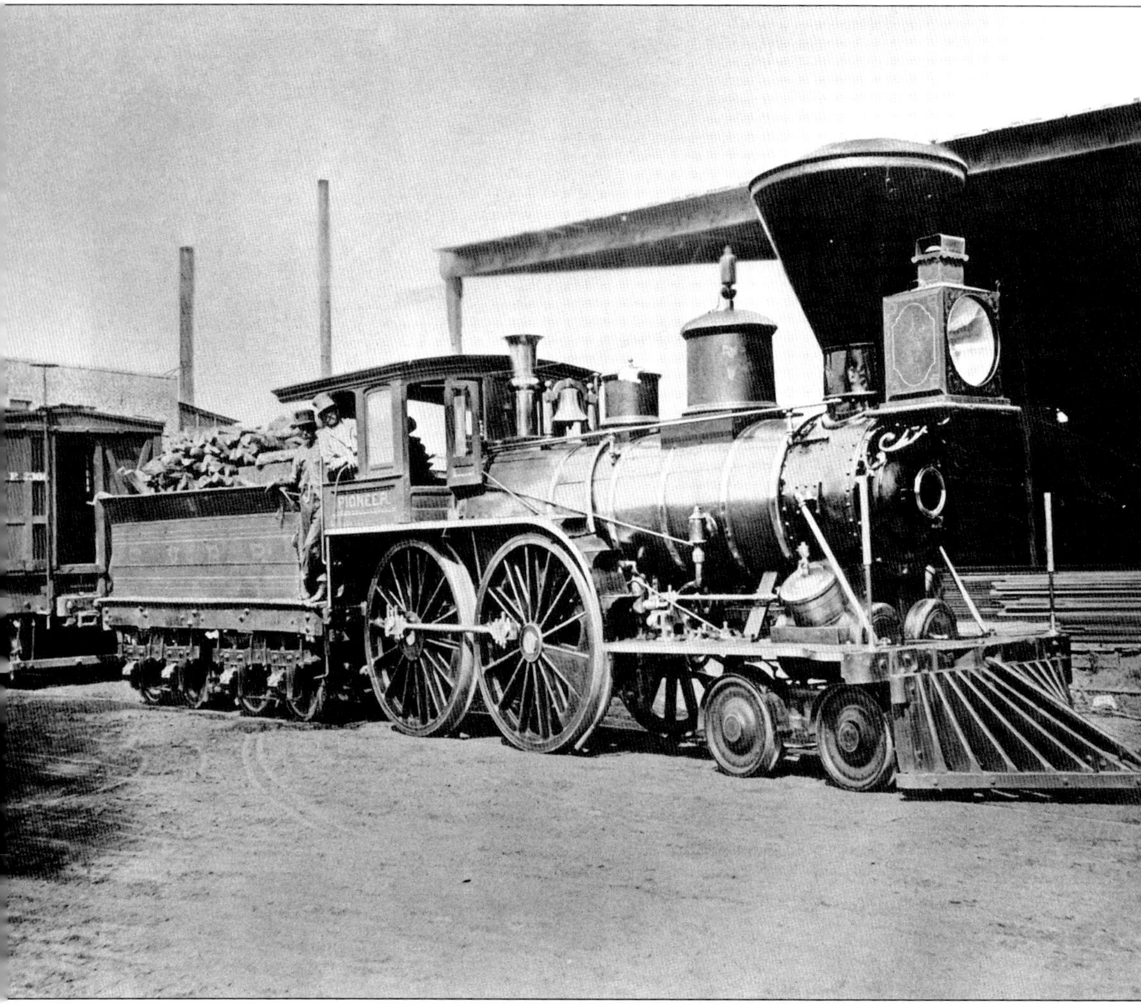

Starting in 1856, the Sacramento Valley Railroad began running its Folsom line from present-day Old Sacramento east up the R Street corridor and then on to the city of Folsom. The R Street portion of the railroad facilitated the distribution of goods produced by businesses such as the California Winery and Buffalo Brewing Company. In the years that followed, many more industrial operations would follow and establish themselves along the R Street corridor.

In 1850, John Frink Richardson arrived in Sacramento from New York. Around 1873, the year this portrait was taken, Richardson settled in Poverty Ridge, where he operated a successful dairy. (Courtesy of the Sacramento Room.)

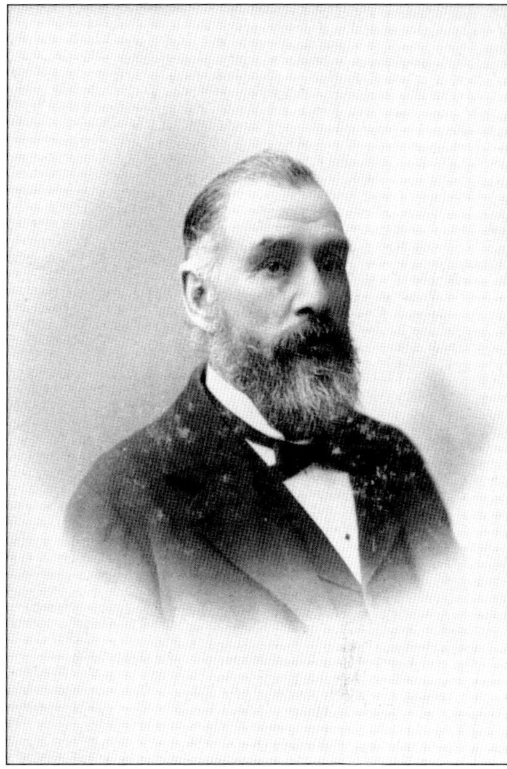

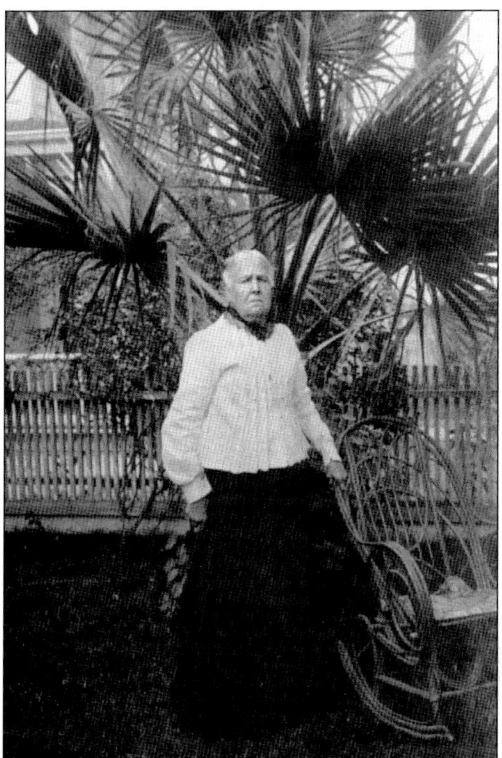

Elizabeth Richardson immigrated to the United States from England in the 1840s, settling in Sacramento just as the Gold Rush got underway in 1849. Originally a hotel keeper along the riverfront, the twice-widowed Elizabeth married prominent dairyman John Frink Richardson in 1878. The couple resided in Poverty Ridge for the next 30 years. After living a total of 60 years in Sacramento, Elizabeth died at the age of 97. (Courtesy of the Sacramento Room.)

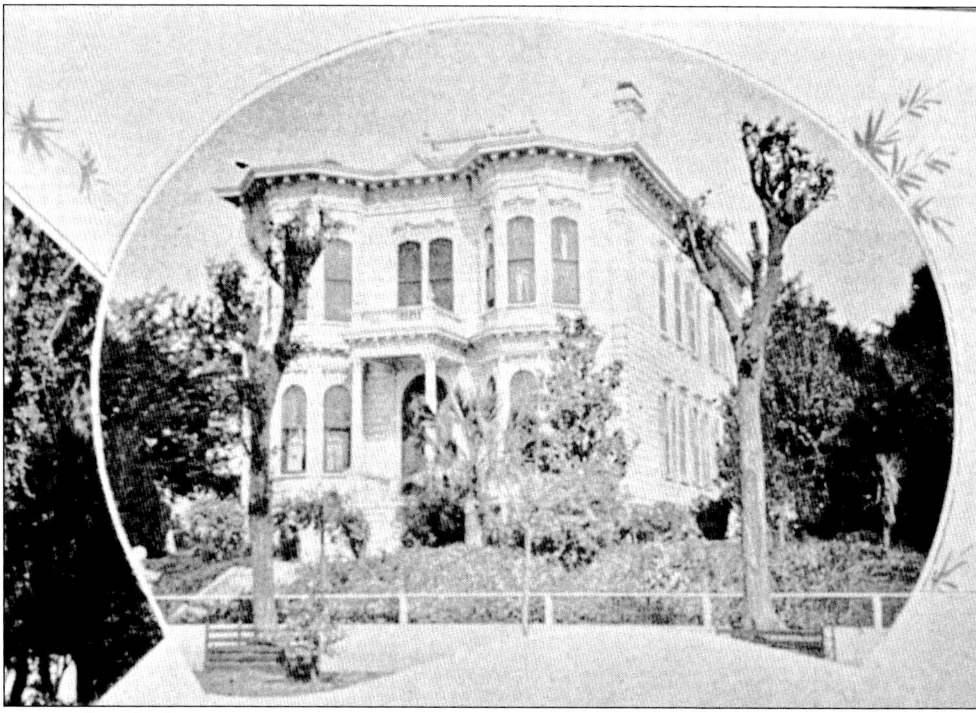

Pictured is the beautiful c. 1873 Italianate residence of John and Elizabeth Frink Richardson at the southeast corner of Twenty-First and T Streets. The Richardsons were the owners of the Pleasant Hill Dairy, which was also in Poverty Ridge just south of their home. In the 1870s, a handful of successful cattle ranchers and dairy farmers began to build elegant homes on Poverty Ridge. (Courtesy of CSL.)

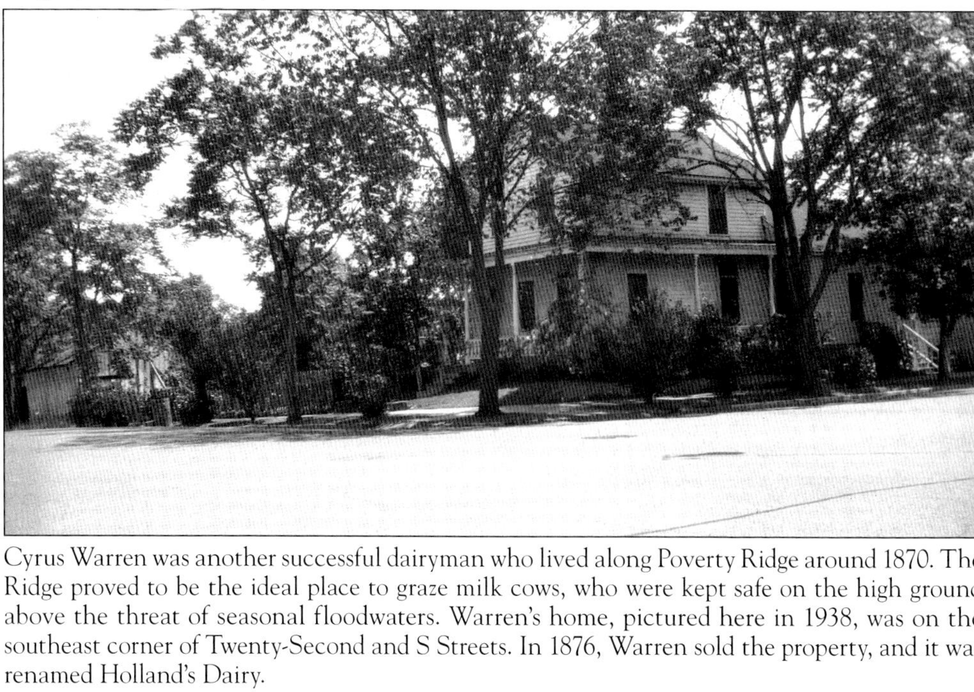

Cyrus Warren was another successful dairyman who lived along Poverty Ridge around 1870. The Ridge proved to be the ideal place to graze milk cows, who were kept safe on the high ground above the threat of seasonal floodwaters. Warren's home, pictured here in 1938, was on the southeast corner of Twenty-Second and S Streets. In 1876, Warren sold the property, and it was renamed Holland's Dairy.

A pioneer of 1850, Frederick Cox became one of the wealthiest men in Northern California. Early on, Cox invested in cattle ranching and agricultural real estate, including the San Juan and Haggin land grants (present-day Fair Oaks and Carmichael). Cox also served as a member of the California State Senate from 1882 to 1886 and was later president of the California State Bank. The Cox family built an elegant residence in Poverty Ridge during the 1870s. (Courtesy of CSL.)

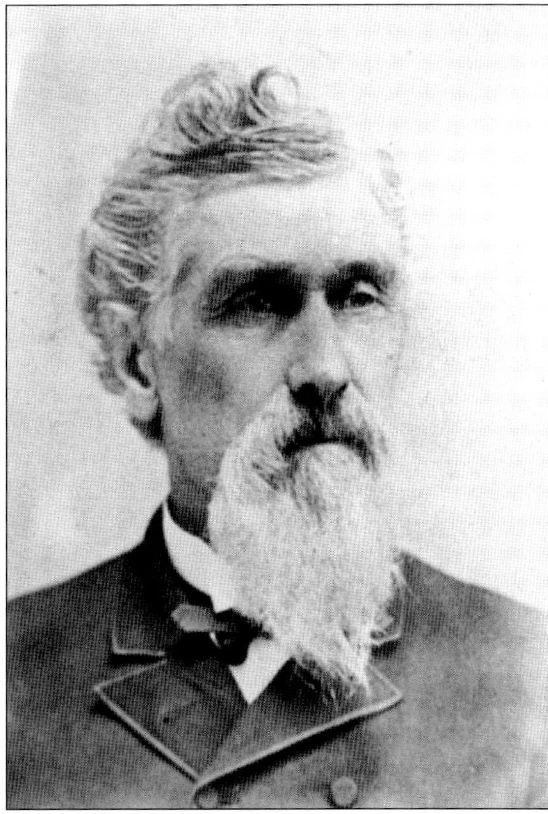

Pictured is the Frederick and Jennie Cox residence, which was located on T Street between Twentieth and Twenty-First Streets. The Sacramento Valley Railroad is depicted along the R Street levee in the foreground. In the late 19th century, two of the Coxes' daughters, Jennie Cox Peltier and Freda Cox, also built private residences on their family's land in Poverty Ridge. (Courtesy of CSL.)

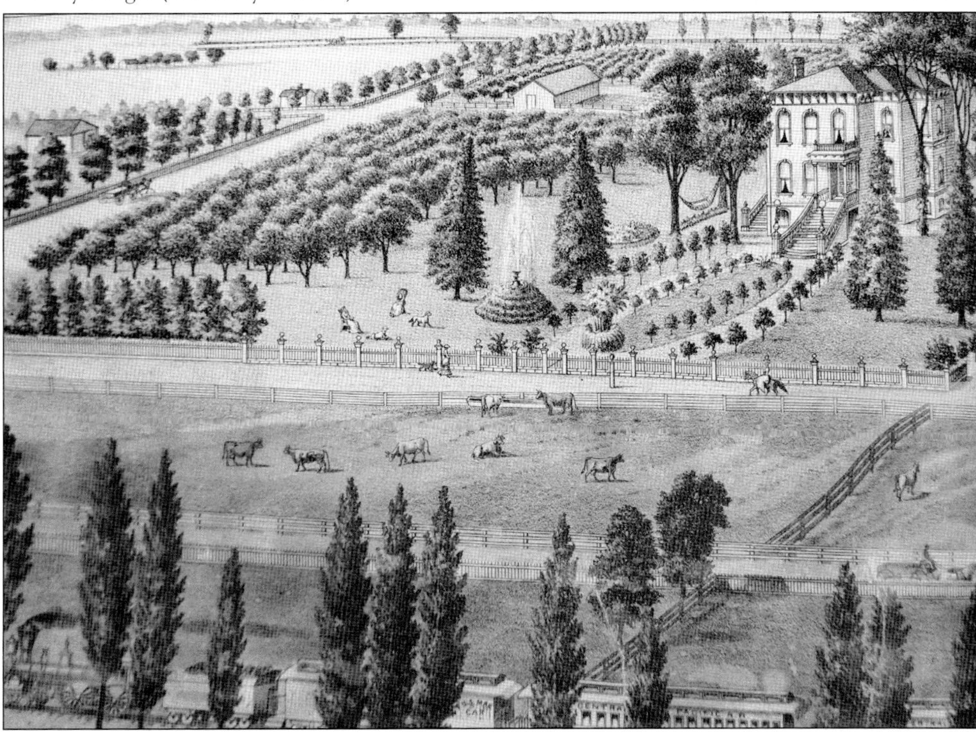

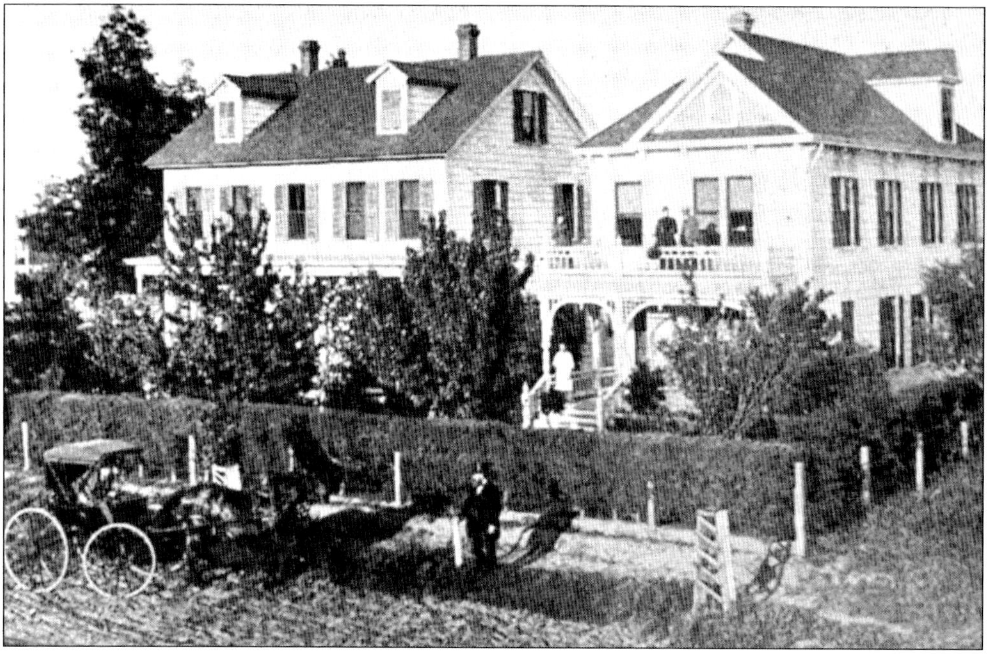

Between 1882 and 1885, Dr. Gustavus L. Simmons acquired a small private hospital at Twenty-Second and S Streets in Poverty Ridge and named it the Ridge Home Sanitarium. The institution promoted itself as being "well situated in the highest and healthiest section of the city." It was managed by a trained matron and nurses under the guidance of leading area physicians. The Ridge Home also offered a place to receive and recover from complex surgeries performed by some of Sacramento's leading surgeons. (Courtesy of CSL.)

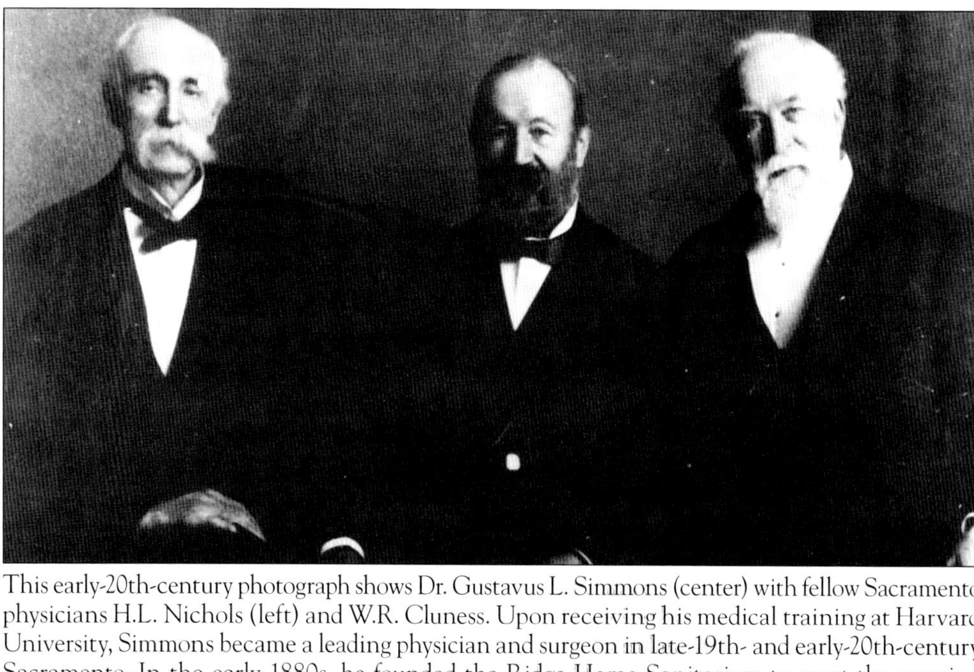

This early-20th-century photograph shows Dr. Gustavus L. Simmons (center) with fellow Sacramento physicians H.L. Nichols (left) and W.R. Cluness. Upon receiving his medical training at Harvard University, Simmons became a leading physician and surgeon in late-19th- and early-20th-century Sacramento. In the early 1880s, he founded the Ridge Home Sanitarium to meet the growing surgical needs of the Sacramento region.

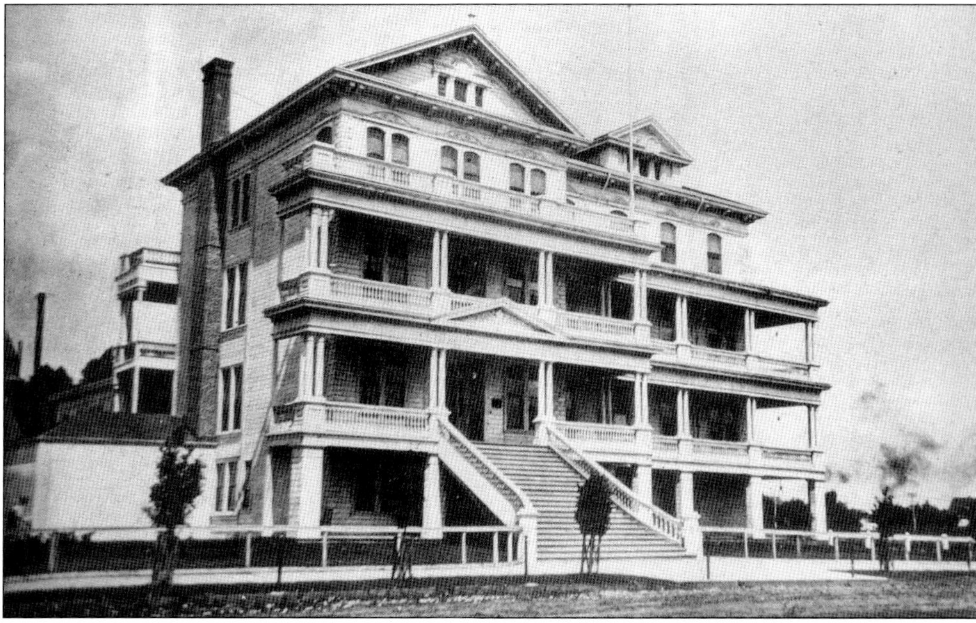

In 1895, Dr. G.L. Simmons convinced the Sisters of Mercy to take over the Ridge Home Sanitarium and to assist with the expansion of surgical and recovery services. In 1896, the sisters assumed ownership of the property and broke ground on a new 30-room hospital on adjacent land. Their new institution, Mater Misericordiae Hospital, was the precursor to the modern Mercy Hospital. (Courtesy of the Sacramento Room.)

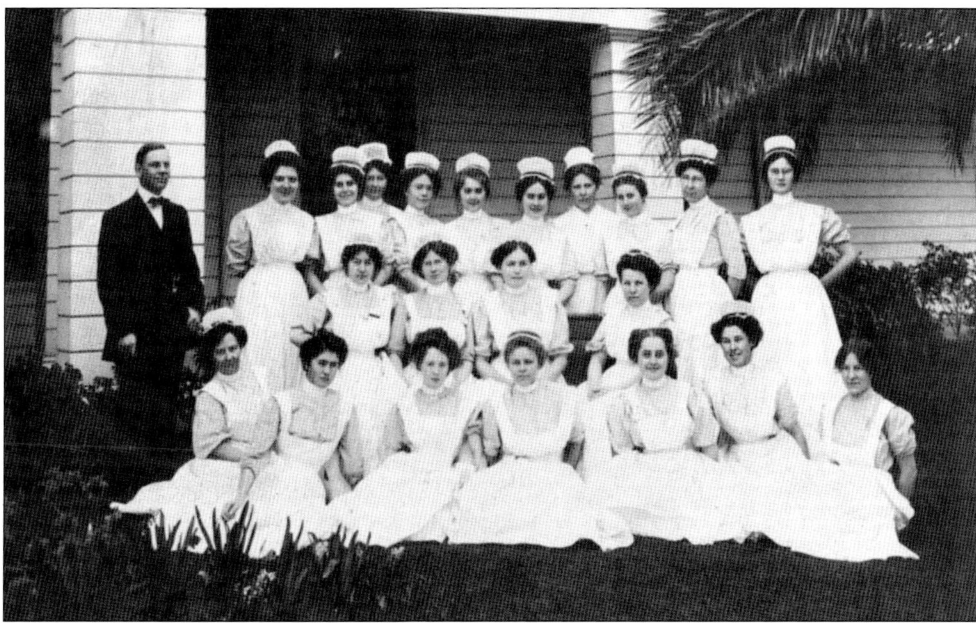

Founded in 1897, Mater Misericordiae expanded upon the previous work of the Ridge Home, converting the old hospital into residences for the elderly and providing more specialized medical care. This c. 1915 photograph shows the Mater Misericordiae nurses in front of the hospital at Twenty-Second and R Streets. Mercy Hospital, as it is now called, remained at Poverty Ridge until 1925. (Courtesy of the Sacramento Room.)

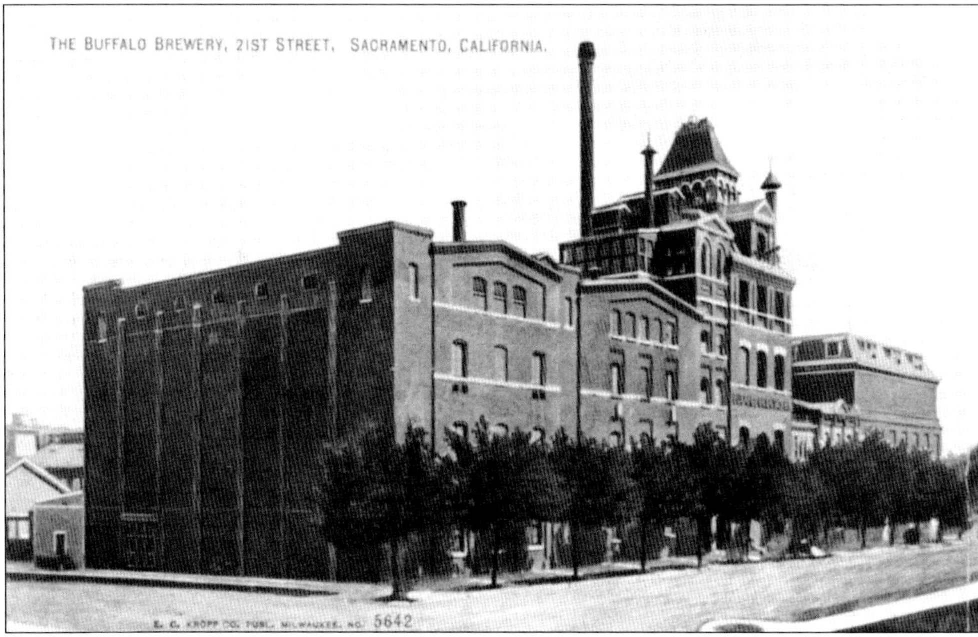

In 1888, brewing pioneer Herman Grau broke ground on the Buffalo Brewery at the 21st and 22nd blocks of Q and R Streets in Poverty Ridge. It was the largest brewery west of the Mississippi, with an initial capacity of 60,000 barrels annually. (Courtesy of the Sacramento Room.)

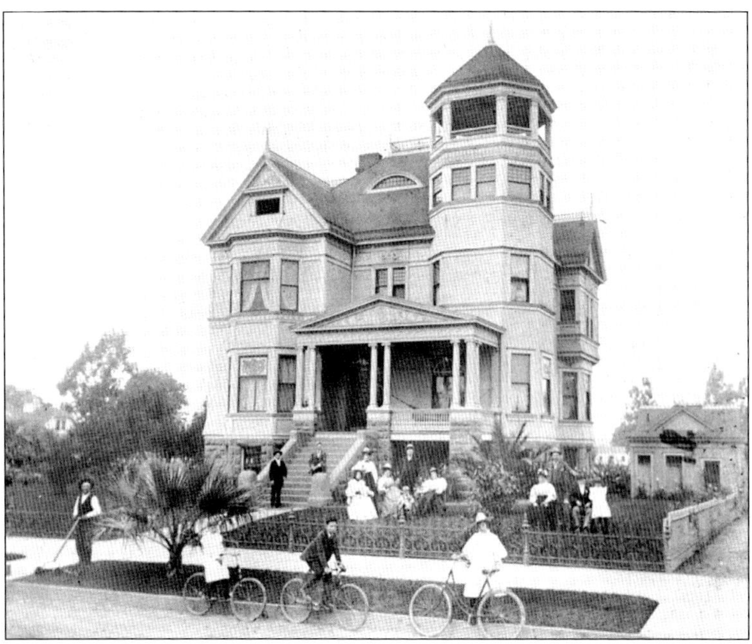

Not long after opening the Buffalo Brewery, Herman and Bertha Grau built this impressive Queen Anne–style home at 2200 Twenty-First Street in Poverty Ridge. This c. 1895 photograph shows the Grau family posing in front of their stately residence. From the tower of the home, Herman Grau could easily keep an eye on his brewing operations just four blocks to the north.

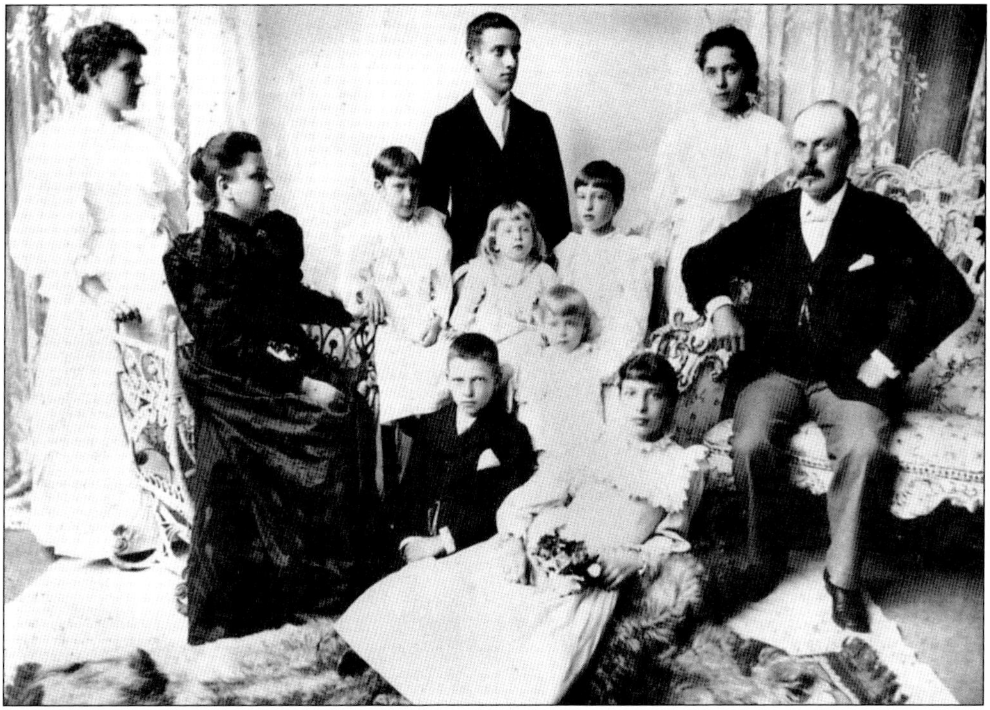

Buffalo Brewing president Herman Grau and his wife, Bertha, had a total of nine children. In 1894, the Graus built a stately home at Twenty-First and V Streets in Poverty Ridge. This c. 1890 family portrait shows Herman and Bertha with their three sons and six daughters.

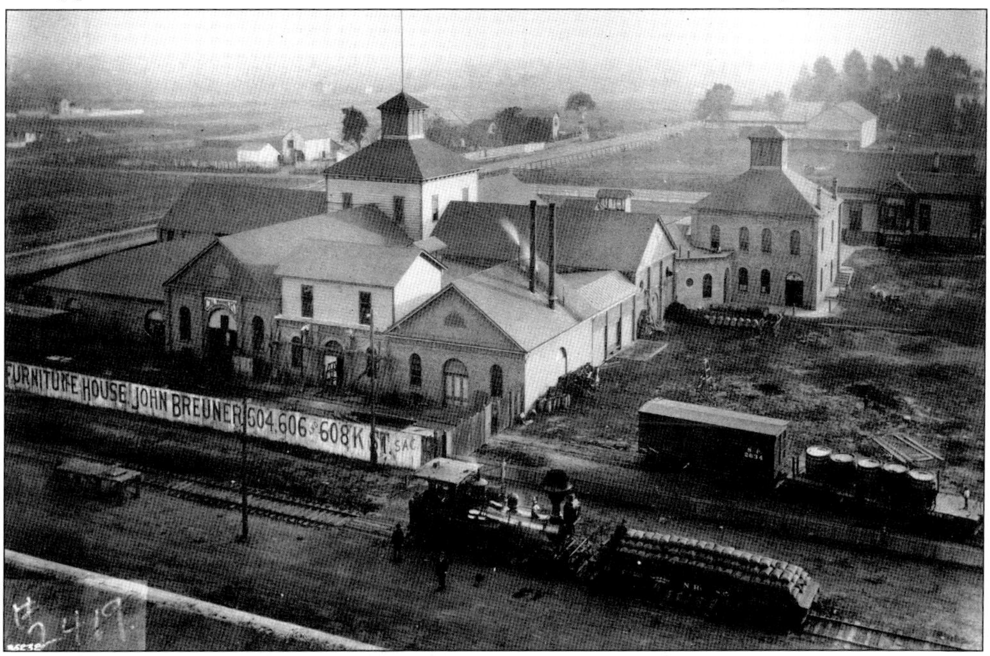

In 1890, Portuguese pioneer Manuel Silva Nevis opened the Pioneer Winery at Twentieth and R Streets and the California Winery at Twenty-First and S Streets. Nevis was an early Sacramento vintner who also established vineyards in the present-day Pocket area. (Courtesy of CSL.)

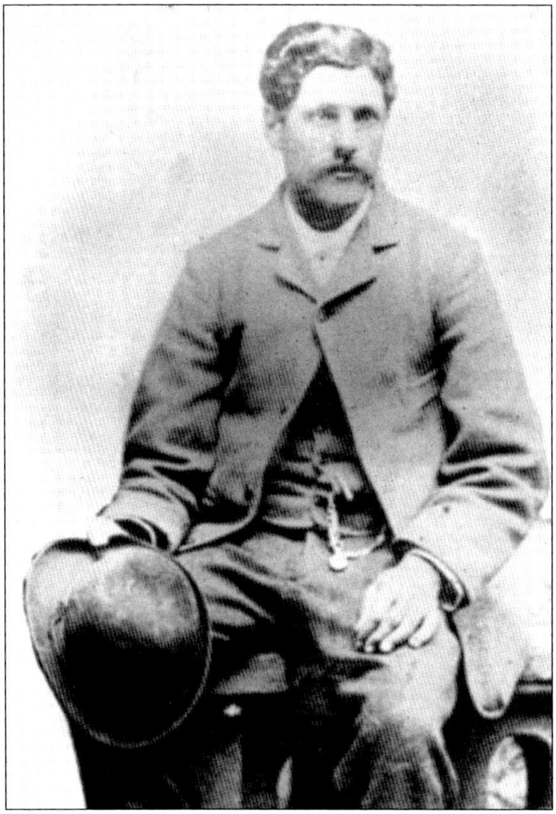

Manuel Silva Nevis was an emigrant from the island of Pico in the Azores and an early settler of the farming community that flourished in Sacramento's modern-day Pocket. Nevis was also a wine grape grower, vintner, and the proprietor of early Sacramento wineries including the California and Pioneer Wineries, which he established on the 20th and 21st blocks of R and S Streets in the early 1890s. (Courtesy SPHCS.)

Poverty Ridge vintner Manuel Silva Nevis was also a master carpenter and built a stately Queen Anne–style home about a block north of the winery for his wife, Emma, and their five children. The Nevis home originally sat at 1830 Twenty-First Street but was later moved to its current location at 1822 Twenty-First Street. As of 2020, the former Nevis family home houses the Edgar Institute. (Courtesy SPHCS.)

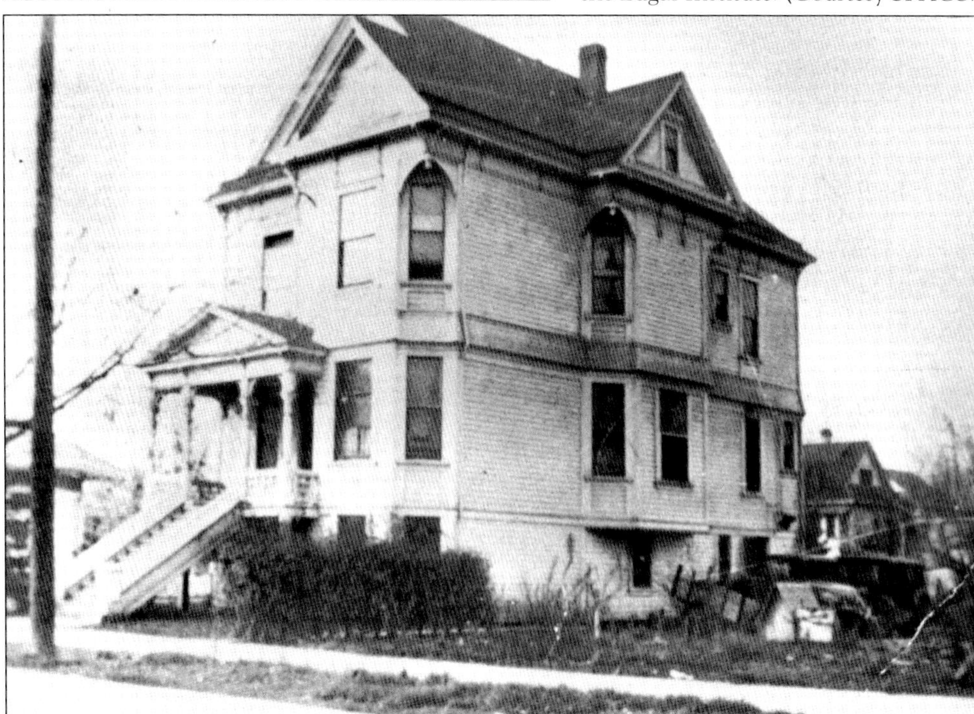

Three

Poverty Ridge and the Aspiration of Sutter Terrace

In the last three decades of the 19th century, affluent Sacramentans such as Sen. Frederick Cox, John Frink Richardson, and Herman Grau purchased land and erected elegant, stately residences on Poverty Ridge. Gold Rush pioneer John Stevens and renowned educator and textbook author E.P. Howe also moved their families to the Ridge. Around 1890, in order to reflect the status of these latest pioneer residents, a relatively brief attempt was made to rechristen Poverty Ridge with a name befitting the affluence of its wealthy tenants: Sutter Terrace.

With the removal of the R Street levee, development increased, and many of the wealthiest families in Sacramento became tied to addresses in the briefly renamed Sutter Terrace district. From the late 19th century through 1920, the area became the most fashionable and exclusive neighborhood in the city of Sacramento. In 1910, *Sacramento Bee* publishers C.K. and Ella McClatchy commissioned Rudolph Adam Herold, arguably the most prolific architect in Sacramento at the time, to design a beautiful residence atop the Ridge for their young family. In 1913, Herold also built a personal residence next door to the McClatchy home.

California's first woman banker and the director of the board of the Bank of Sacramento, Mary Ross-Roan, also built her dream home at the southwest corner of Twenty-Second and T Streets. Many other entrepreneurs, politicians, lawyers, and physicians soon followed.

In the first several decades of the 20th century, the children of these affluent Sacramento pioneer families grew up living and playing with one another in Poverty Ridge. When they reached adulthood, many of them married into other neighborhood families and built homes of their own upon the Ridge, creating a multigenerational community of old friendships strengthened by marriages.

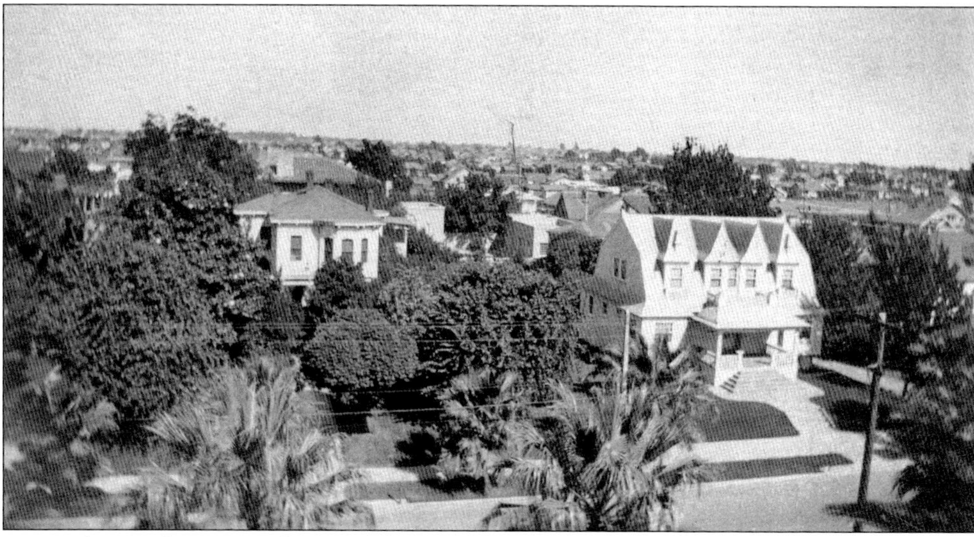

Pictured around 1920 are the Poverty Ridge homes of E.P. Howe Sr. (left) at 2201 Twenty-First Street and E.P. Howe Jr. (right) at 2215 Twenty-First Street. In 1872, Howe served as principal of Sacramento High School. The following year, he opened Howe's High School and Normal Institute, which became a well-respected private school throughout the region. Four generations of Howe family members became educators and lawyers in the Sacramento region and beyond.

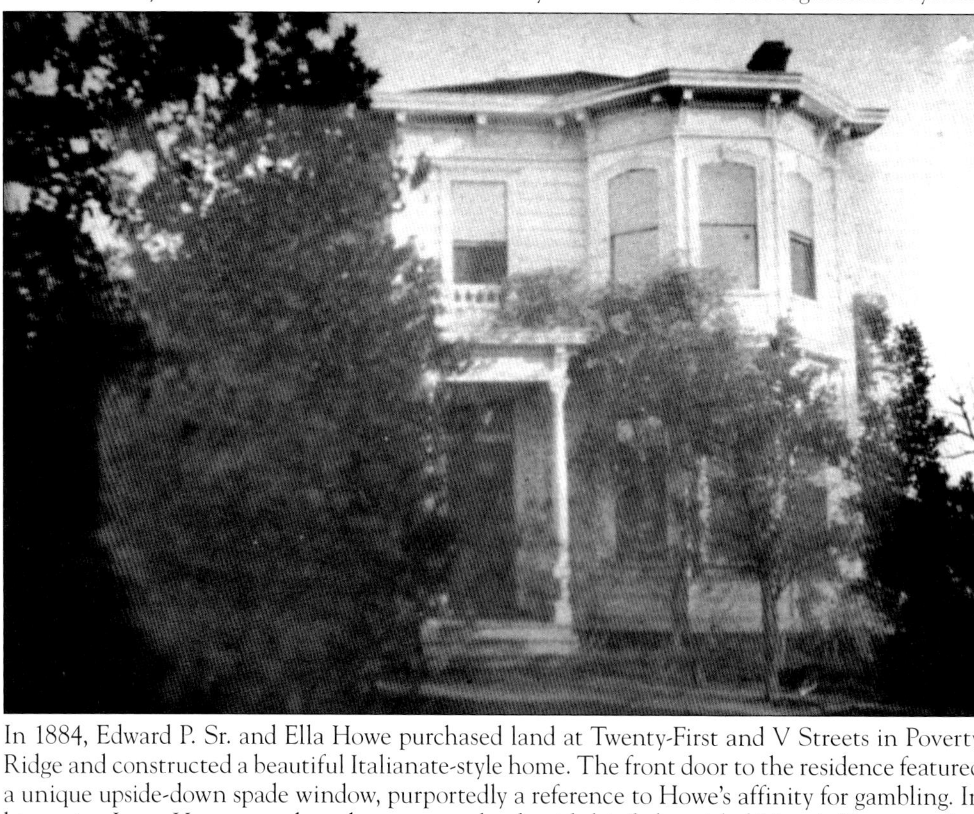

In 1884, Edward P. Sr. and Ella Howe purchased land at Twenty-First and V Streets in Poverty Ridge and constructed a beautiful Italianate-style home. The front door to the residence featured a unique upside-down spade window, purportedly a reference to Howe's affinity for gambling. In his native Iowa, Howe coauthored a grammar book with his father titled *Howe's Grammar* that became one of the most widely distributed English textbooks in 19th-century America.

This early-20th-century portrait shows Edward Page Howe Jr., who, like his father, was an educator and administrator at the Howe family's private school. In 1890, he and his wife, Luella Slack Howe, built a Colonial Revival and shingle-style home next door to his parents at 2215 Twenty-First Street. In 1982, the property was listed in the National Register of Historic Places.

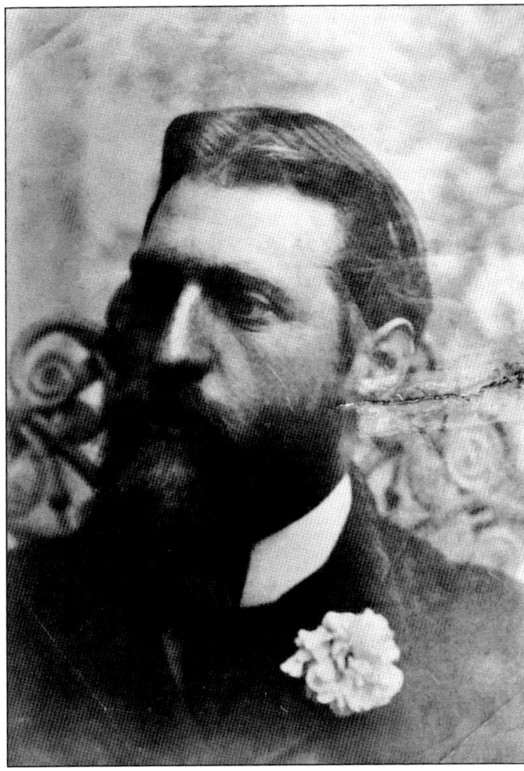

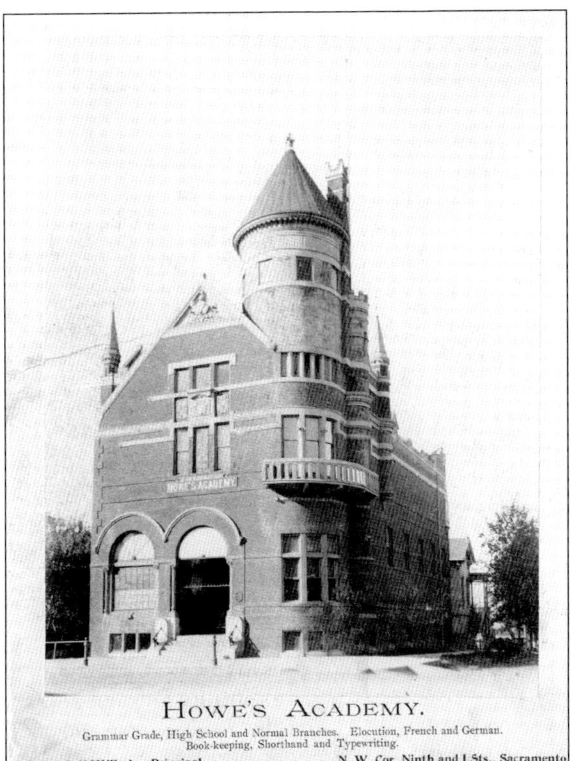

E.P. Howe Jr. eventually became principal of Howe's Academy, a school that provided education from elementary grades to high school. Courses offered included elocution, French, German, bookkeeping, shorthand, and typewriting. The school changed locations several times throughout the years, eventually landing at 831 I Street as Howe's Normal Academy and Business College. That building was later demolished to make way for the new federal courthouse. (Courtesy of the Sacramento Room.)

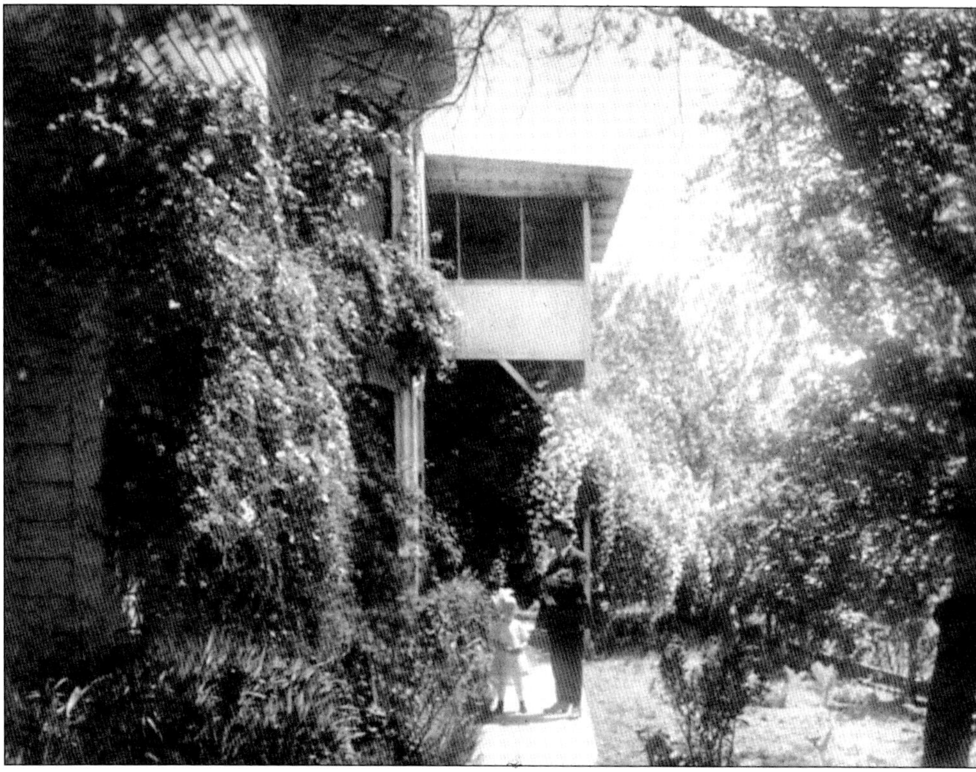

Pictured around 1900 as a little girl in the yard of her grandparents' Poverty Ridge home, Helen Margaret Howe was the only child of E.P. Jr. and Luella Howe. She was raised next door to her grandparents at 2215 Twenty-First Street. Helen went on to study education at Mills College in Oakland. She graduated in 1930 and became the fourth generation of educators in the Howe family.

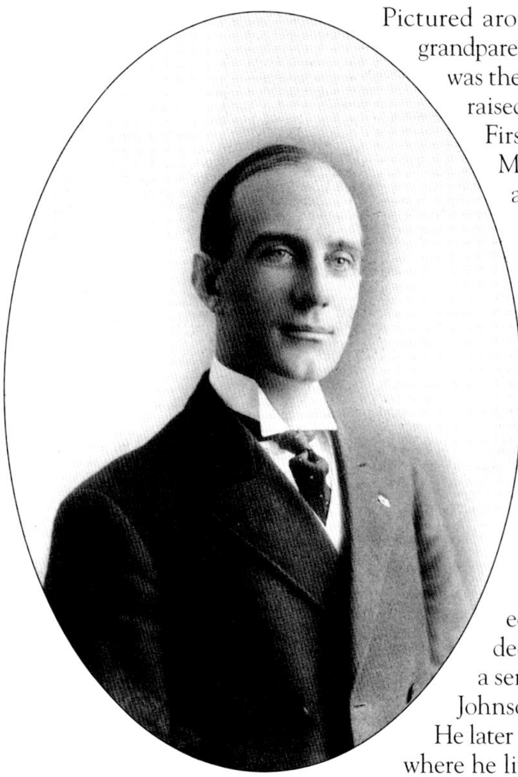

S. Luke Howe was one of Ella and E.P. Howe Sr.'s three sons. Instead of pursuing a career in education, both S. Luke and his brother William decided to study law. S. Luke eventually became a senior partner in the firm of Howe, Hibbitt, and Johnson. He also served as Sacramento city attorney. He later assumed ownership of 2201 Twenty-First Street, where he lived until his death in 1945.

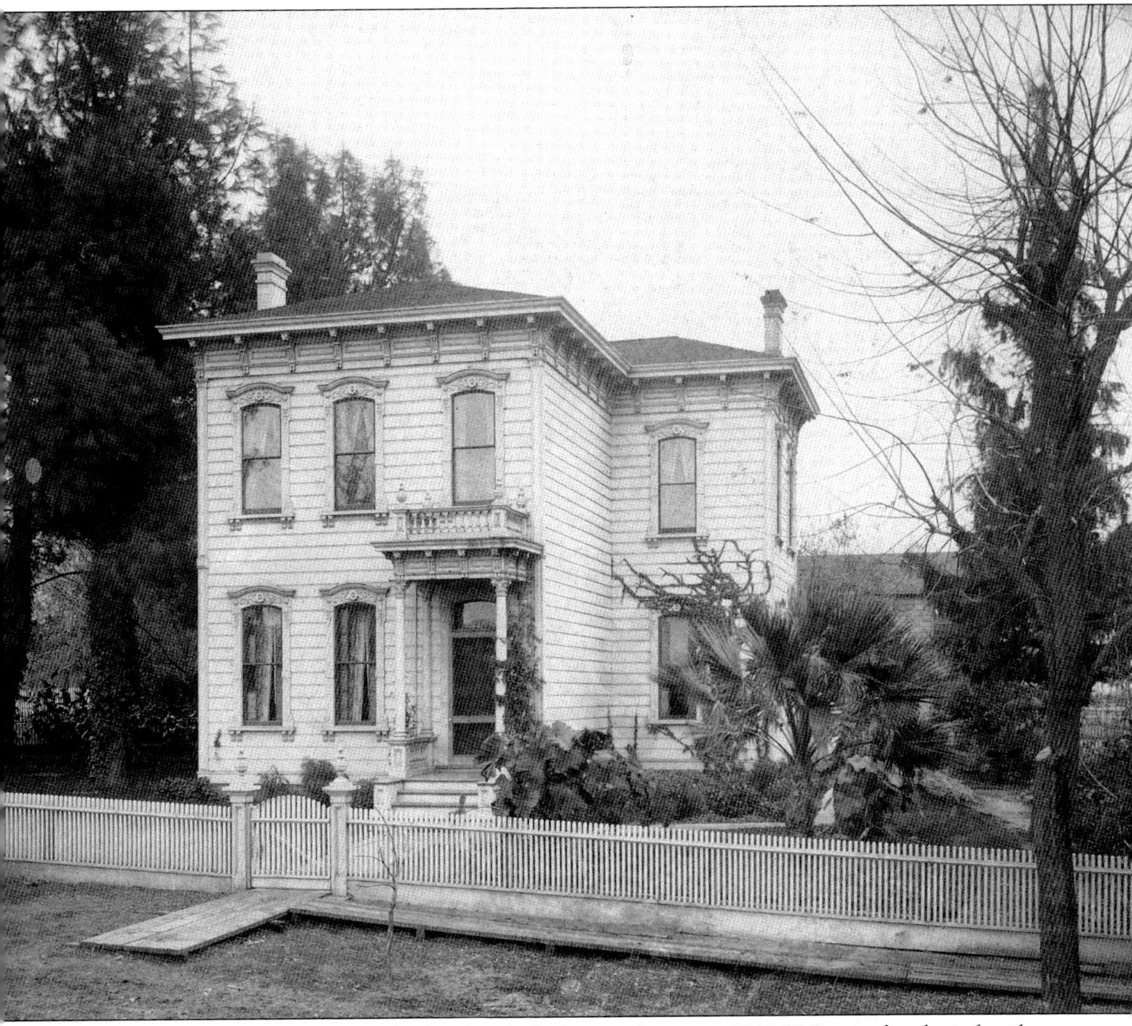

In 1882, John and Eliza Stevens built a lovely Italianate home at 2110 U Street for their family of four children. The property was celebrated for its lush gardens, which used to extend the full half-block of U Street between Twenty-First and Twenty-Second Streets. John Stevens was a celebrated citizen of Sacramento as well as an early California pioneer, arriving with his family via the isthmus of Panama in 1855 and taking up work as a carpenter and teamster in the young city. Stevens later served as the vice president of the Friend and Terry Lumber Company, president of the Pioneer Box Company, and surveyor of city streets. Stevens later championed the installation of sidewalks at Poverty Ridge. As of 2020, this lot was believed to be the largest intact pioneer-era parcel remaining in the central city and the oldest remaining home in Poverty Ridge. (Courtesy of CSL.)

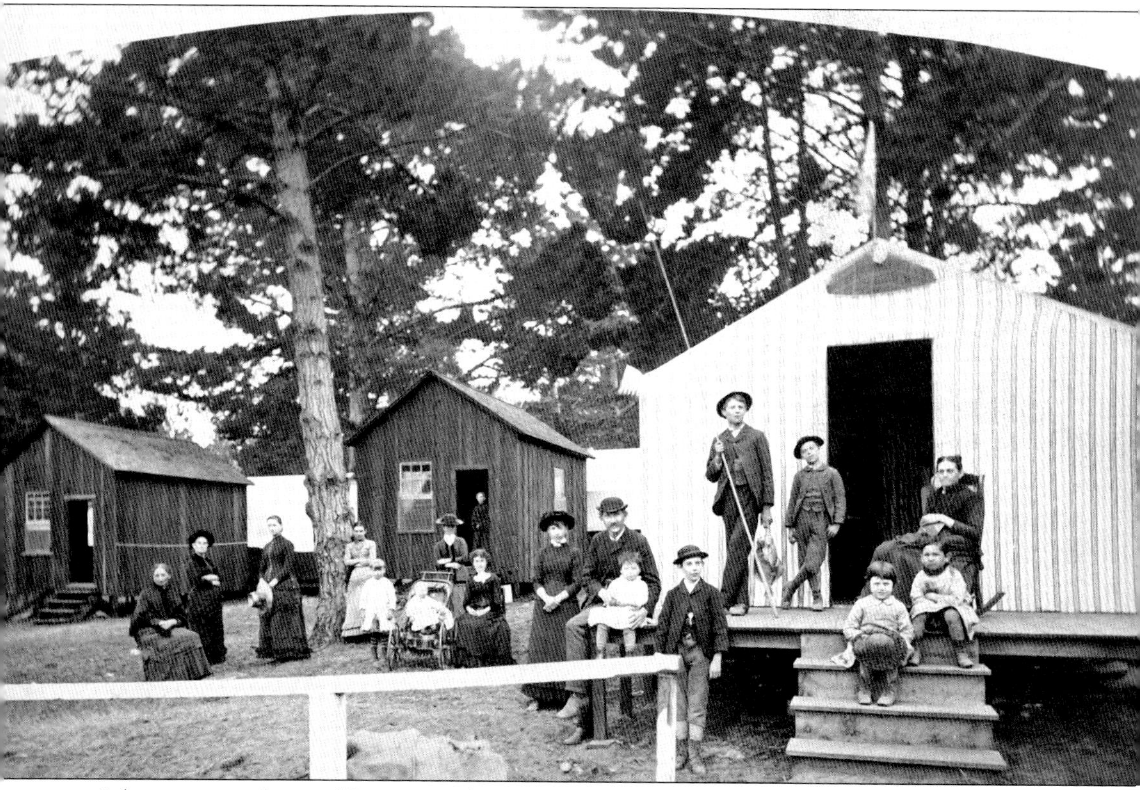

Like many residents of Poverty Ridge, the Stevens and Howe families were good friends and neighbors. Both families developed Italianate-style residences along Twenty-First Street during the 1880s. This c. 1882 photograph shows the Howe and Stevens families camping together at the Howes' coastal property in Pacific Grove, California. E.P. Howe Jr. is seen holding a fishing pole. William Howe stands next to the open door. Ella Howe sits in a rocking chair. S. Luke Howe stands on the ground next to the steps. The Howes' daughter Ella sits on the lower step, and her little boyfriend sits next to her. John Stevens is believed to be the man holding the child in his lap. The members of the Stevens family are toward the cabins to the left.

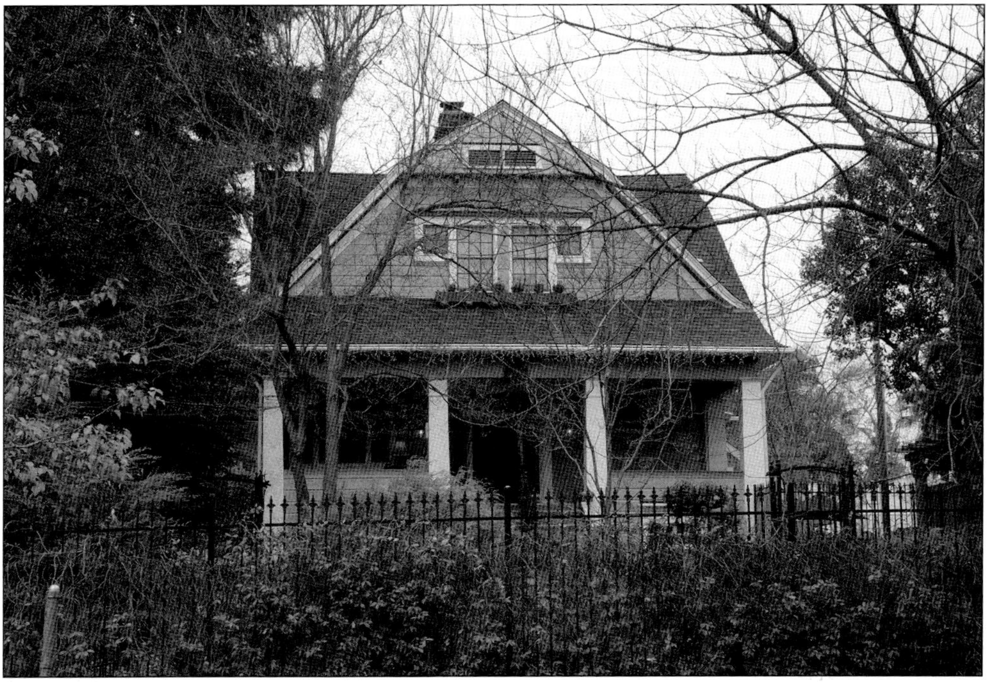

This is the c. 1900 delta Queen Anne–style home of Civil War hero Brig. Gen. T.W. Sheehan and his wife, Mollie, at 2122 Twenty-Second Street. In 1866, Sheehan settled in Sacramento, where he served as a deputy sheriff and later as the manager of the *Sacramento Daily Union* newspaper. The Sheehans had five children. Their daughter Rose Sheehan became supervisor of kindergartens for the city and for most of her life lived at 2122 Twenty-Second Street. The Sheehan family built at least three other homes in Poverty Ridge. (Author's collection.)

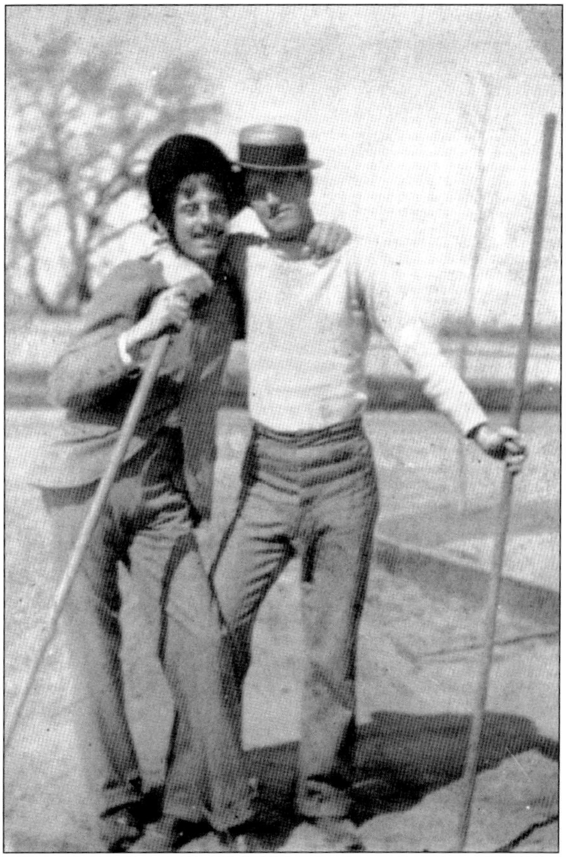

This portrait demonstrates just one example of the unique friendships between the children of the pioneer families of Poverty Ridge. Edgar M. Sheehan (left) and William S. Howe are pictured at the river in 1894 holding long poles. The Sheehans lived within a block of the Howe family, and their children grew up together. Edgar Sheehan later became president of the California Winery, and William Howe became a respected area attorney.

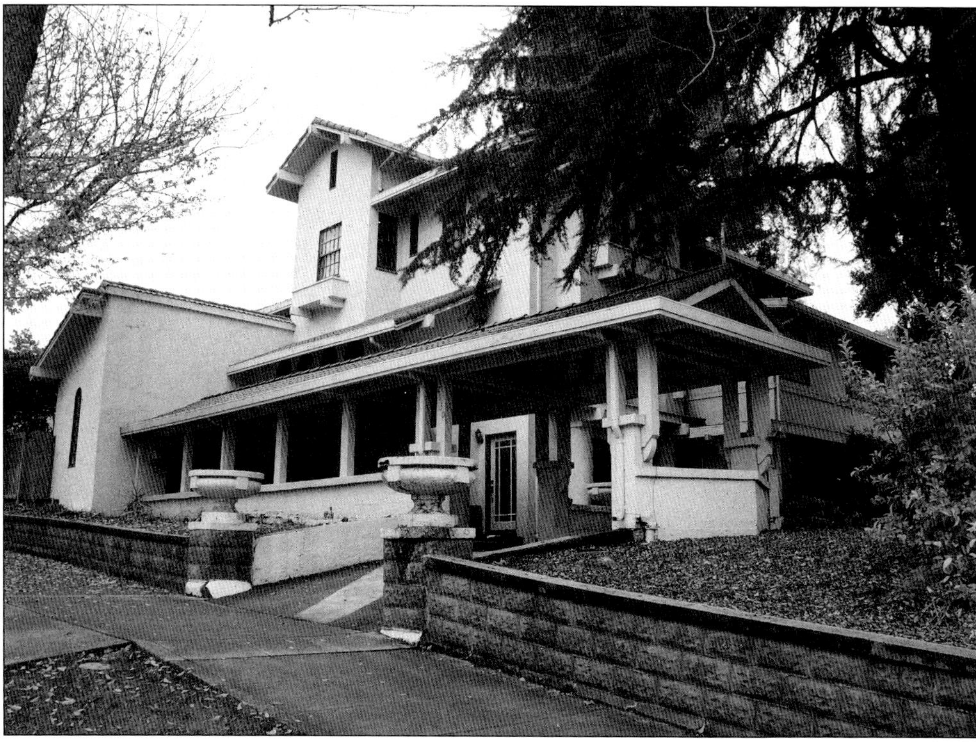

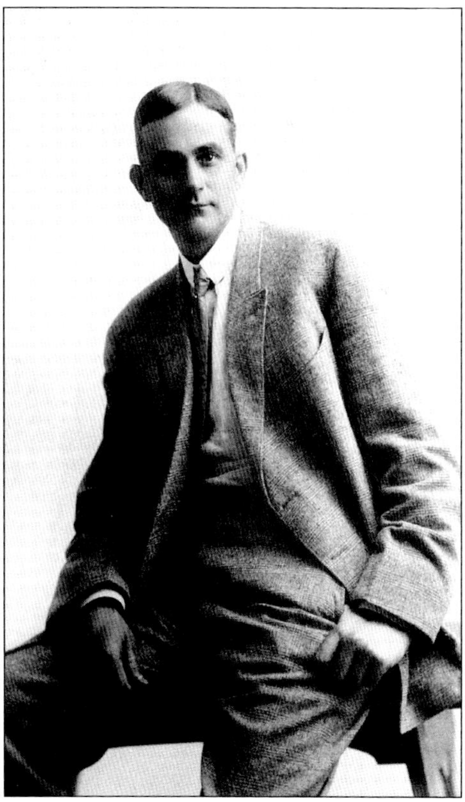

Completed in 1898, this Spanish Revival–style home at 2130 Twenty-Second Street was constructed by A.A. Merkley upon his marriage to Molly Sheehan, daughter of T.W. Sheehan. The Merkley-Sheehan wedding took place at one of the Sheehan residences across the street with 200 people in attendance. Rose Sheehan, Molly's sister, lived next door at 2122 Twenty-Second Street. (Author's collection.)

This c. 1904 photograph shows A.A. "Vin" Merkley, who built this Spanish Revival–style residence at 2130 Twenty-Second Street. Merkley made his living in real estate as co-owner of the firm Merkley, Chittenden, and Keller. He also served a term as Sacramento County tax collector.

This iconic Queen Anne–style home, with its towering turret and unique stained-glass windows, is at 1931 Twenty-First Street and is believed to be the most photographed single-family home in the city of Sacramento. It was constructed in 1903 by Fred and Caroline Mason, proprietors of Mason's Steam Laundry as well as Mason's Haberdashery. Both of the Masons lived in the home until their deaths. (Author's collection.)

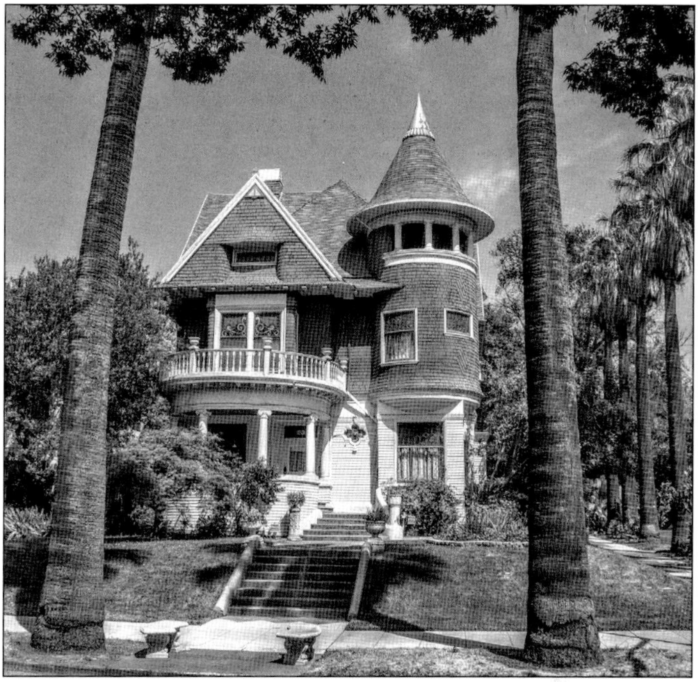

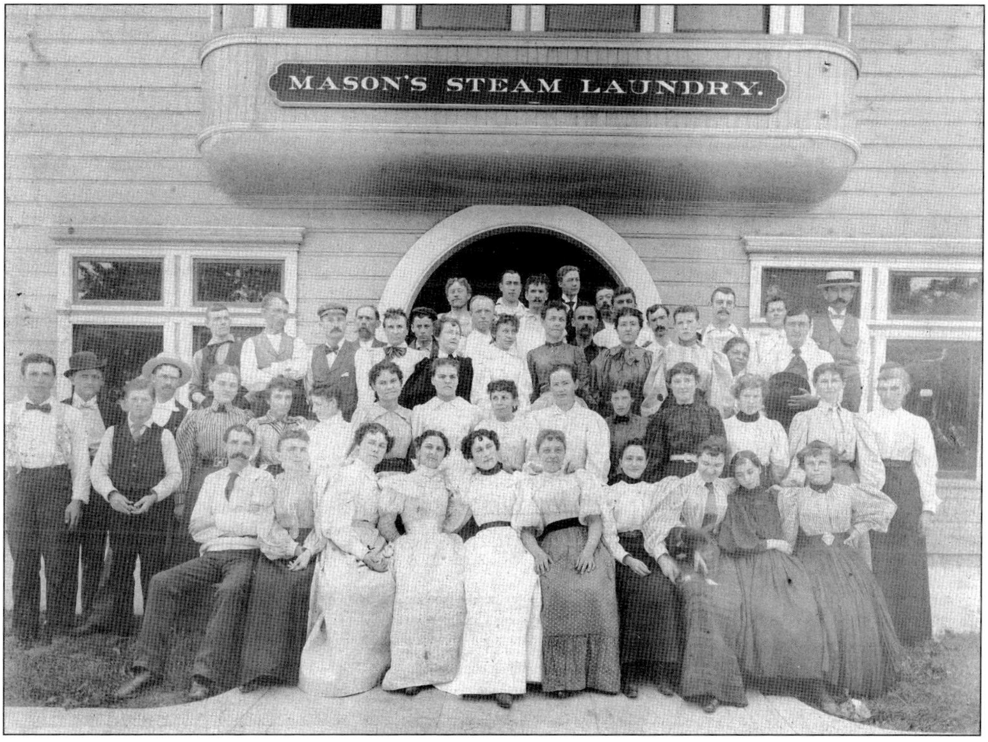

This c. 1893 photograph shows the staff of Mason's Steam Laundry at Twenty-First and O Streets. The enterprising Fred and Caroline Mason built a majestic home at 1931 Twenty-First Street. After Fred's death, Caroline continued to operate and grow their businesses for another 40 years until passing away in the home in 1942. (Courtesy of the Sacramento Room.)

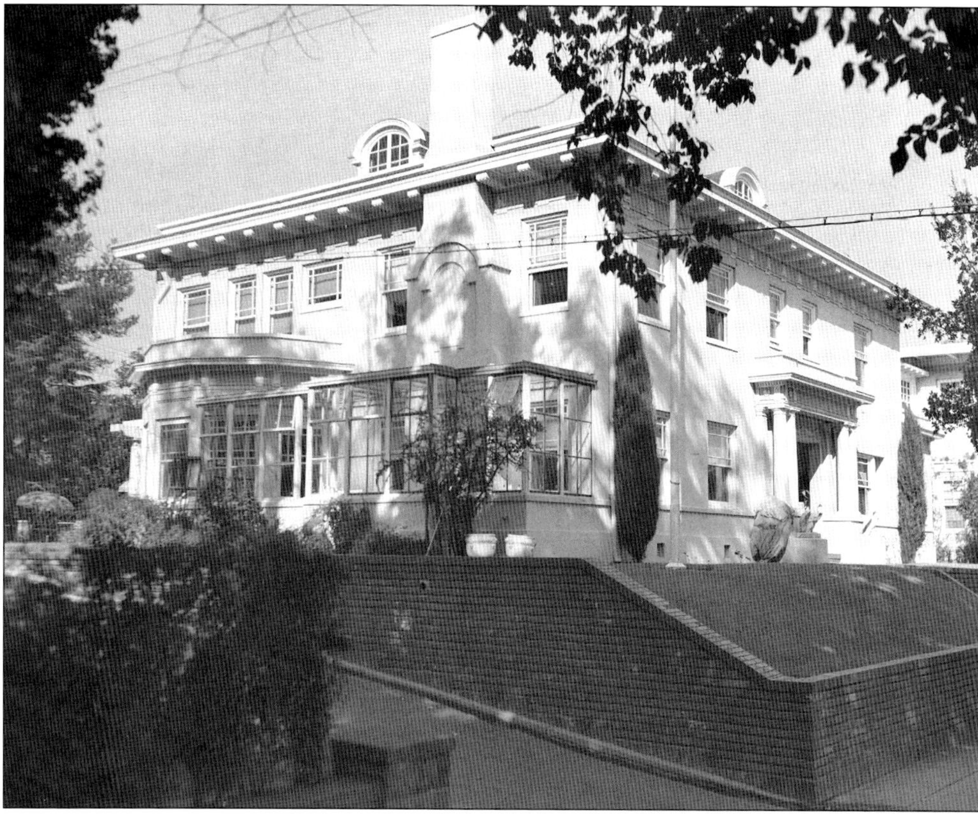

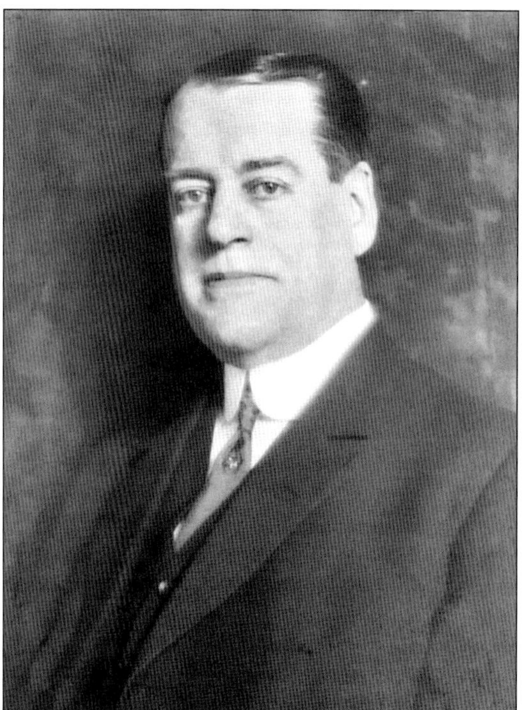

In 1910, *Sacramento Bee* publisher and editor C.K. McClatchy and his wife, Ella, constructed a residence at 2112 Twenty-Second Street. The home was designed in the Beaux Arts and Colonial Revival styles by famed local architect Rudolph Adam Herold. The McClatchy family business—currently known as the McClatchy Company—is the recipient of over 54 Pulitzer Prizes for excellence in journalism. Arguably no other family has made a greater or more positive historical impact on the neighborhood.

Charles Kenny "C.K." McClatchy was one of the two sons of original *Sacramento Bee* editor James McClatchy. Upon his father's death in 1883, C.K. became editor and, eventually, owner of the paper. Under C.K.'s leadership, the newspaper continued to thrive. A man of the people, C.K. continued James McClatchy's legacy of support for progressive causes, including trust-busting and workers' rights. (Courtesy of CSL.)

In 1885, C.K. McClatchy married Ella Kelly. In the years that followed, Ella and C.K. welcomed three children: Charlotte, Carlos, and Eleanor. Carlos was responsible for the *Bee's* expansion into the lucrative Fresno and Modesto markets. Carlos's premature death in 1933 meant that C.K. and Ella's youngest daughter, Eleanor, would lead the company for the following 40 years.

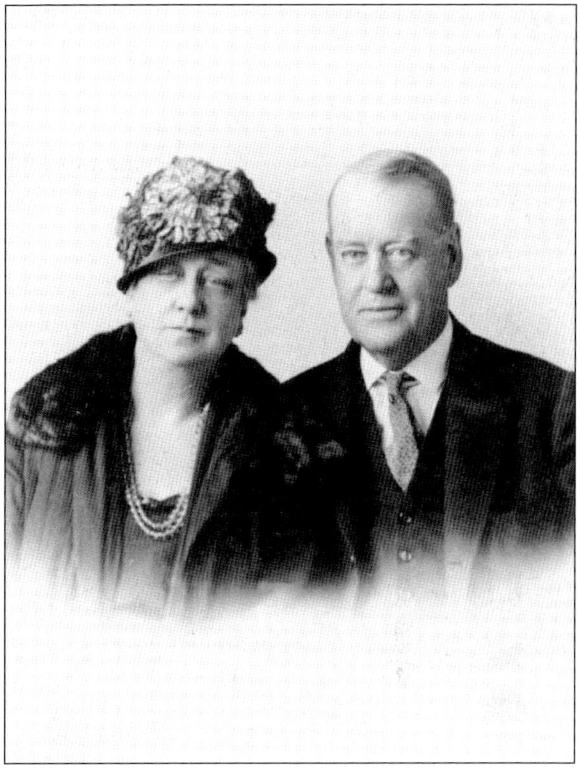

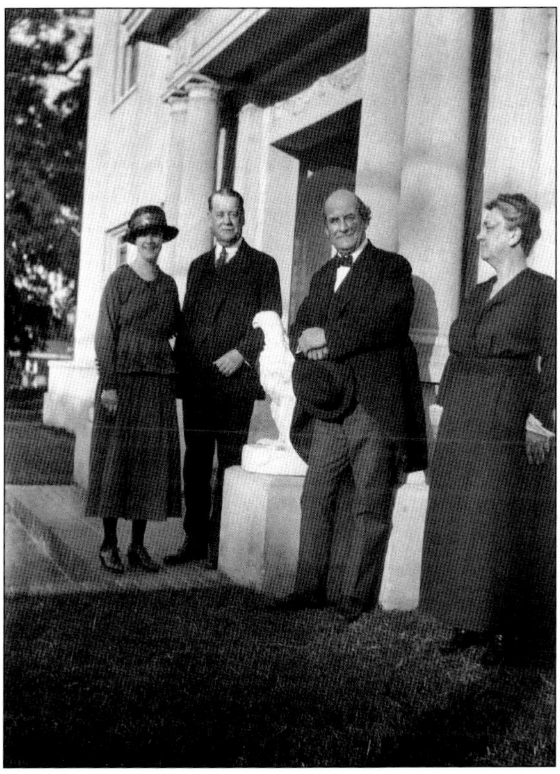

At their Poverty Ridge home, the McClatchys entertained many notable public figures, including politicians, musicians, and artists. Pictured around 1920 in front of their home are, from left to right, Eleanor and C.K. McClatchy, former presidential candidate and US secretary of state William Jennings Bryan, and Ella McClatchy.

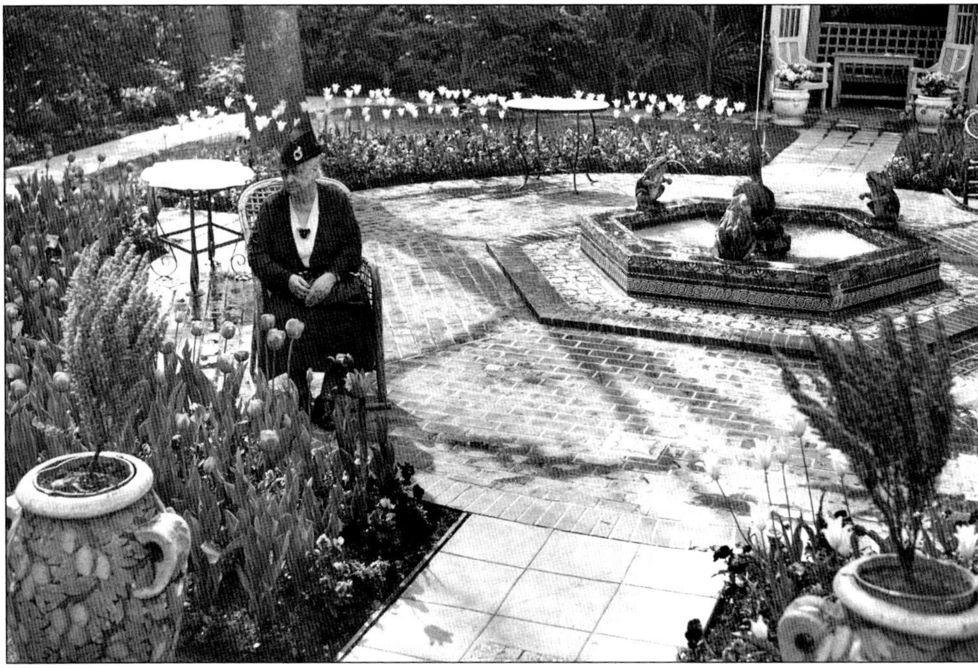

This late 1930s photograph shows Ella K. McClatchy resting in the beautiful gardens behind her home at 2112 Twenty-Second Street. The backyard of Ella and C.K.'s residence was adjacent to the gardens of their daughter Eleanor's home at 2124 U Street.

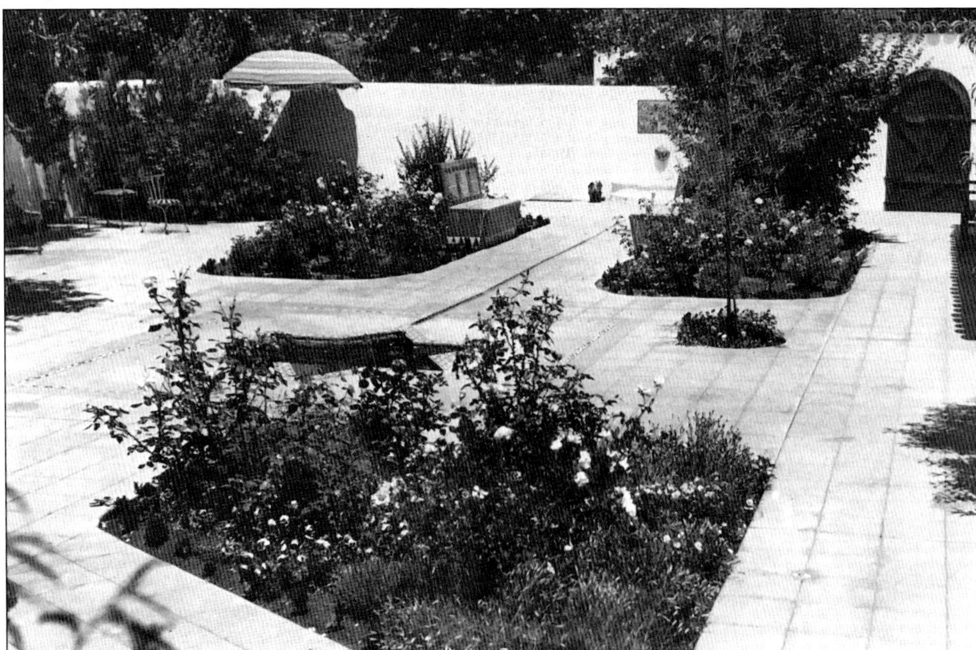

This c. 1933 photograph shows the gardens of the McClatchy family properties at 2112 Twenty-Second Street and 2124 U Street. In keeping with the style of Eleanor McClatchy's residence, the garden exhibits a blend of Spanish Revival and Moorish architectural details. Notice the Moorish reflecting pool at the center of the courtyard. (Courtesy of CSL.)

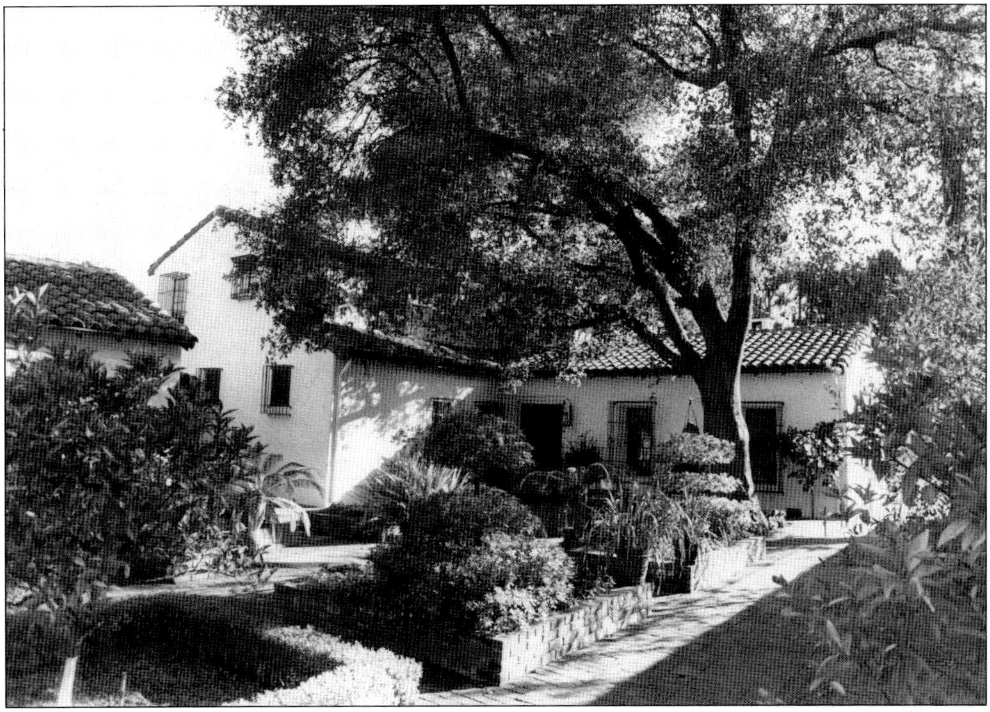

Ella McClatchy maintained beautiful gardens at her Poverty Ridge residence. In time, the family also acquired the parcel adjoining their gardens to the west. In the 1930s, at her father's behest, Eleanor McClatchy returned to Sacramento from New York in order to helm the family business. She made her home in this beautiful Spanish Revival residence at 2124 U Street. Through the years, Eleanor would host guests in the backyard gardens between the two McClatchy homes.

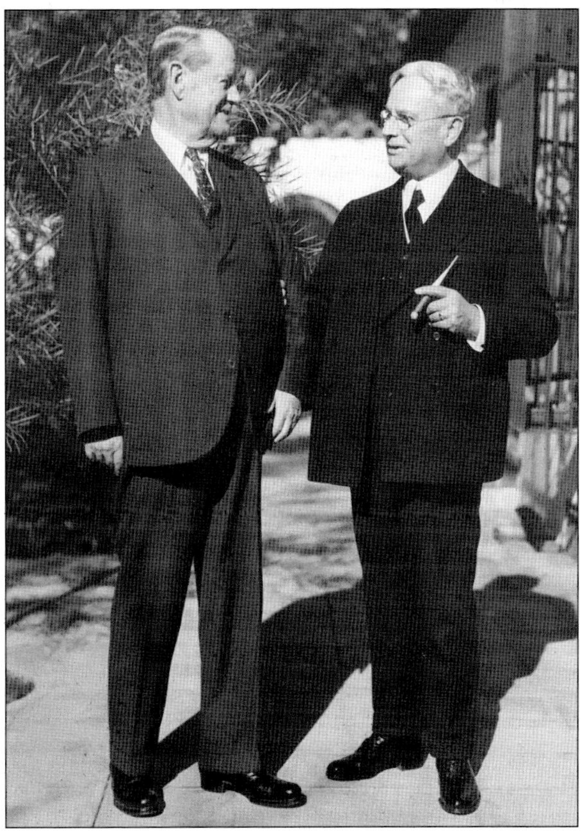

In this c. 1930 photograph taken in the McClatchy gardens are US senator and former California governor Hiram Johnson (right) and C.K. McClatchy. The two men were dear friends and maintained regular correspondence throughout their lives. Senator Johnson's widowed father, Sen. Grove Johnson, also lived in Poverty Ridge just a couple of blocks from the McClatchy residence. (Courtesy of CSL.)

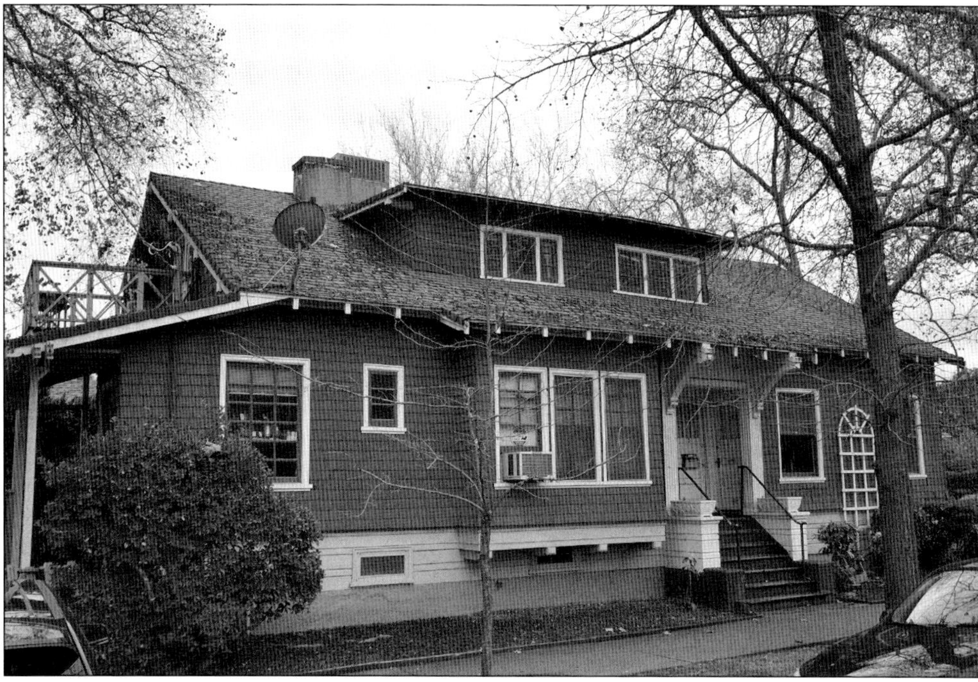

The Arts and Crafts–style home at 1929 Twenty-Third Street in Poverty Ridge was built in 1915 and likely intended as a retirement home for state senator Grove Johnson, father to California governor and US senator Hiram Johnson. Today, the Johnson home has been converted to multifamily housing. However, most of the original exterior architectural details remain intact. (Author's collection.)

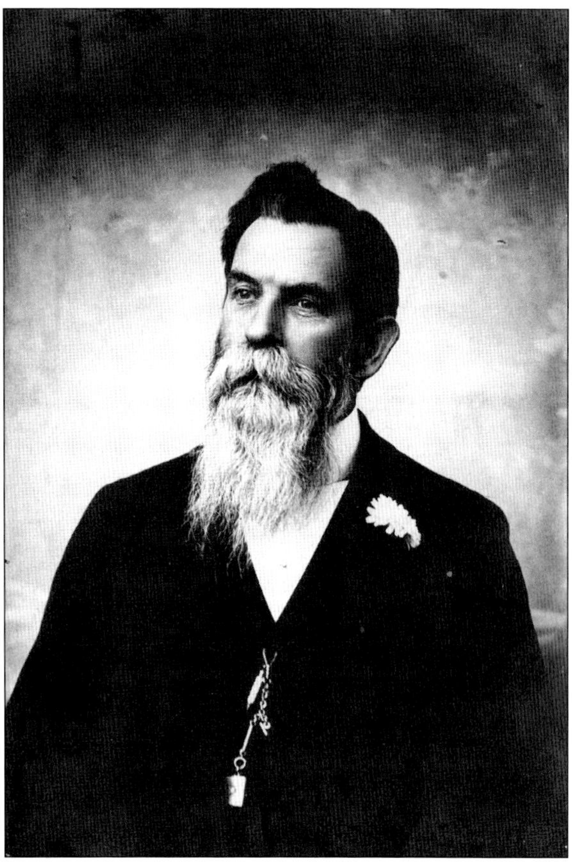

Beginning in 1915, widower Grove Johnson lived at the northeast corner of Twenty-Third and T Streets in Poverty Ridge. Johnson arrived in California in 1865 and quickly established himself as a prominent Sacramento attorney. In 1877, he won a seat in the California State Assembly, where he served until 1879. Grove Johnson also served in the California State Senate and later in the US Congress. (Courtesy of CSL.)

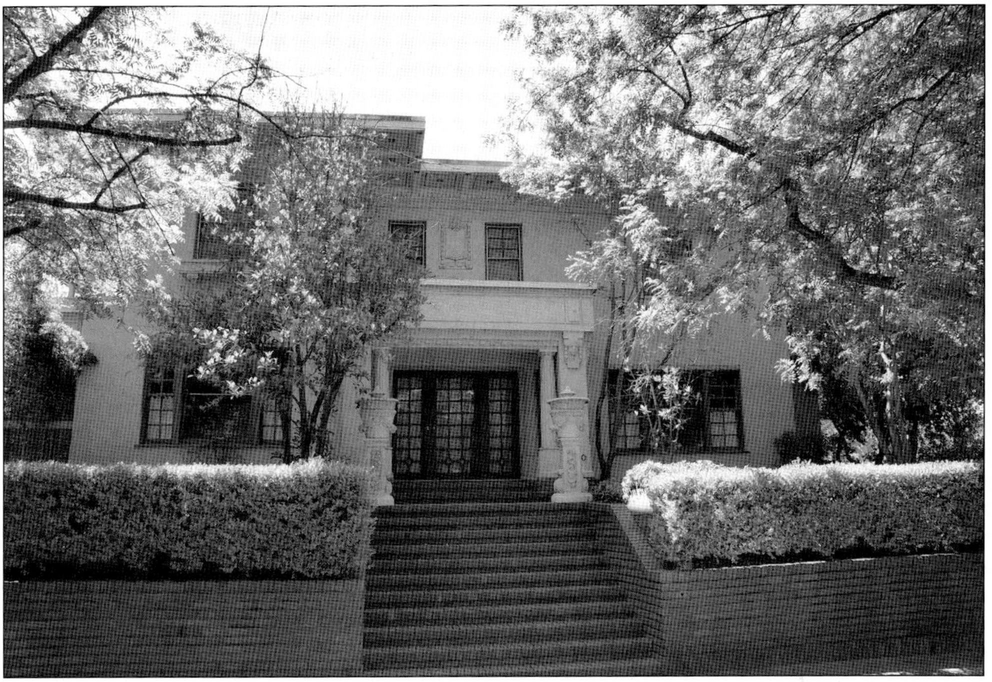

Between 1911 and 1913, famed Sacramento architect Rudolph Adam Herold designed and built his family residence at 2100 Twenty-Second Street, adjacent to the McClatchy family home, which he also designed. The residence is a unique blend of Frank Lloyd Wright and Viennese Secession architectural styles. In the decades following the Great Depression, the McClatchy family acquired the former Herold residence as accommodations for visiting journalists, artists, and musicians.

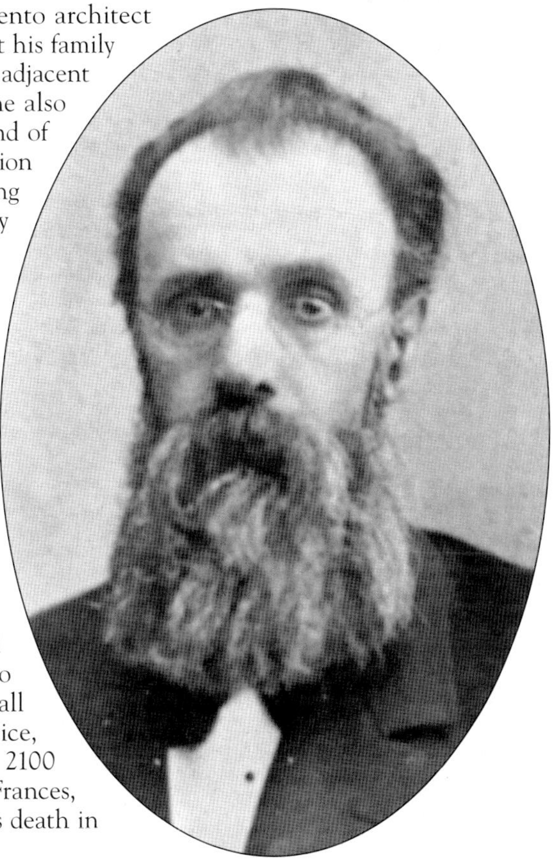

Rudolph Herold, pictured around 1925, was arguably Sacramento's most prolific architect of the early 20th century. Herold designed such buildings as the Sacramento City Hall, the Masonic Temple, the Marshall School, and the Sacramento Hall of Justice, as well as his own personal residence at 2100 Twenty-Second Street. He and his wife, Frances, occupied the home until a year before his death in 1926. (Courtesy of CSL.)

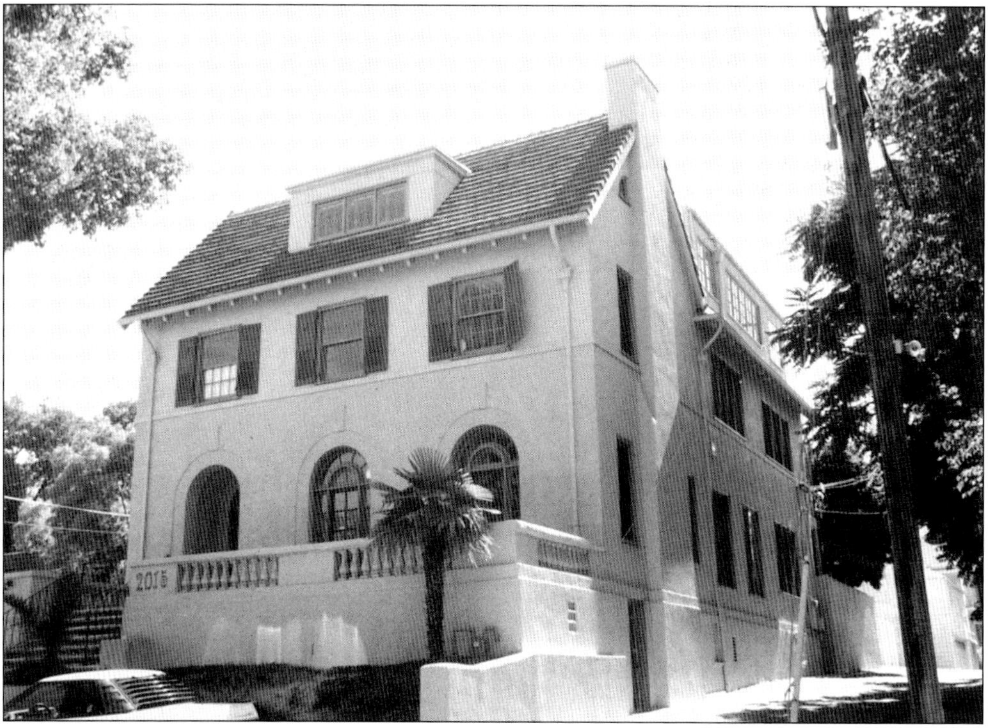

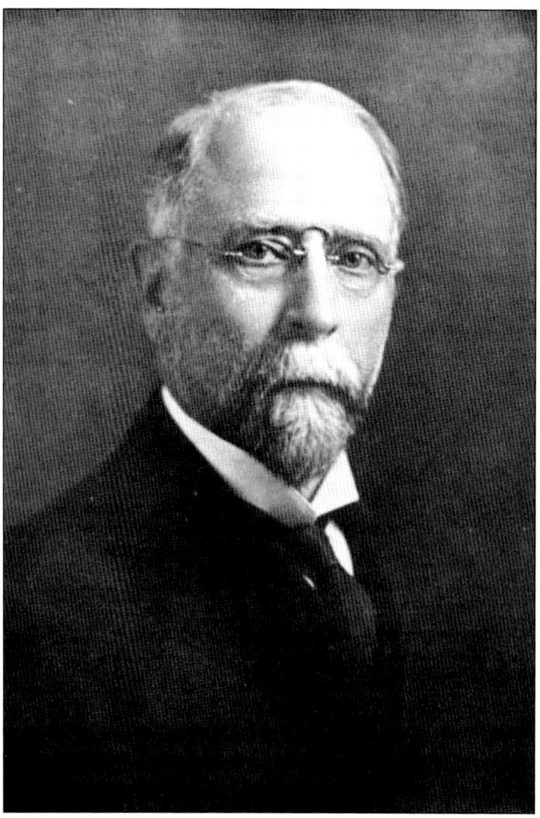

Around 1914, Dr. Wallace A. Briggs and his wife, Ella, erected this elegant 6,000-square-foot Beaux Arts mansion in the French country style at 2015 Twenty-First Street. Dr. Briggs came from a family of celebrated Northern California physicians. His brother William Ellery Briggs was also a Sacramento doctor. Wallace Briggs lived in the home until his death in 1927.

Wallace A. Briggs, pictured around 1900, spent years intermittently traveling the United States and Europe to study the most cutting-edge medical procedures. He was considered one of the most capable physicians and surgeons in the western United States at the time. During his career, Dr. Briggs was appointed to the California State Board of Health and served as the president of the Sacramento Society for Medical Improvement. (Courtesy of CSL.)

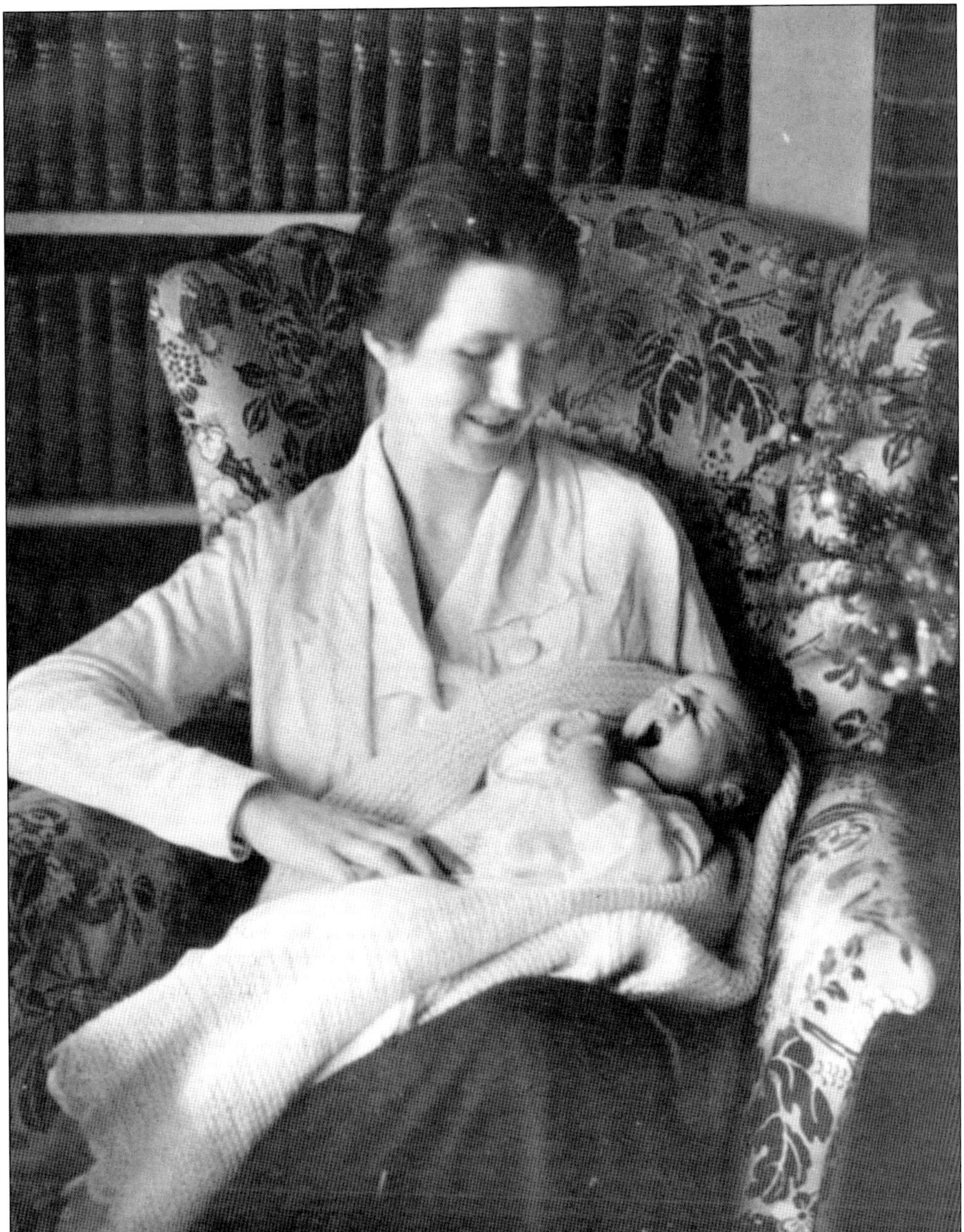

At the turn of the 20th century, several old Sacramento pioneer families living in Poverty Ridge became connected by marriage. Phebe Briggs was the daughter of Dr. William Ellery Briggs and the niece of Dr. Wallace A. Briggs of 2015 Twenty-First Street. In 1918, Phebe, a graduate of Vassar College, was wed to Carlos McClatchy, the only son of Ella and C.K. McClatchy. The couple had three sons, one of whom is pictured with Phebe in this undated photograph. Carlos and Phebe's sons, under the tutelage of their aunt Eleanor, would later grow up to help lead the McClatchy media empire.

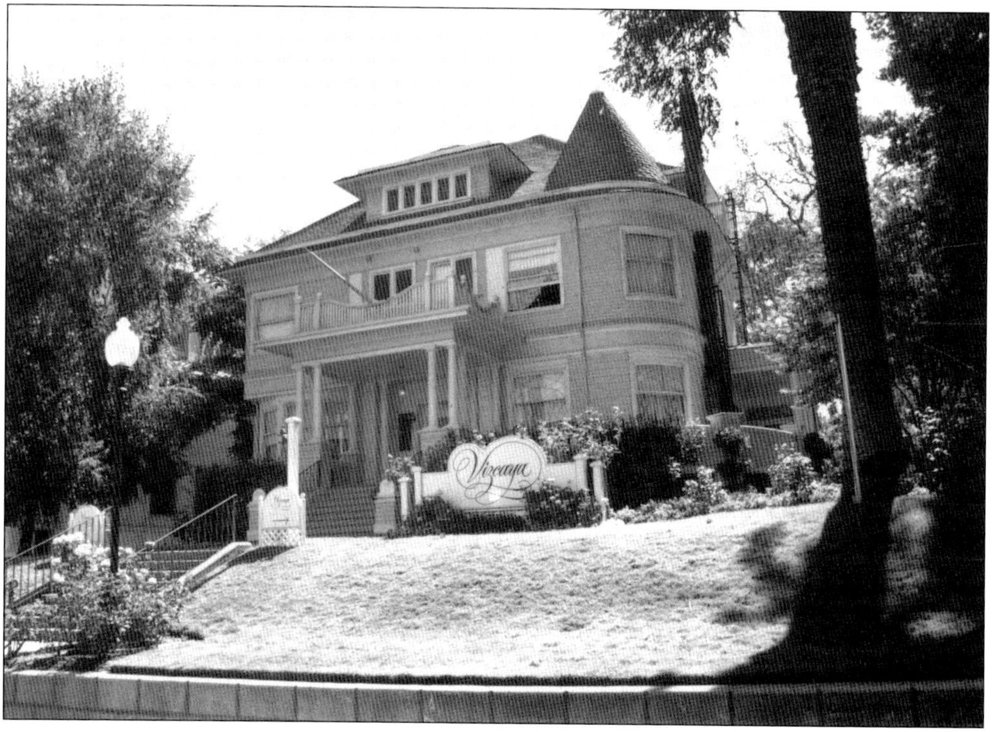

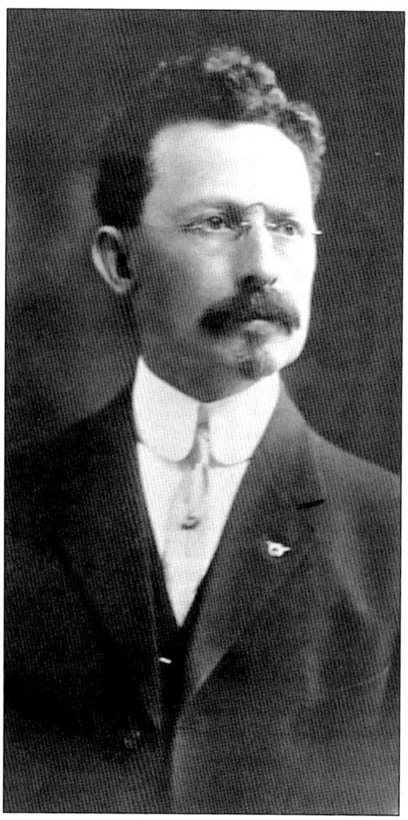

Built in 1899 for native Sacramentan Philip S. Driver and his wife, Elizabeth, this Colonial Revival mansion also exhibits elements of Craftsman and shingle architectural styles. The property was later converted into the Driver Mansion bed-and-breakfast and event center. Today, it is a wedding, event center, and bed-and-breakfast known as Vizcaya.

Philip Driver was the son of Elisha Driver, an original pioneer of 1849. Philip lived his entire life in Sacramento and grew up to become one of the most highly successful and respected attorneys in the county at the time. He also cofounded the law firm of Driver and Driver with his brother B. Frank Driver. Philip served as a member of the Sacramento Board of Education. He died at his Twenty-First Street home in 1923. (Courtesy of CSL.)

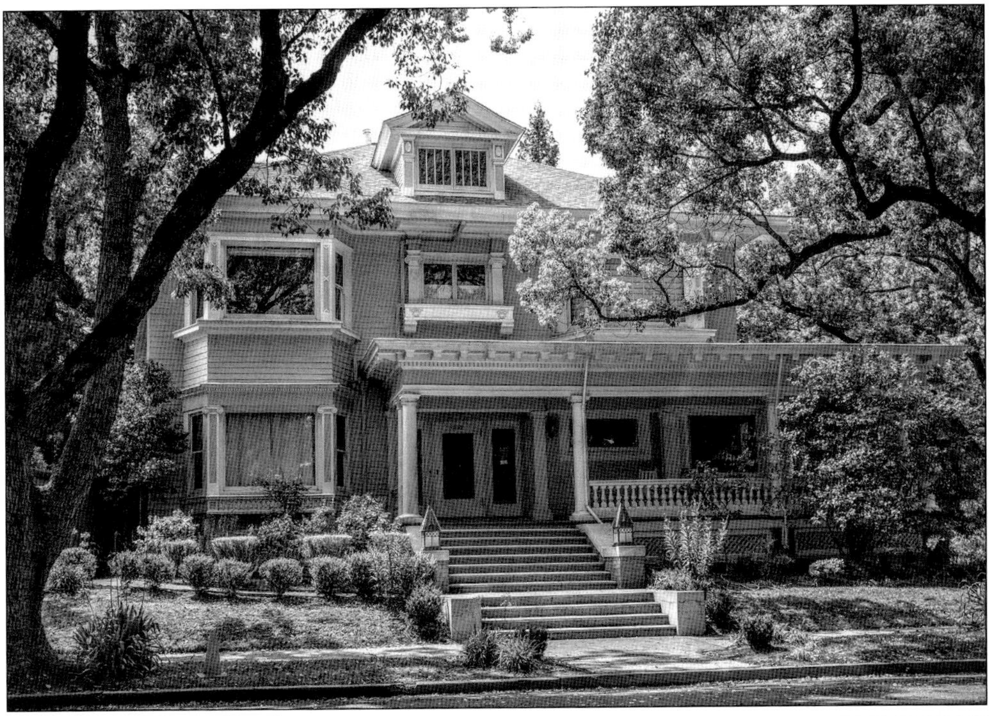

This magnificent Colonial Revival mansion at 2000 Twenty-Second Street was designed by Seadler & Hoen in 1911 for William and Mary Ross-Roan. Mary was the director of the board of the Bank of Sacramento. She passed away in the home in 1917 at the age of 69. In the late 1940s, the residence was acquired by Genevieve and J. Frank Didion. Today, it is known as the Didion Home. (Author's collection.)

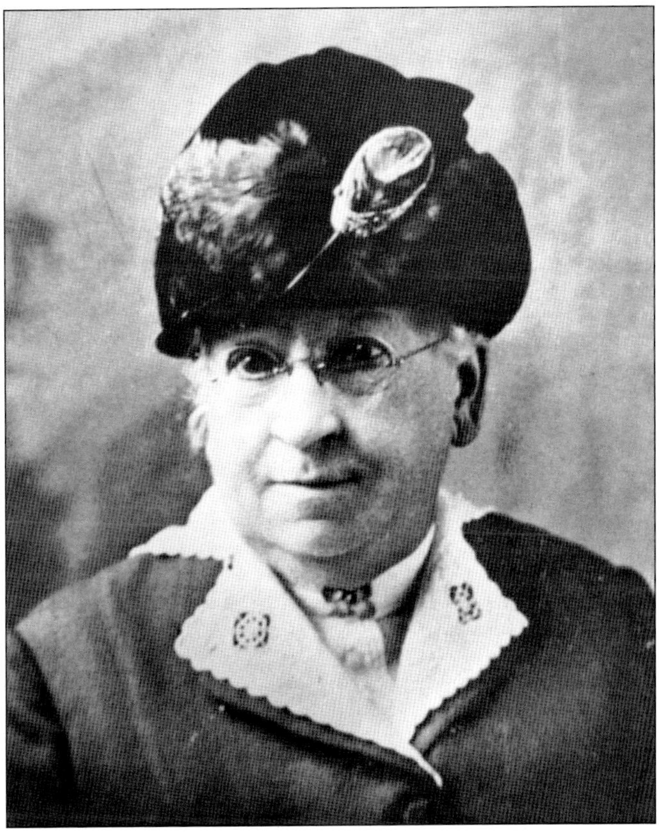

Mary Ross-Roan became known, with respect, as "the woman banker," a title she held for 30 years as one of the only women in banking in the United States at the time. Under Ross-Roan's leadership, Sacramento women were permitted, for the first time, to open their own personal bank accounts. (Courtesy of CSL.)

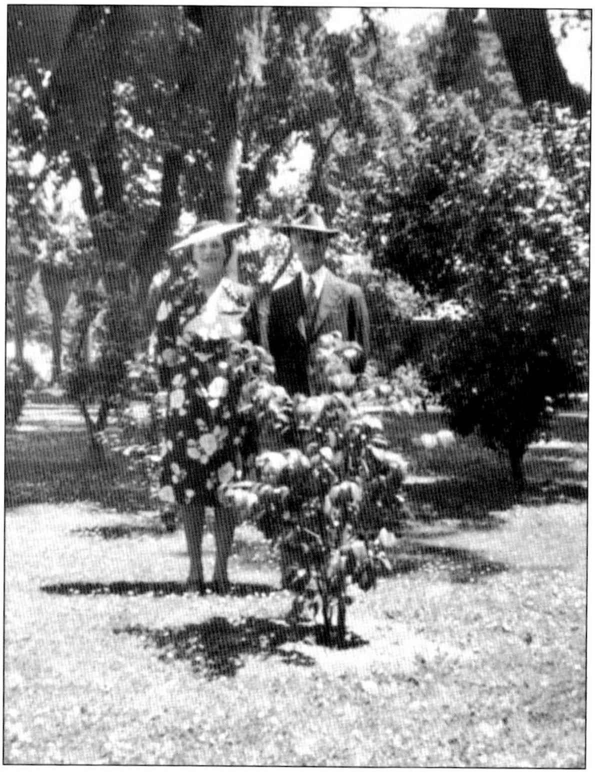

The Ross-Roan home was purchased in the 1940s by Joseph Frank and Genevieve Didion, pictured around 1950. J.F. Didion was the Sacramento County tax and license collector. Genevieve Didion was a celebrated civic activist and longtime member of the Sacramento Board of Education. Their daughter Mary Didion Armstrong continued to live in the home for many years after their deaths.

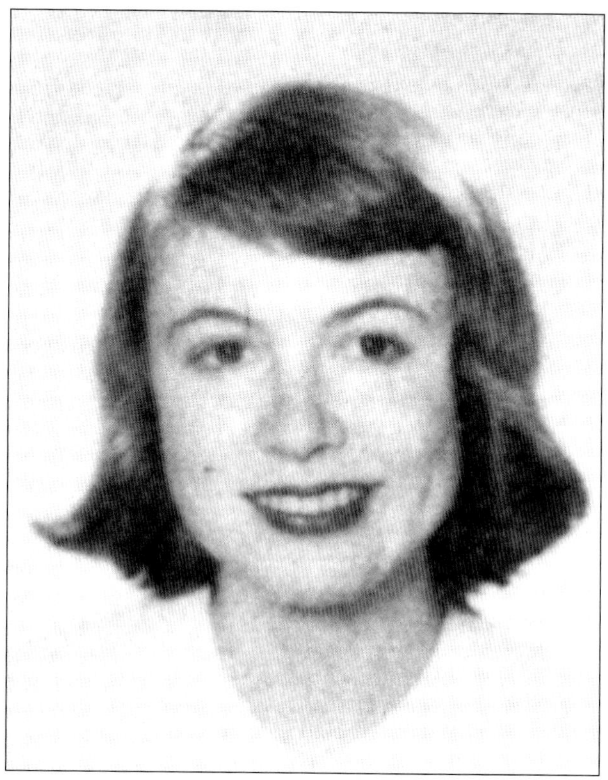

National Book Award recipient Joan Didion, pictured here in 1952, lived in the home of her grandfather J. Frank Didion at 2000 Twenty-Second Street for her last two years at McClatchy High School. Joan famously received her rejection letter from Stanford while living at the home (she later had the letter framed and keeps it as a memento). After graduating from Berkeley, Didion went on to become a literary icon. (Courtesy of Golden Nugget.)

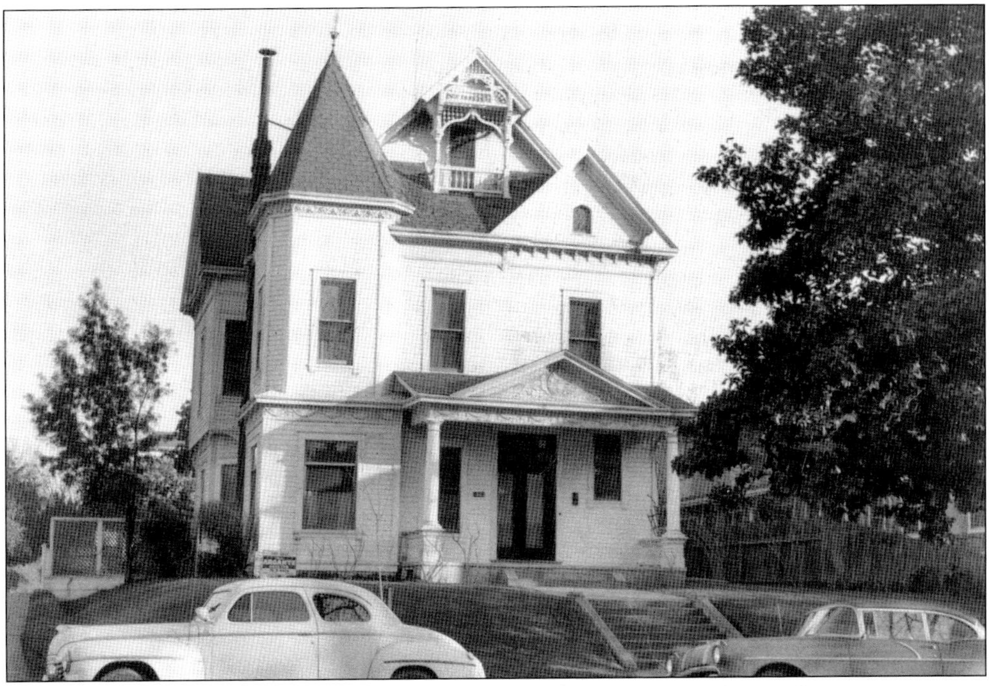

This c. 1958 photograph shows the Queen Anne–style home at 1903 Twenty-First Street that was built in 1898 by Charles S. Robb. His daughter Myrtle and her new husband, Daniel W. Carmichael, occupied the home shortly after its completion. Robb and his wife, Candace, lived with the Carmichaels for several years at this address. Eventually, the Robbs constructed a home at 2030 Twenty-Third Street.

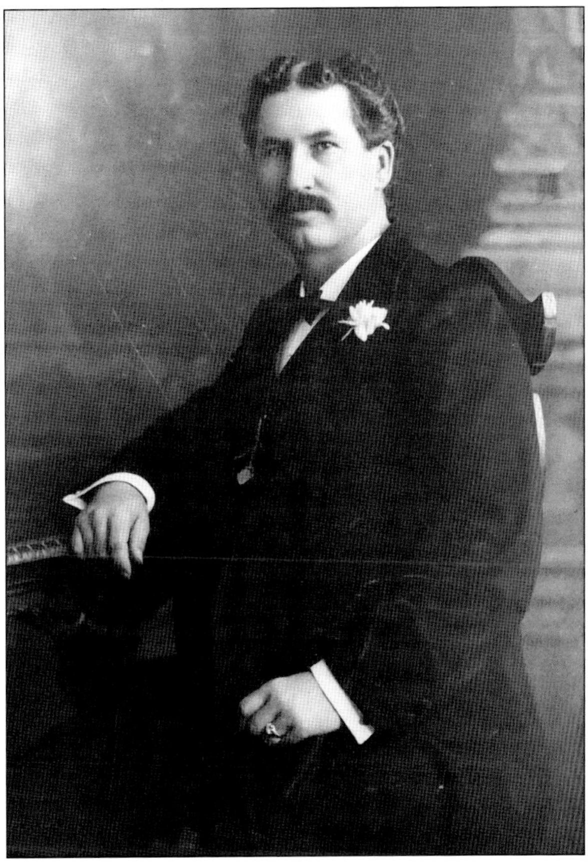

Daniel Carmichael served as the mayor of Sacramento from 1917 to 1919 and was a representative in the state assembly. He was also a major land developer, having established the community of Carmichael in 1910 through his real estate company, Curtis, Carmichael, and Brand. (Courtesy of CSL.)

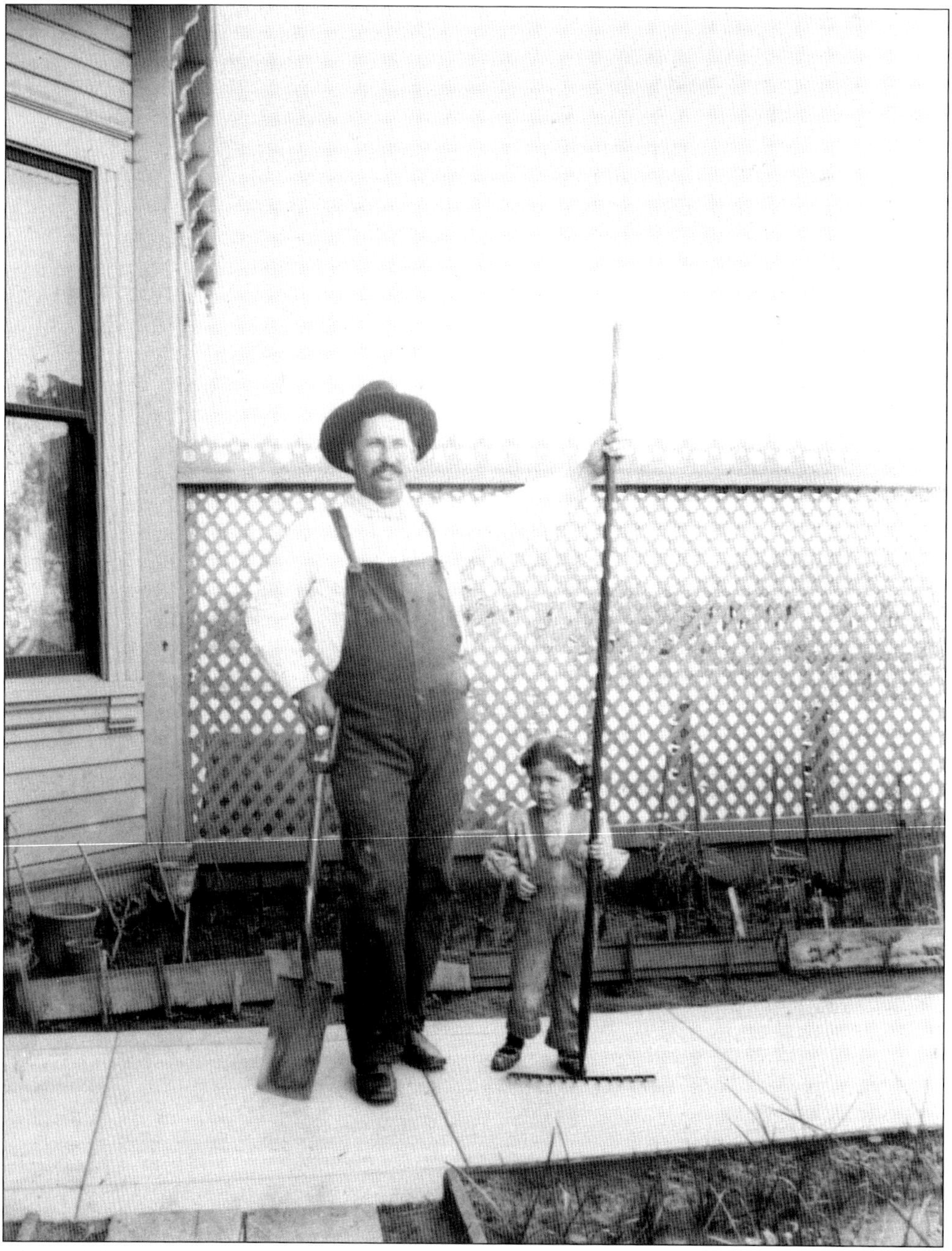

This c. 1898 photograph shows Daniel W. Carmichael dressed and ready to do yard work in the side garden of his new home at 1903 Twenty-First Street with two- or three-year-old Ruth Sheldon, whose father was a cousin to Carmichael's wife, Myrtle Robb Carmichael. The Carmichaels lived in two different homes in Poverty Ridge, first at 1903 Twenty-First Street (occupied today by law offices), and later at 2030 Twenty-Third Street (the home of Myrtle Carmichael's parents).

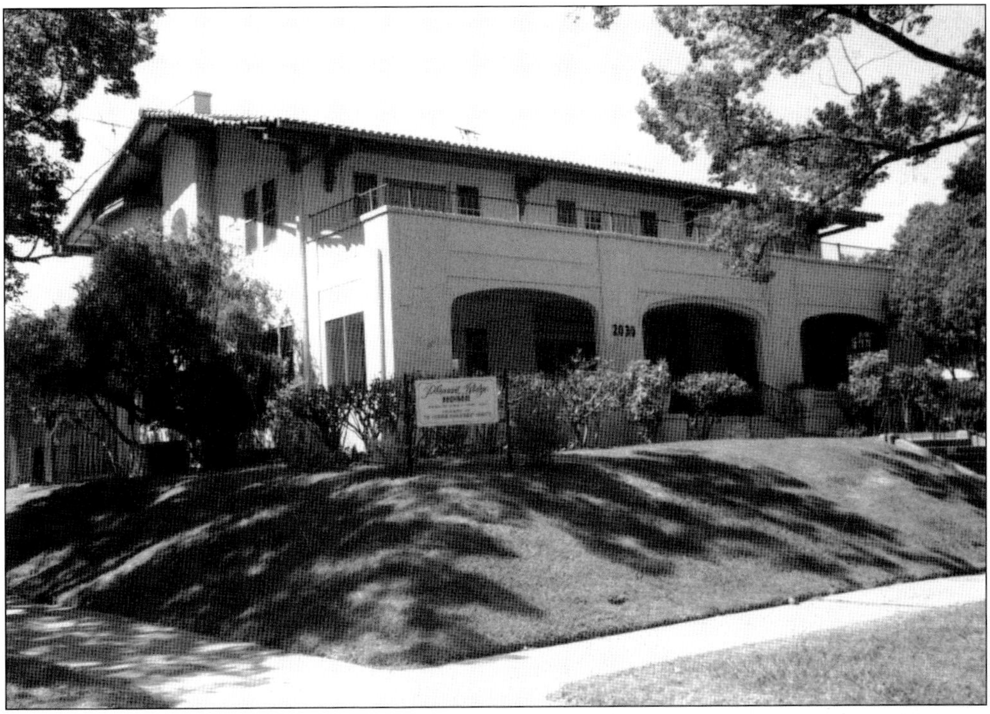

Constructed in 1911, the home at 2030 Twenty-Third Street was designed in the Mission Revival and Prairie School architectural styles. It was built by Charles and Candace Robb; their daughter Myrtle and her husband, Daniel Carmichael, also moved into the home in 1911.

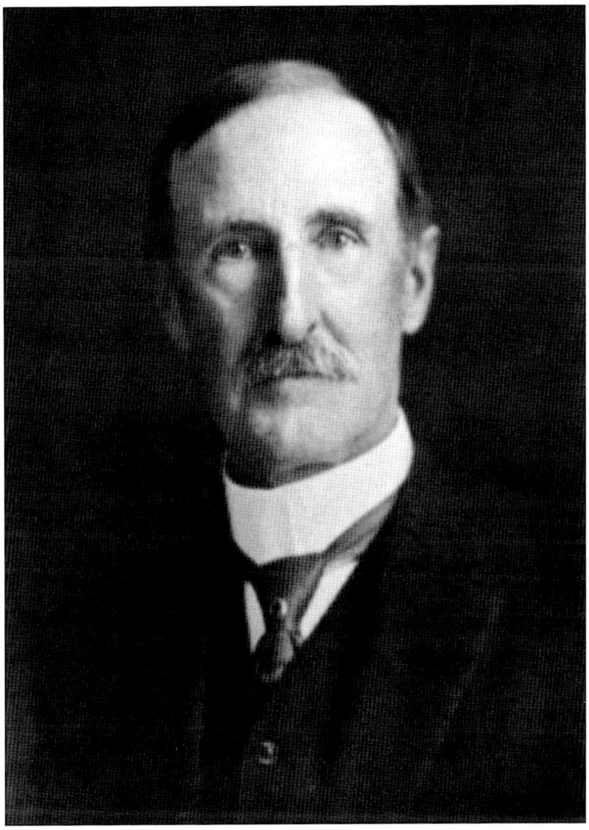

Charles Robb built two homes in Poverty Ridge. The first, at 1903 Twenty-First Street, was deeded to his daughter Myrtle and her husband, Daniel Carmichael. The second was constructed in 1911 as a home for Charles, his wife, Candace, and their youngest daughter, Mollie. The Robbs arrived in Sacramento in 1875. A former train conductor for the Southern Pacific, Charles invested his savings wisely, and in 1909 was able to retire from the railroad in order to completely focus on his extensive portfolio of oil, land, and real estate investments. (Courtesy of CSL.)

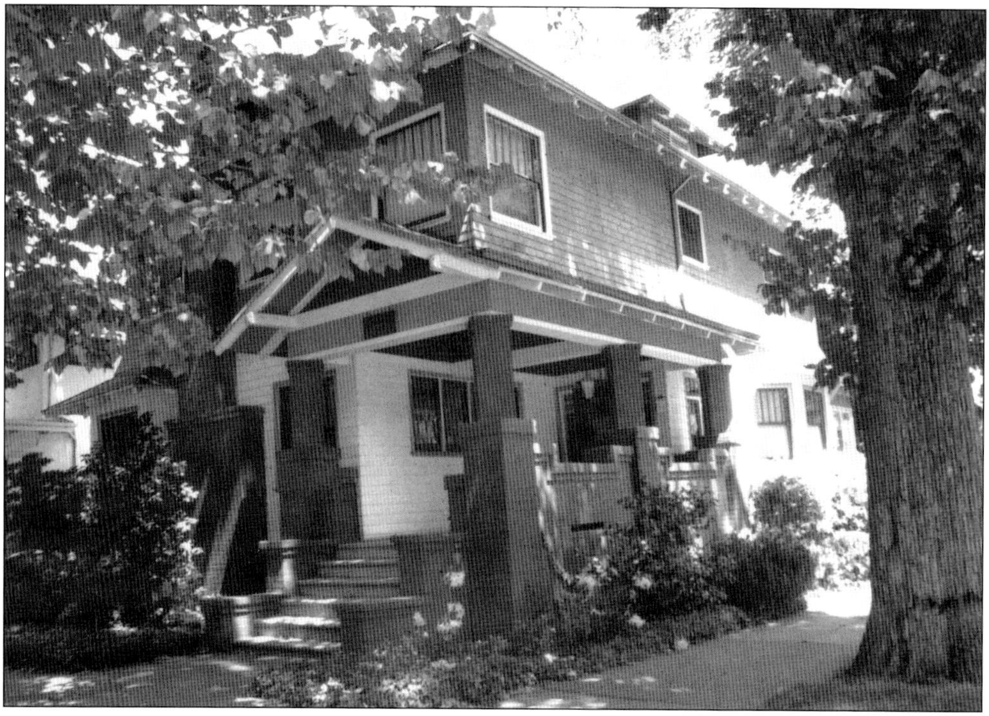

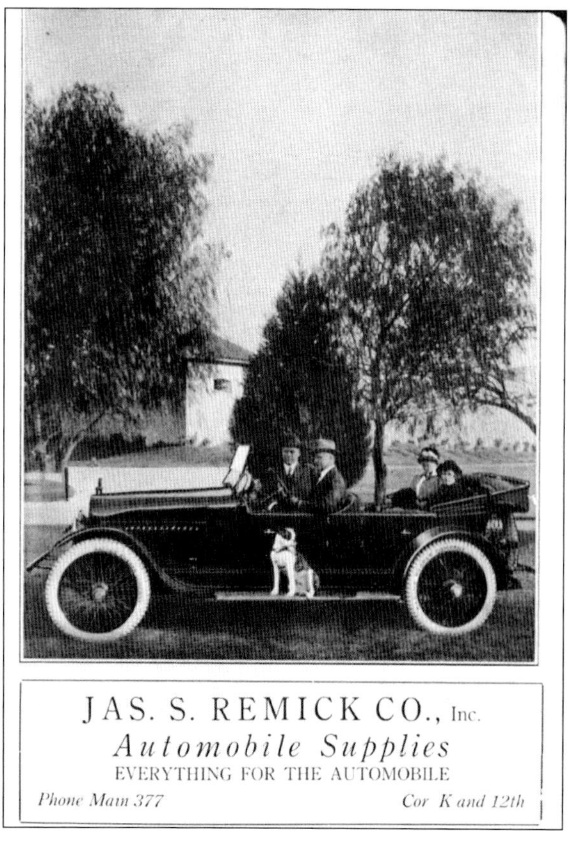

This handsome Craftsman home at 1931 Twenty-Second Street was built by Mr. and Mrs. James S. Remick between 1908 and 1909. Remick was a salesman for Hall-Luhrs & Company, a Sacramento grocery at 914 Second Street. He later founded and became president of the James S. Remick Company, which sold automobile parts.

This c. 1915 advertisement is for the James S. Remick Company. The Remick family built their Craftsman home at the intersection of Twenty-Second and T Streets in Poverty Ridge.

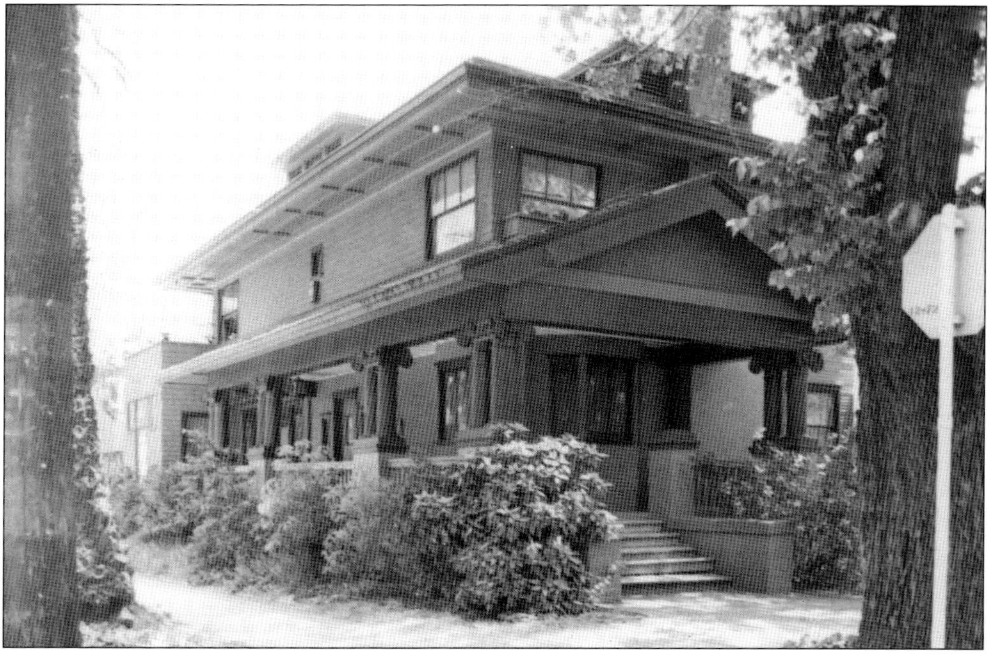

The beautiful home at 2200 T Street was designed in an interesting blend of Prairie and Colonial Revival architectural styles with Craftsman elements. The residence was built around 1910 and was owned by Frank D. Ryan, a native Sacramentan born to a Gold Rush–era pioneer family. Ryan was employed by the Capitol Banking and Trust Company and later opened the popular confectionery Ryan's Candy Company at 725 K Street.

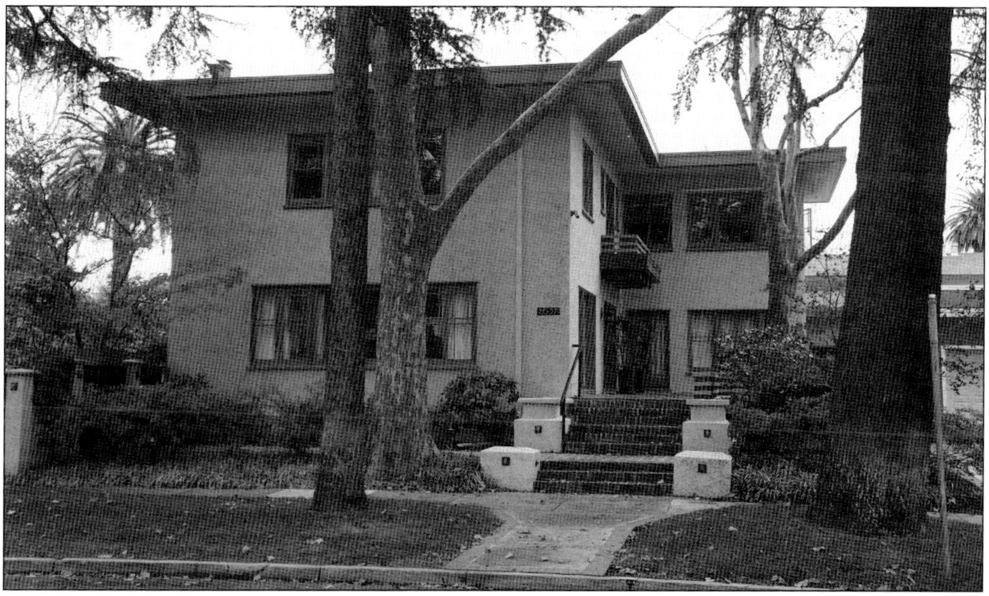

In 1915, the contracting firm of Murcell and Haley constructed the Prairie School–style homes at 2009 and 2015 Twenty-Third Street, forming a court between the pair. In 1917, Sacramento Superior Court judge Peter J. Shields and his wife, Carolee, purchased 2009 Twenty-Third Street. The couple lived in the home for most of their lives. Judge Shields passed away at the property after his 100th birthday. (Author's collection.)

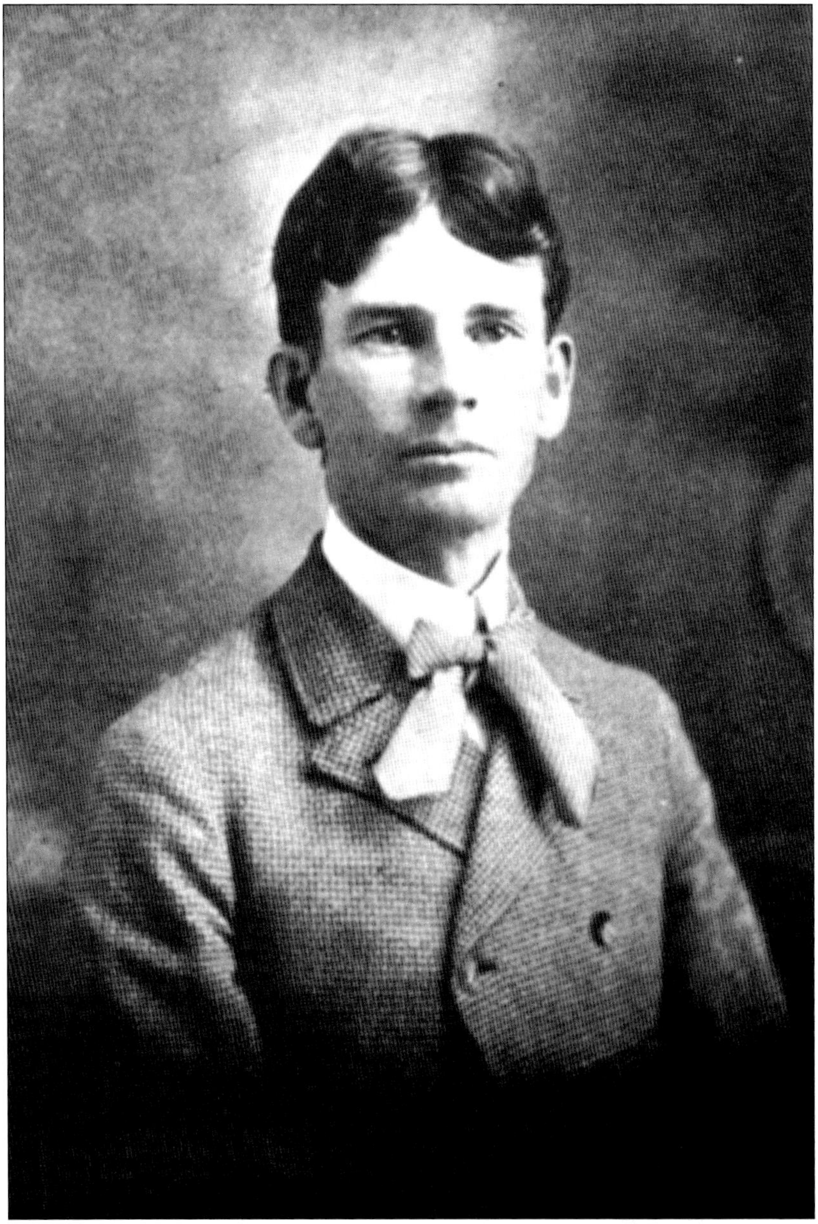

Longtime Poverty Ridge resident Judge Peter J. Shields was born on a ranch along the American River in modern-day Rancho Cordova. Shields's father had purchased the ranch with gold nuggets that he had personally excavated during the early days of the Gold Rush. Judge Shields led a long life of public service, serving as the private secretary to Gov. James H. Budd, secretary of the state agricultural society, and a law partner to Hiram W. Johnson. At the age of 38, he was elected to the superior bench in Sacramento, and served longer than any other superior judge in state history. Having been raised on a ranch, Shields had a deep love for all things agricultural. For many years, he won gold medals at the state fair for the livestock that he raised on his ranch. As one of the founders of the University of California at Davis, he maintained a lifelong interest in the school and in youth. The main library at UC Davis as well as the street running along its north side were named in honor of Judge Shields.

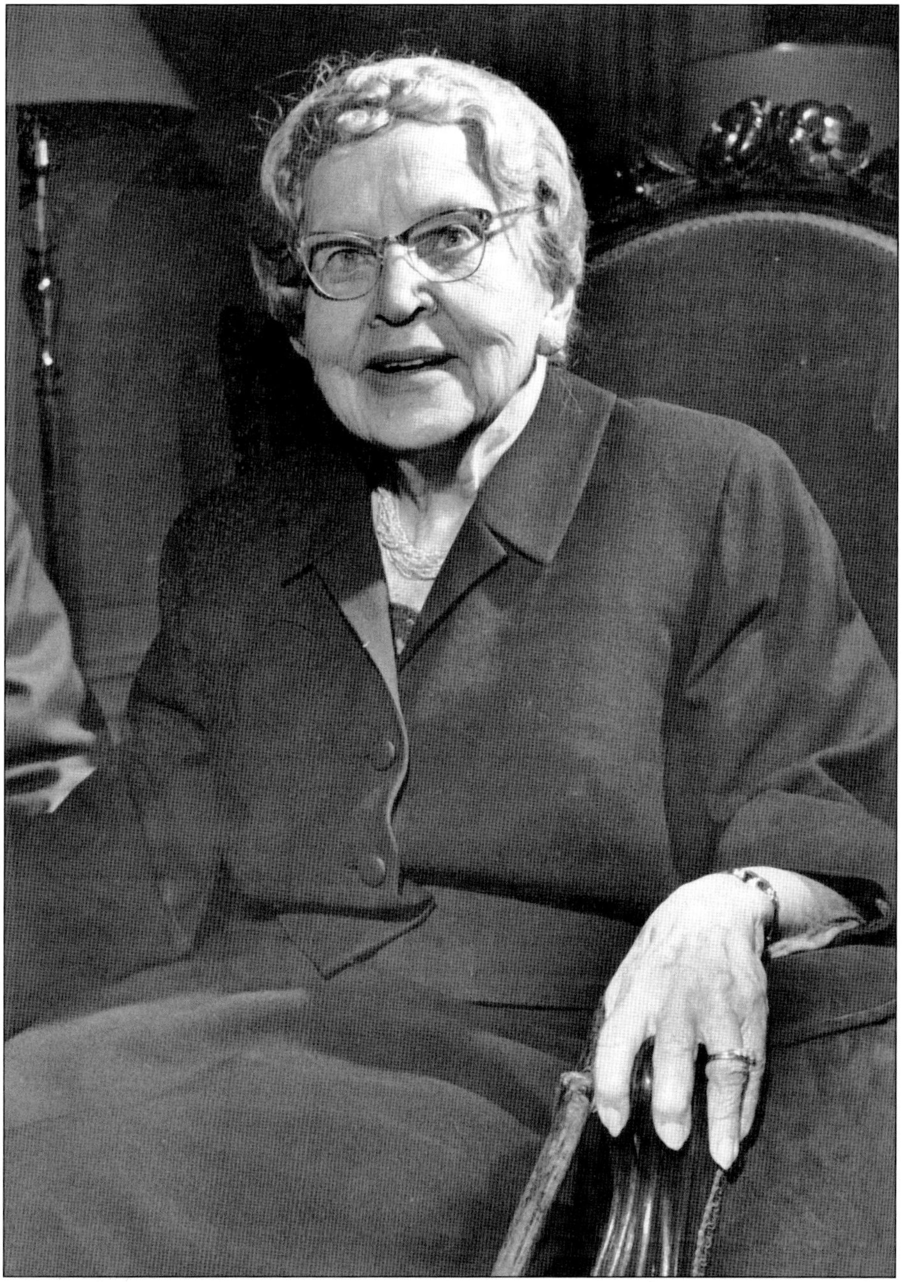

Carolee Shields was born in Sacramento in 1871. She met the future judge Peter Shields at a New Year's Eve party in 1900. Peter proposed to Carolee at McKinley Park just a few weeks later, and the two were married the following year. The couple would ultimately celebrate 61 years of marriage. Judge Shields reportedly never showed any interest in streetcars or buses and walked to work downtown every day for most of his 49 years on the bench. Carolee received her driver's license early on in their marriage and would drive Peter to their cattle ranch, where he grew up, as well as to civic events throughout the county. Carolee loved to garden and spent many hours tending to the trees and flowers in her yard. She continued to live in her Poverty Ridge home at 2009 Twenty-Third Street until passing away in 1971.

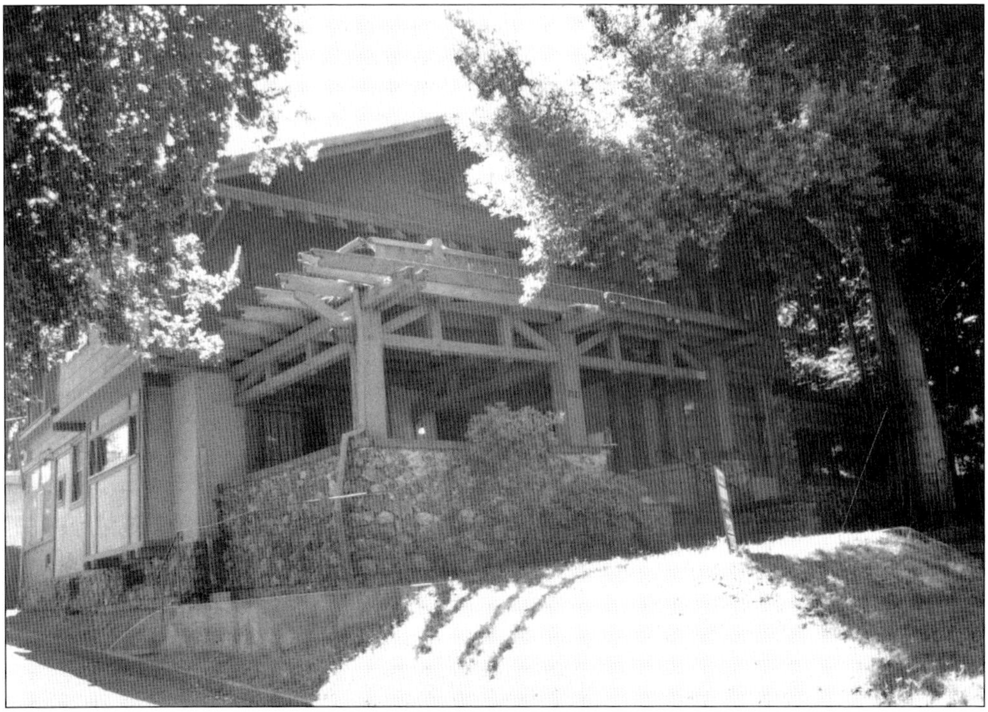

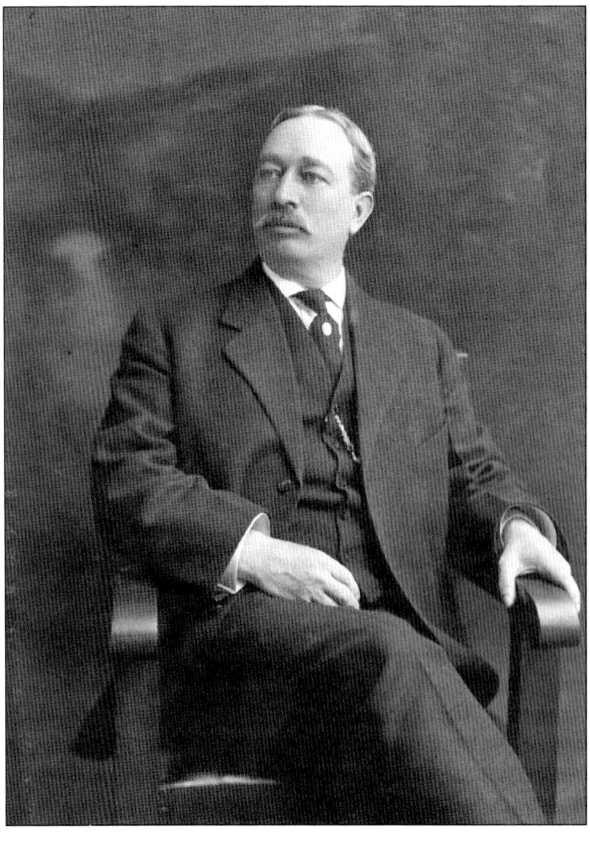

This Greene Brothers–style Craftsman bungalow at 2121 Twenty-First Street was built around 1911 for James and Kate Gillis. James Gillis was the California state librarian as well as the president of the California Library Association. After his death in 1917, the residence remained in the Gillis family. Their daughter Mabel, who also became California state librarian, lived in the home until her passing in 1961.

James Louis Gillis served as the 16th California state librarian from 1899 until his death in 1917. He felt strongly that the resources of the state library should be made more readily available to all Californians. In 1903, he created the Department of Traveling Libraries, which created over 200 mobile libraries with more than 10,000 volumes sent out across California. He also created the state library's Books for the Blind department. (Courtesy of CSL.)

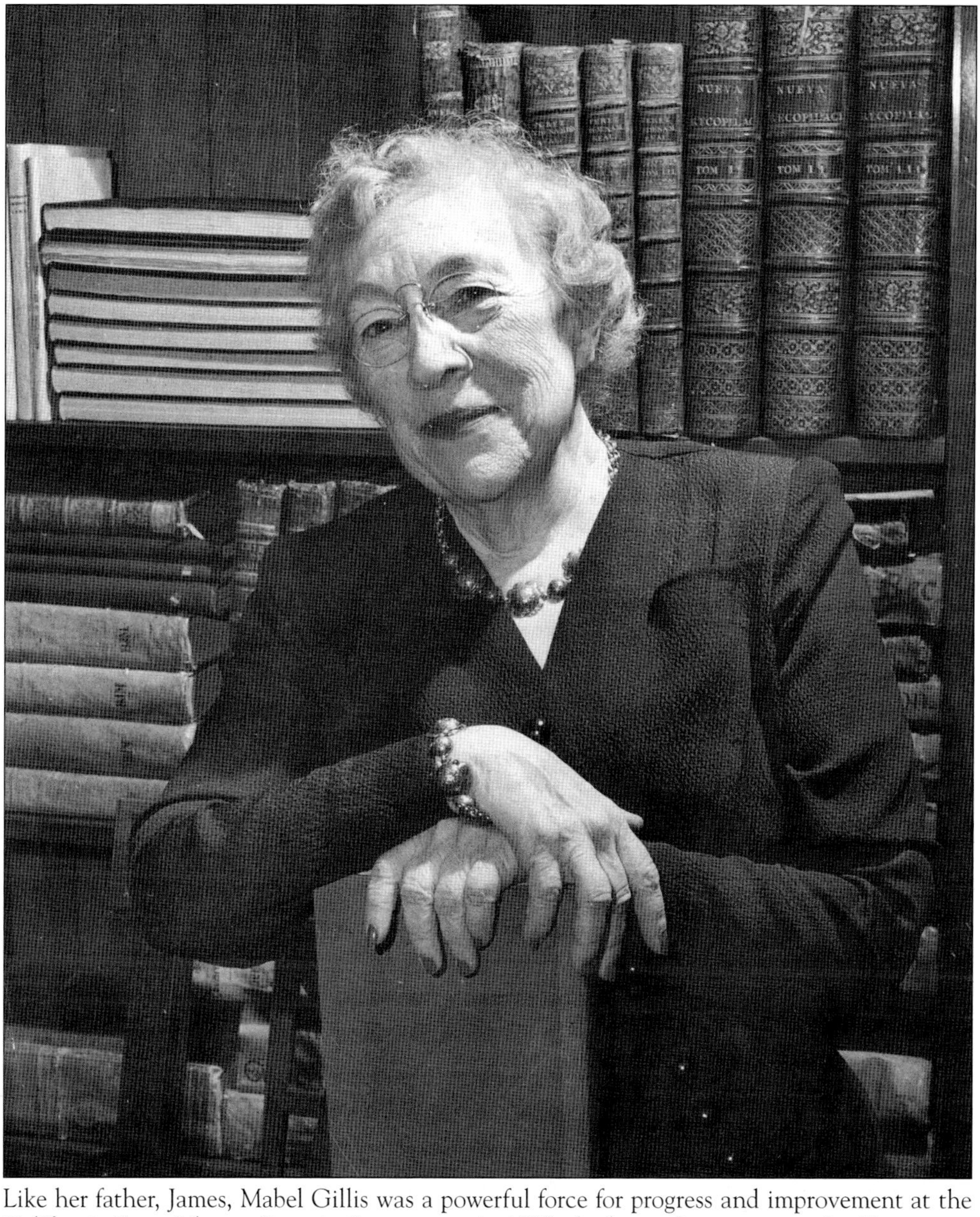

Like her father, James, Mabel Gillis was a powerful force for progress and improvement at the California State Library. Born in Sacramento in 1882, she began her tenure at the library as a young adult. After helping to establish services for visually impaired readers, she was assigned to lead the Books for the Blind department. In 1930, Gillis was appointed state librarian, the first woman to hold the post in state history. In this role, she shined as an example and a mentor to many young female professionals entering the state library system at the time. Expanding upon her father's work, Gillis organized annual conferences and introduced additional certifications for county library professionals statewide. She also improved the state library's catalog network, which for the first time allowed branches across California to share millions of books. At the local level, Gillis took a keen interest in collecting historic photographs from her neighbors in Poverty Ridge and archiving them in the state history department. Mabel Gillis retired in 1952 and spent the last decade of her life in the Gillis family home at 2121 Twenty-First Street. (Courtesy of CSL.)

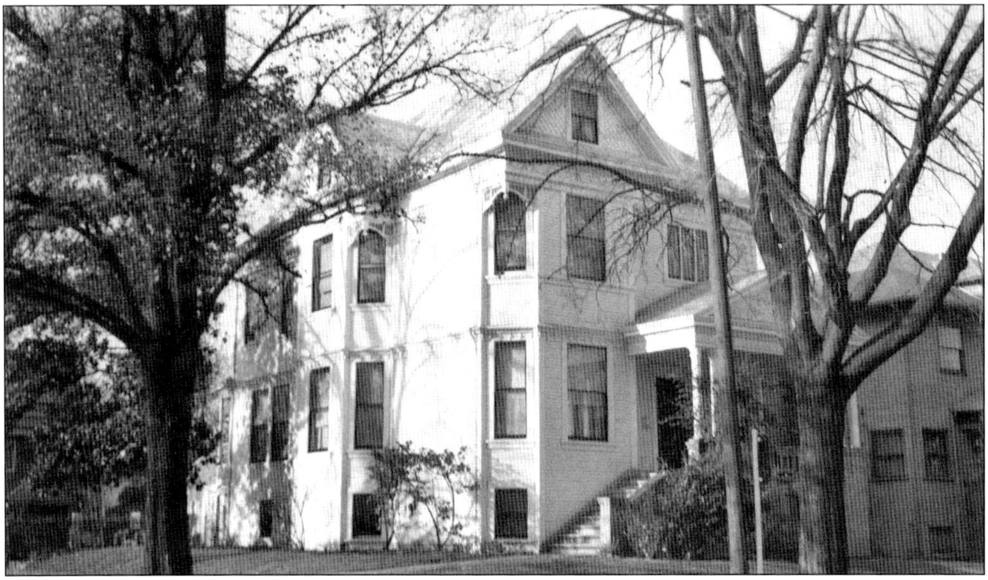

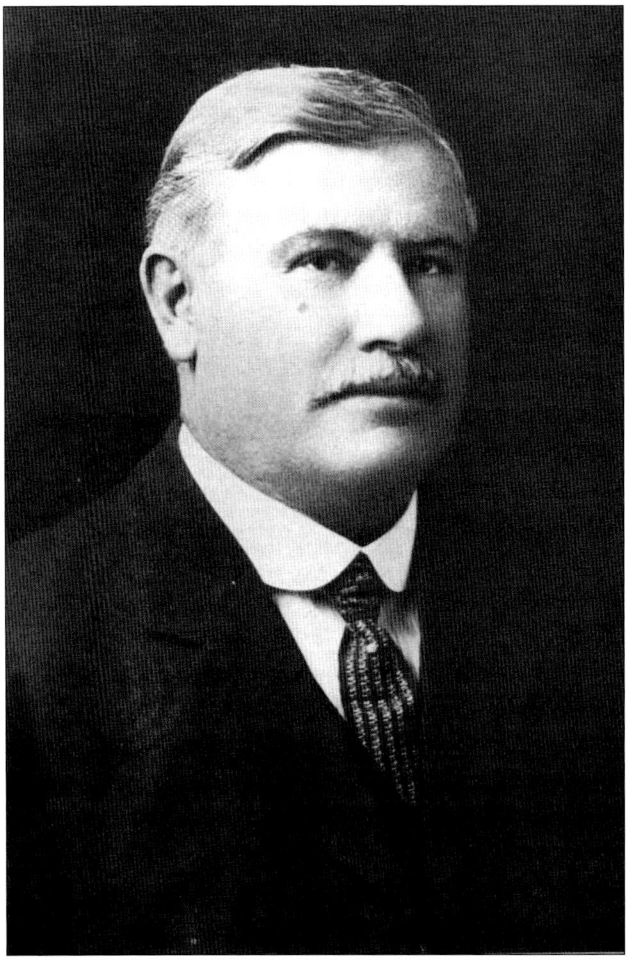

Built in 1897 for Dr. William F. Wiard, this Queen Anne–style home on the northwest corner of Twenty-Second and T Streets originally had the address of 1930 Twenty-Second Street. The address was later changed to 2131 T Street. Judge Charles McLaughlin purchased the home in 1907 and continued to reside there until 1931. The property was used in the 1970s to house the Sigma Phi Epsilon fraternity for California State University–Sacramento.

For many years, Judge Charles McLaughlin owned and lived in the Queen Anne–style home at 2131 T Street. (Courtesy of CSL.)

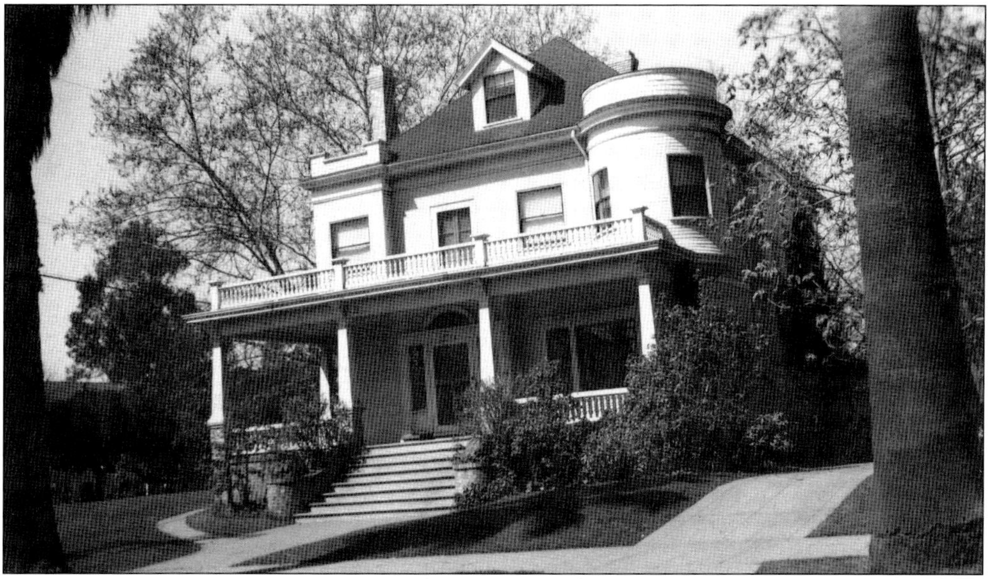

Between 1911 and 1913, A.E. Clark of the Morrill and Clark Building & Construction Company purchased land near the intersection of Twenty-First and W Streets and constructed this stately home at 2214 Twenty-First Street. Built as a blend of Colonial and Gothic Revival styles with Palladian elements, the architecture was likely intended to complement the impressive Grau family residence next door. Decades later, the original cupola was removed from the northern tower.

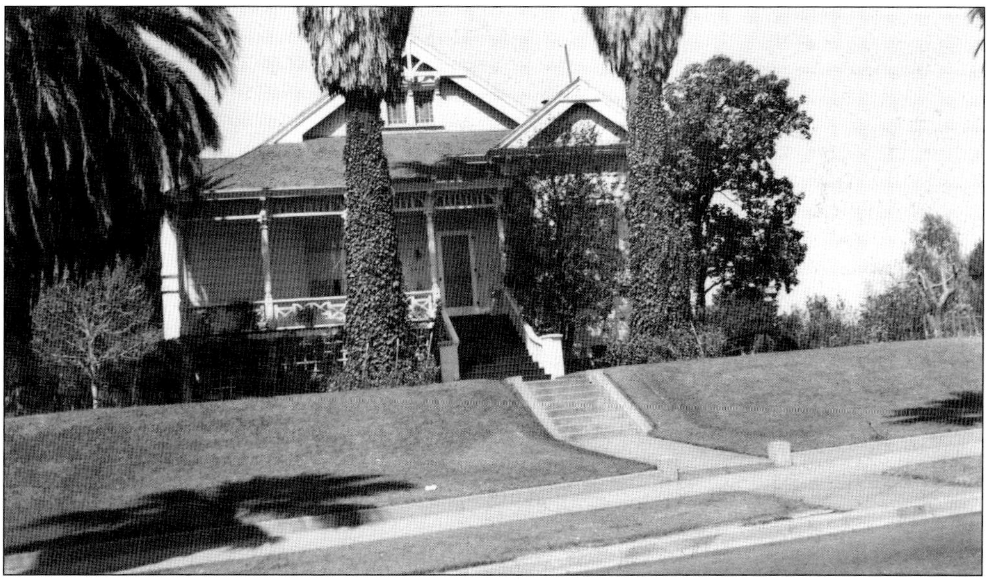

Upon his death in 1906, Gold Rush pioneer Fredrick Cox left the land he owned in Poverty Ridge to his two daughters, Jennie and Freda Cox. Both daughters married and built homes of their own on the land. Jennie Cox and her husband, George Peltier, lived at 2228 Twenty-First Street (pictured in 1940). After their passing, the home was inherited by the Peltiers' only daughter, Jeanette, and her husband, Byron Vandenberg. (Courtesy of CSL.)

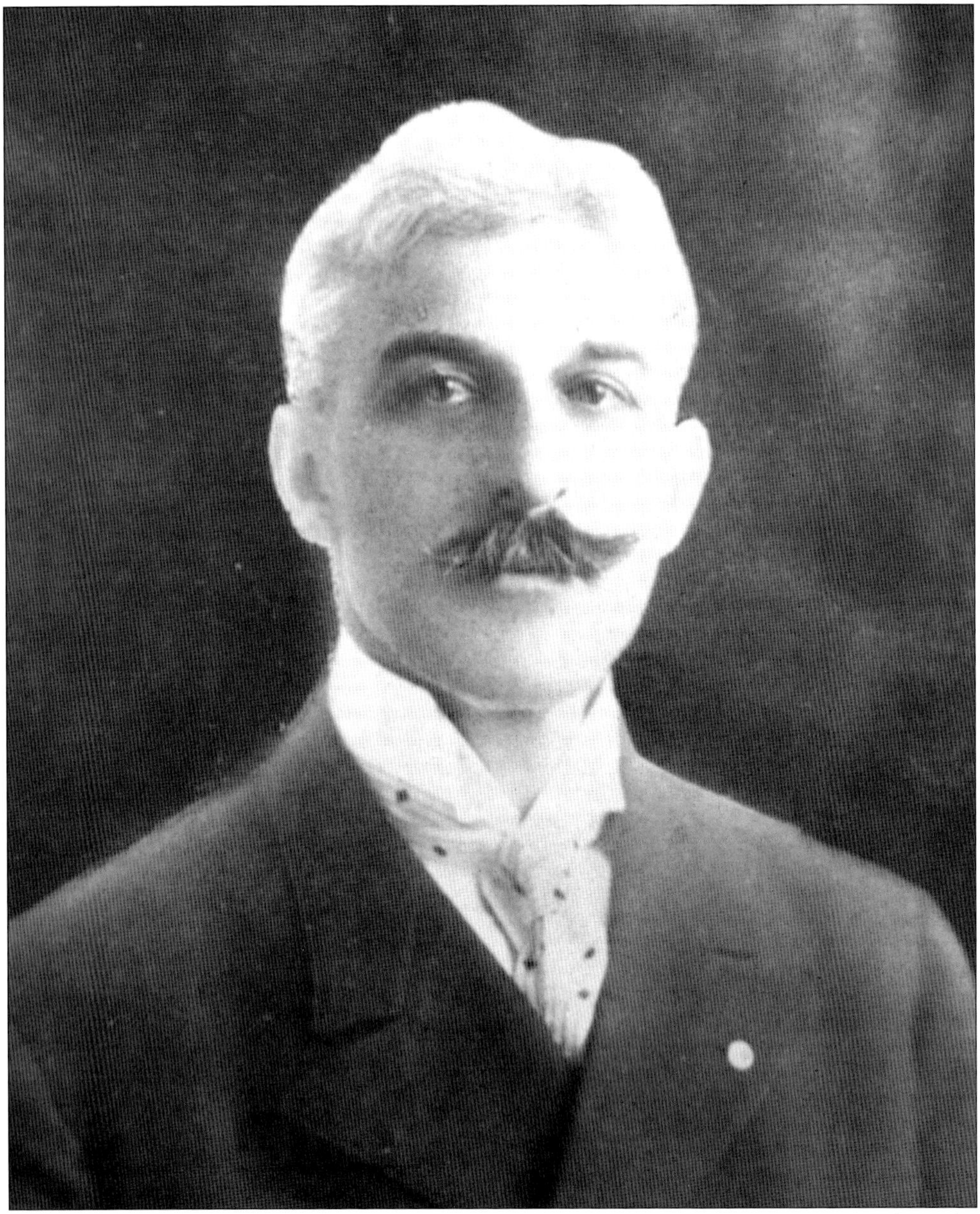

Jennie Cox married George Peltier in 1892 at the Cox family residence in Poverty Ridge. The new couple built their own home at 2228 Twenty-First Street on land deeded to Jennie by her father. George Peltier was one of the most active businessmen in Sacramento County at the turn of the 20th century, serving as the president of the Farmers and Mechanics Bank of Sacramento and vice president of the California National Bank. He owned a newspaper in addition to several local insurance and real estate companies. In 1923, Peltier built Sacramento's most famed movie palace, the Alhambra Theatre. The Peltiers were active philanthropists throughout their lives, and George directed and raised tens of thousands of dollars in relief funds on behalf of the Sacramento chapter of the American Red Cross. Jennie Peltier passed away in 1918, followed by George in 1938. The Peltiers left their home to their daughter Jeanette Peltier Vandenberg, who raised her own family there. (Courtesy of CSL.)

This c. 1912 stucco Craftsman bungalow at 2026 T Street was the home of Freda Cox Short and John Short. The Shorts built their home next door to Freda's childhood home and the residence of her parents, the late Senator Frederick Cox and his wife, Jennie Holdridge Cox. John and Freda named their home Sequoia and lived there until their deaths.

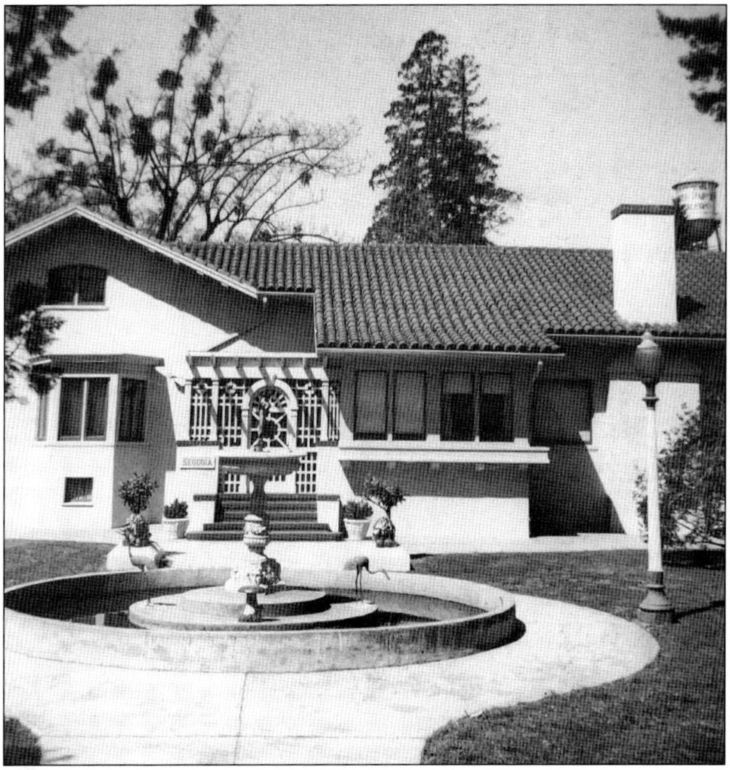

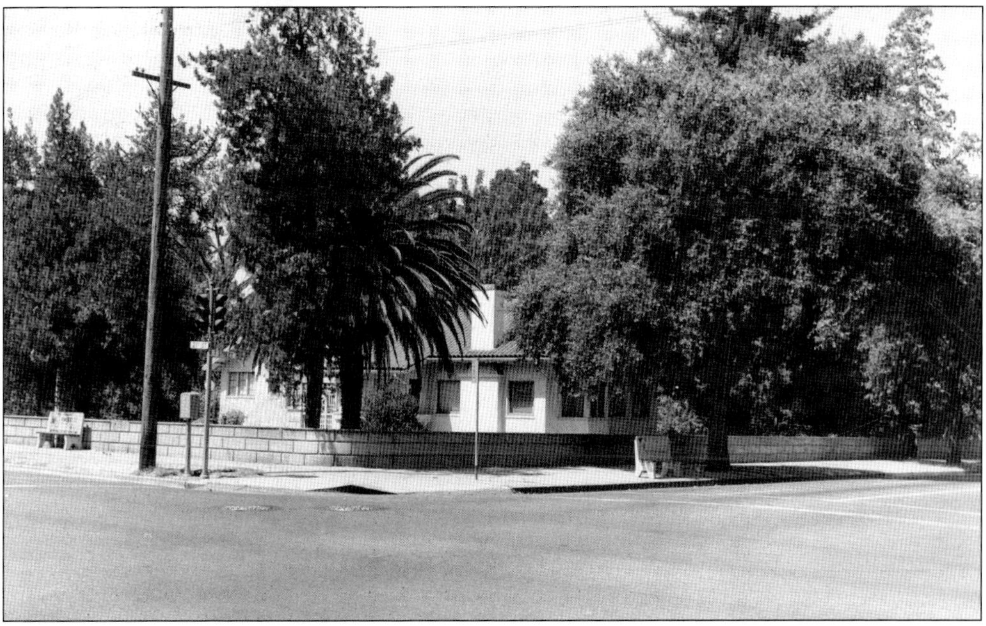

Shown here in 1956, the Cox-Short home was demolished in 1960 and the site turned into a state building. In more recent years, that building was replaced with a well-designed urban infill project known as Tapestri Square. Notice the historic wall surrounding the sunken gardens of the Short residence, portions of which remain standing today around the Tapestri Square brownstones. (Courtesy of CSL.)

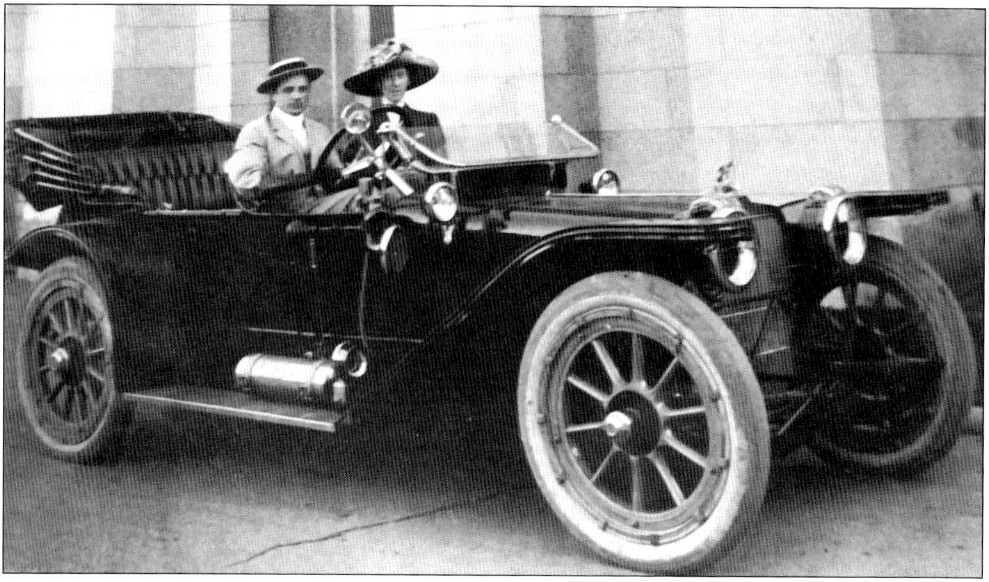

As adults, Freda Cox Short and her sister Jennie Cox Peltier built homes of their own in Poverty Ridge on the land they grew up on as the daughters of the late Senator Cox. Freda and her husband, John E. Short, a cattle rancher, are seen in this c. 1915 photograph of the couple on a road tour. (Courtesy of CSL.)

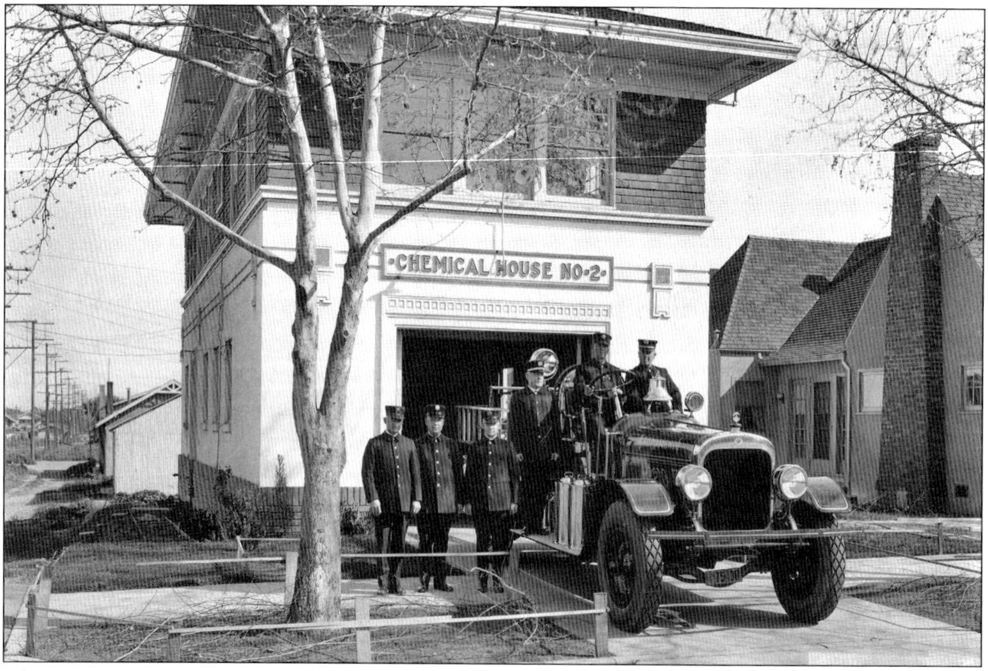

This c. 1925 image shows the Sacramento Fire Department's Chemical House No. 2 at 1917 Twenty-Second Street. Built around 1912, it was one of four chemical houses in the central city at the time. Chemical houses, which were smaller than fire engine houses, contained a mid-sized fire hose that would be attached to a horse-drawn or motorized chemical wagon utilizing soda-acid flame retardants to help control a fire until a larger engine with water hoses could arrive. (Courtesy of CSL.)

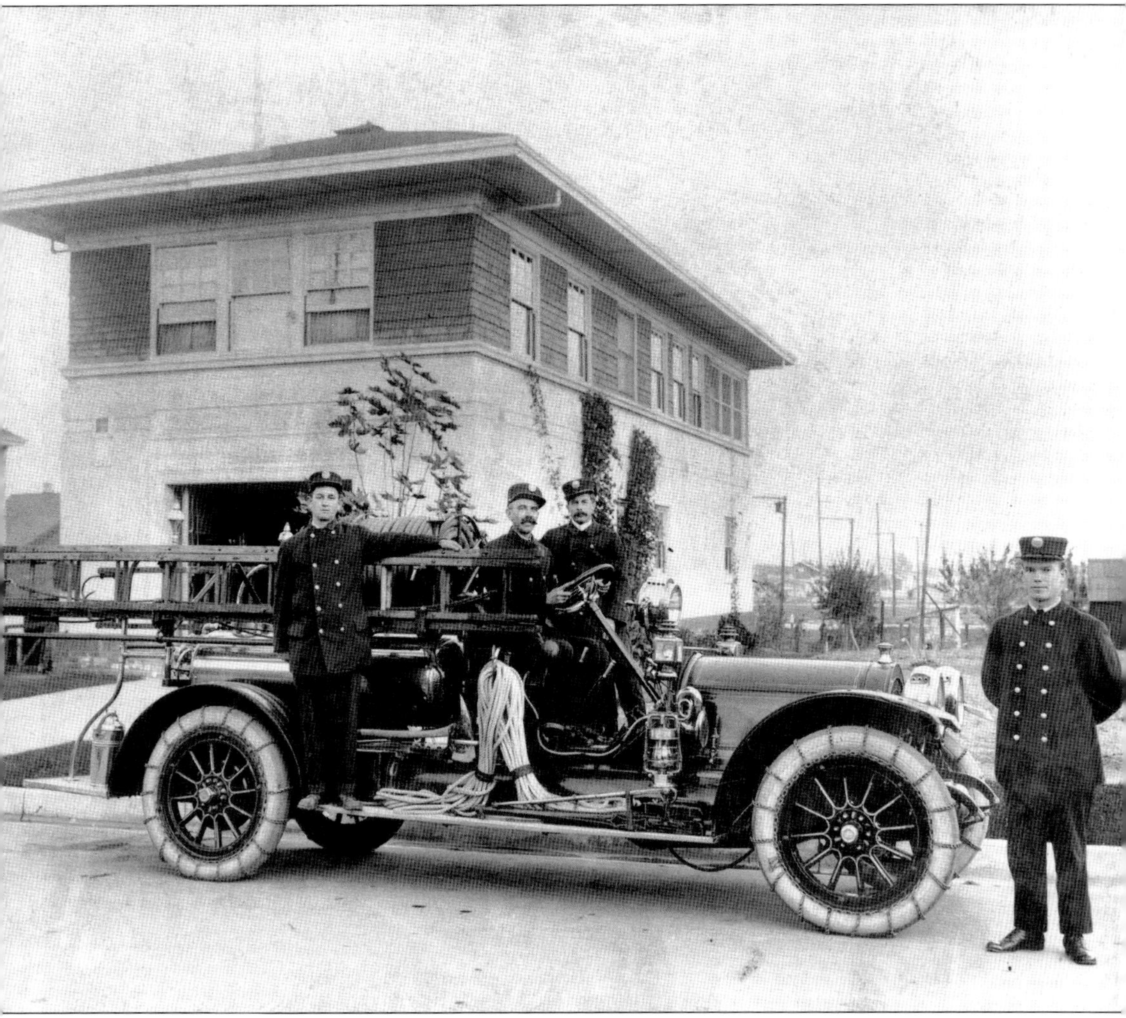

This image from 1918 shows Chemical House No. 2. at Twenty-Second and T Streets. As firefighting technologies improved through the decades, the need for chemical wagons began to decline. By the late 1940s and early 1950s, Chemical House No. 2 was no longer actively used for its original purpose.

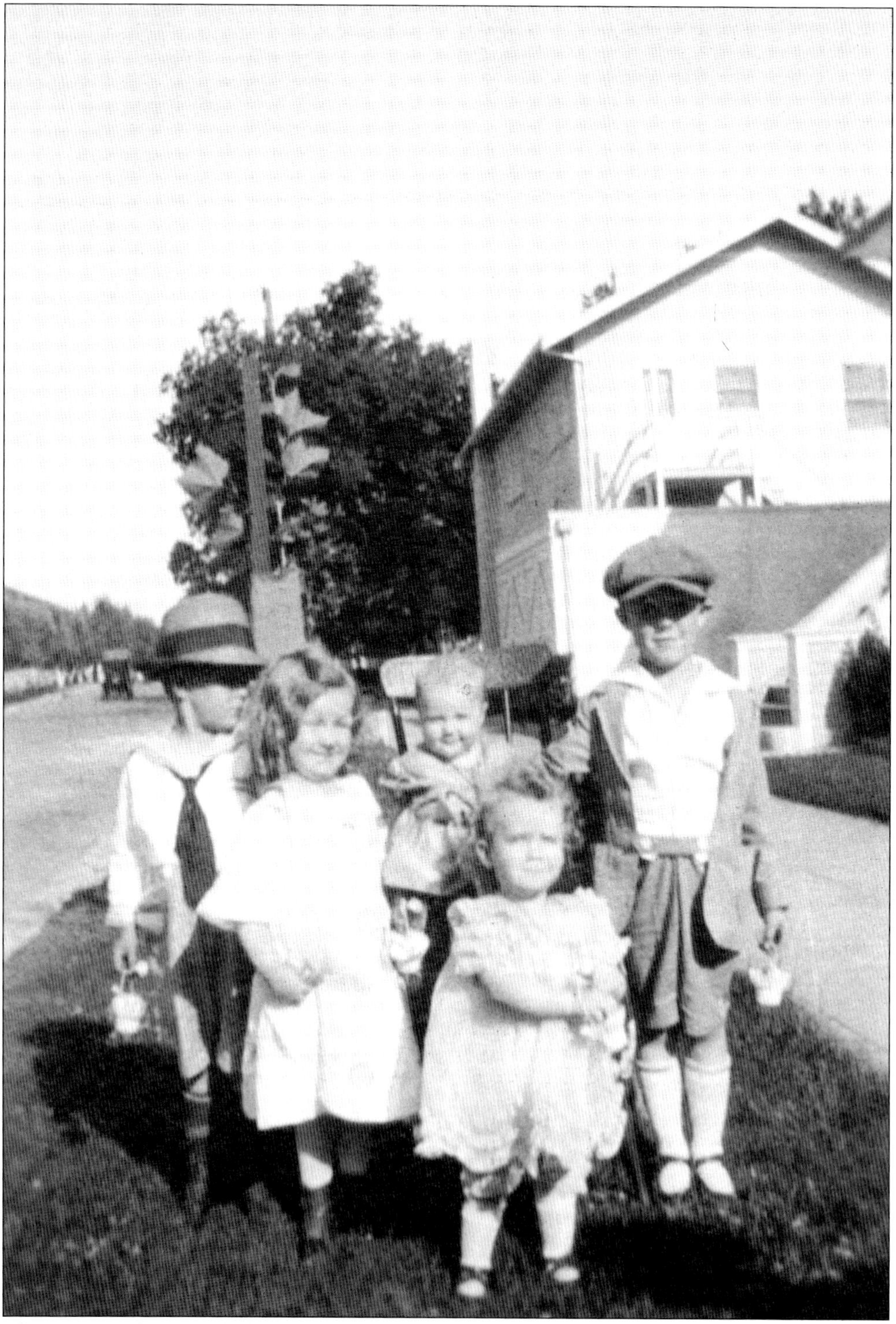

This c. 1923 photograph shows neighborhood children playing in front of the home of Bessie and Karl Bose at 2016 S Street. Three-year-old Bette Robinson is in the front. The back of 1900 Twenty-First Street can be seen in the background.

Four

NEWTON BOOTH, BORN OF A SIMPLE WOODEN SCHOOLHOUSE

In the last decade of the 19th century, working families with small farms dotted the southeast corner of the sparsely populated city grid immediately to the east of Poverty Ridge. Many of these families grew what they needed for themselves and sold surplus produce and poultry when and where they could for extra income.

The breadwinners of these mostly blue-collar households often worked industrial jobs for the railroad as well as for breweries, wineries, and factories along the nearby R Street corridor. The arrival of streetcar service in the 1890s between Sacramento's downtown and the newly developed Oak Park suburb to the southeast made it easier for residents of these neighborhoods to commute to jobs at the Southern Pacific Railroad Yards and other businesses near downtown (the Poverty Ridge and Newton Booth neighborhoods were roughly between Sacramento's downtown and Oak Park).

Notwithstanding developments like the new streetcars, there was limited transportation infrastructure in the areas south of R Street and east of Twenty-Second Street in the late 19th century. During the winter, long before there were almost any sidewalks or pavement in this area, the district was often flooded or mired in mud. The thick winter mud made it difficult for young children to walk to the closest school (Fremont School at Twenty-Fourth and N Streets), and most families in the area did not have the means to regularly buy their children streetcar fare. Parents began to petition city leaders for a schoolhouse.

In 1896, city officials responded by approving the construction of a small, wooden, two-room school at Twenty-Sixth and V Streets. In 1897, the simple schoolhouse was named in honor of California's 11th governor, Newton Booth. By the turn of the century, a reliable streetcar line, paired with a new school and adjacent industrial jobs along the R Street corridor, made the previously overlooked southeast corner of the city an exceptionally attractive place for working Sacramentans to build a home. From 1898 through 1920, the Newton Booth neighborhood, which came to be called after the school at its center, exploded with growth and became a lively and bustling neighborhood of young families pursuing the American Dream and seeking a bright future for their children. One such family—the Boyles, who lived at 2523 U Street—is heavily featured as reasonably representative of many working-class and, in a few cases, upper-middle-class families who called the emerging Newton Booth neighborhood home.

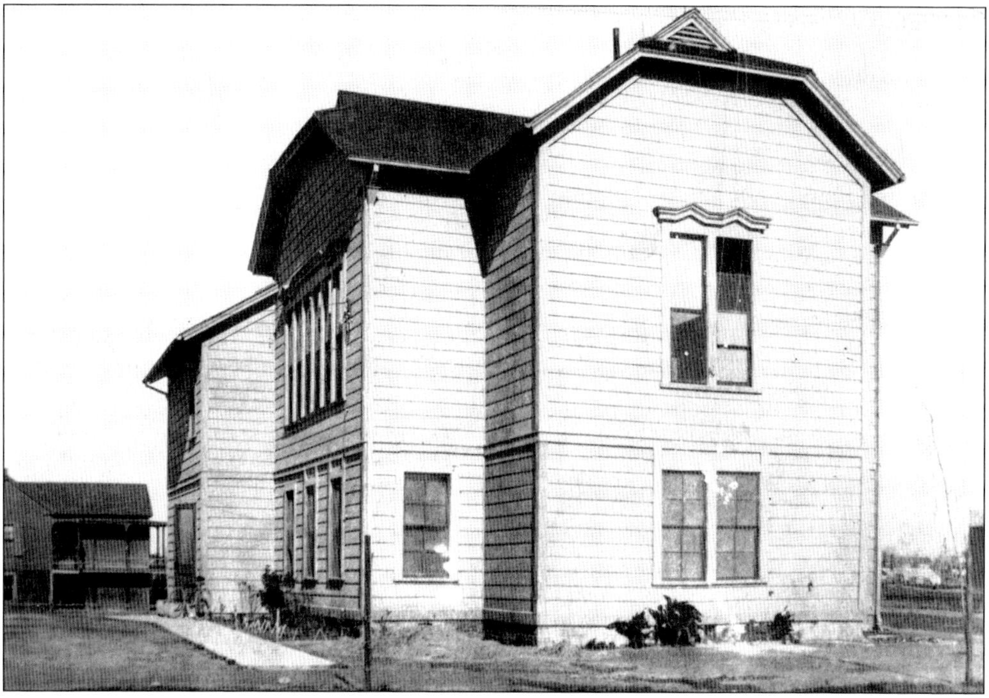

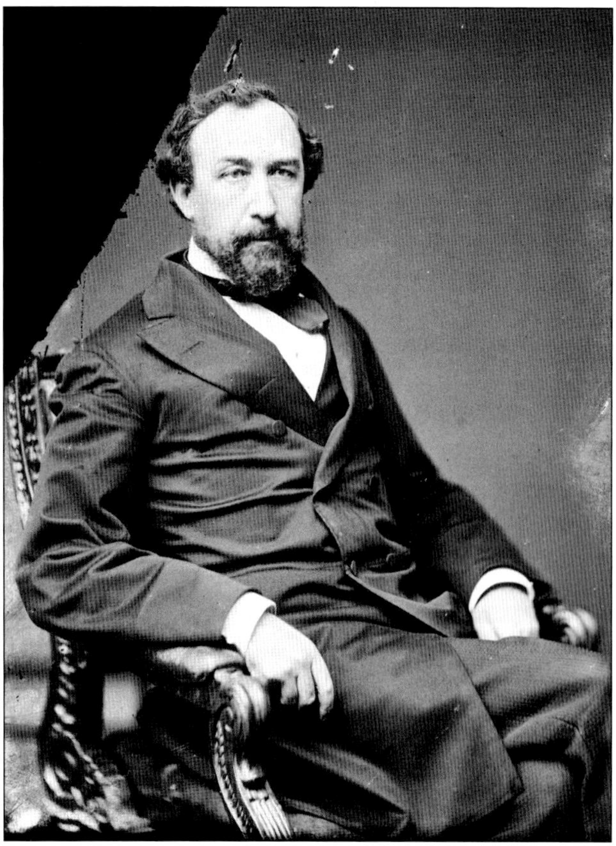

In the 1890s, several working-class families who ran small farms and were employed in industrial jobs at local factories advocated for a school to be built in the area east of Twenty-First Street and south of R Street. The city responded in 1896 by constructing a two-room, wood-framed schoolhouse. In 1897, a year after its founding, the school was christened in honor of California's 11th governor, Newton Booth.

The Newton Booth neighborhood was named for its school. Newton Booth arrived in California in 1850 freshly graduated from law school. Soon thereafter, he opened a wholesale grocery business at Front Street and quickly became one of the wealthiest merchants in the city. Booth was elected governor of California in 1871. (Courtesy of the Library of Congress.)

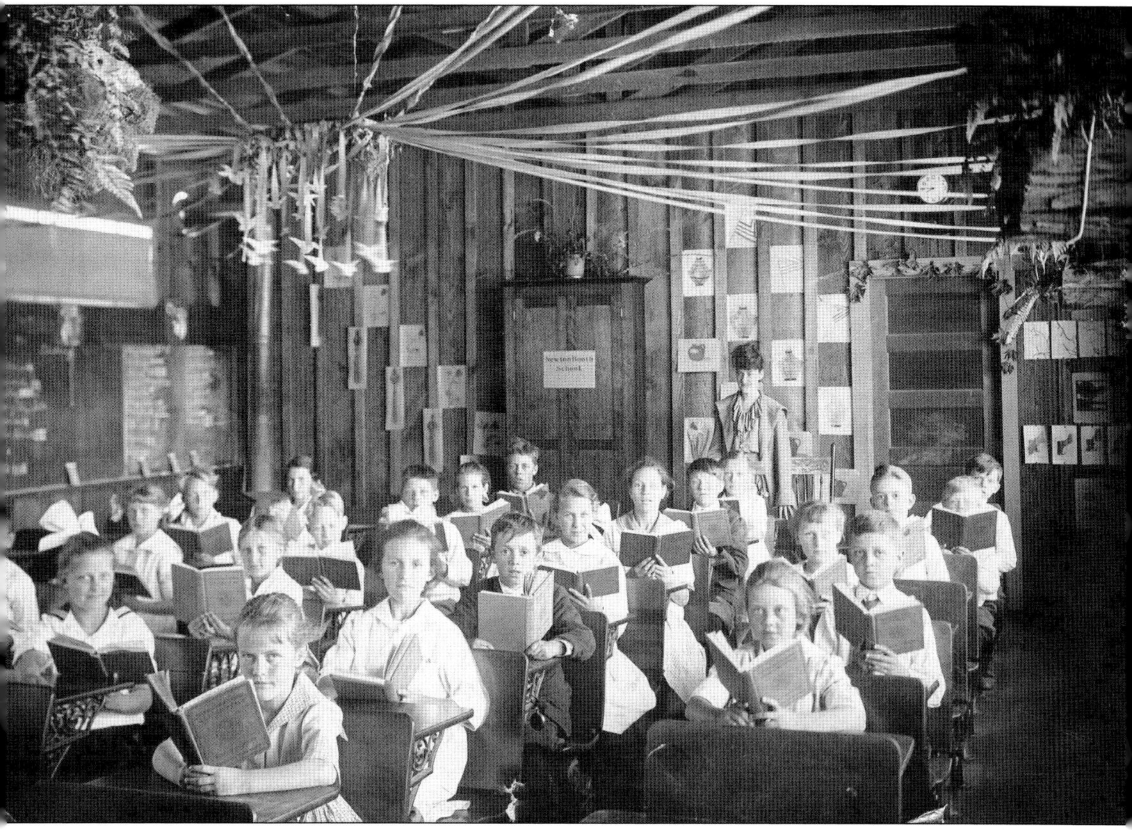

This c. 1917 photograph shows students posing with their textbooks inside the original Newton Booth School, which comprised two rooms. The first room was finished at the time of construction. The second room was left unfinished until enrollment warranted its finishing and service. The teacher standing at the back of the classroom is believed to be Helen Margaret Howe, a fourth-generation educator and the daughter of renowned educator E.P. Howe Jr., who lived at Twenty-First and V Streets. The Newton Booth School served children from the Newton Booth, Poverty Ridge, and adjacent neighborhoods.

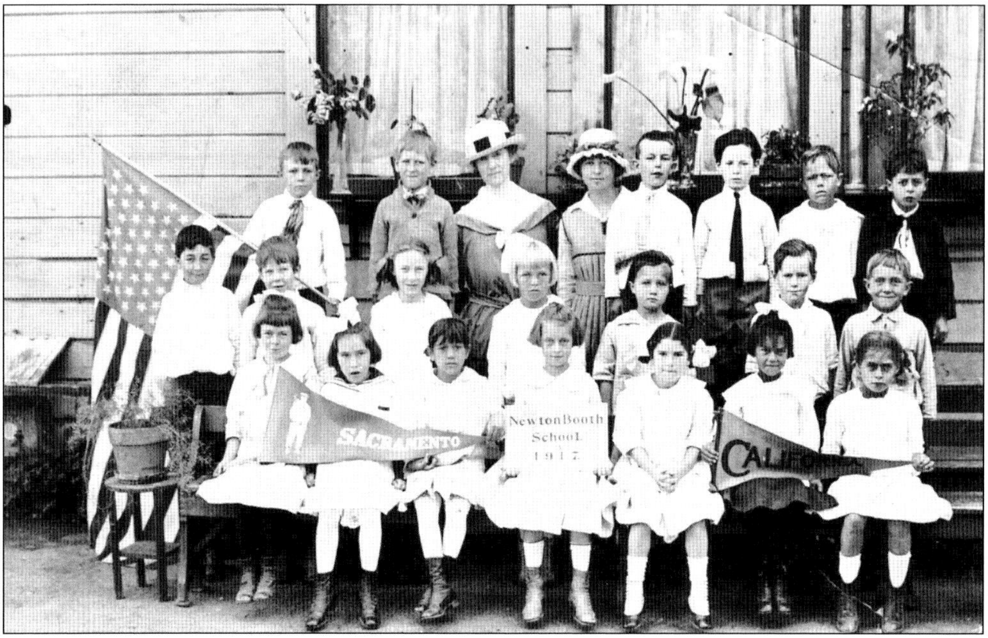

This c. 1917 class photograph features elementary students from the original two-room Newton Booth School. Edgar Boyles Jr., second from right in the second row, lived with his family in the neighborhood at 2523 U Street. He and his two sisters attended Newton Booth School. (Courtesy of Chris Boyles David.)

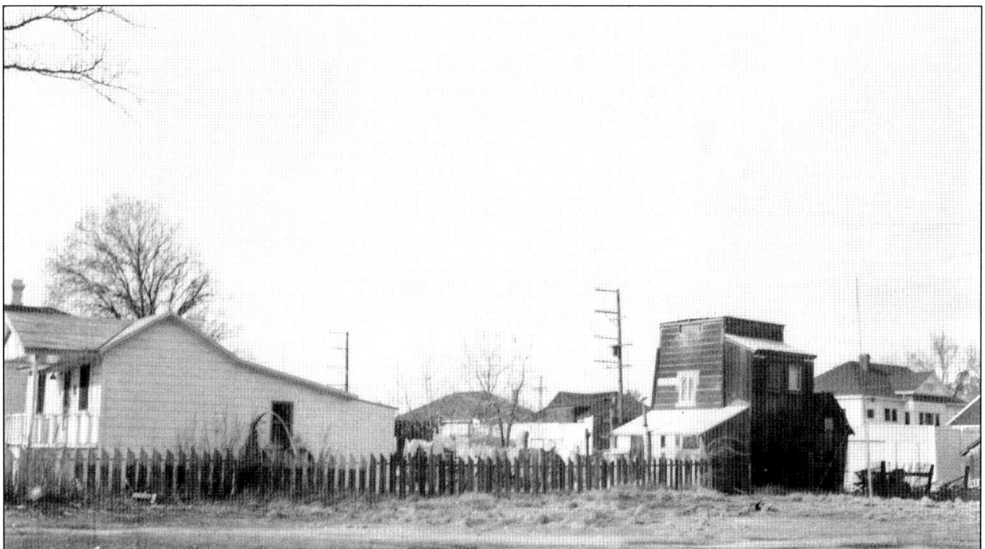

This c. 1939 streetscape shows the remnants of a late-19th-century home with adjacent auxiliary buildings and a water tower that once stood on the northwest corner of Twenty-Eighth and V Streets. In the late 19th century, most families living in the sparsely populated southeast corner of the central city built homes on deep lots and developed small barns, stables, carriage houses, animal pens, and gardens behind the homes.

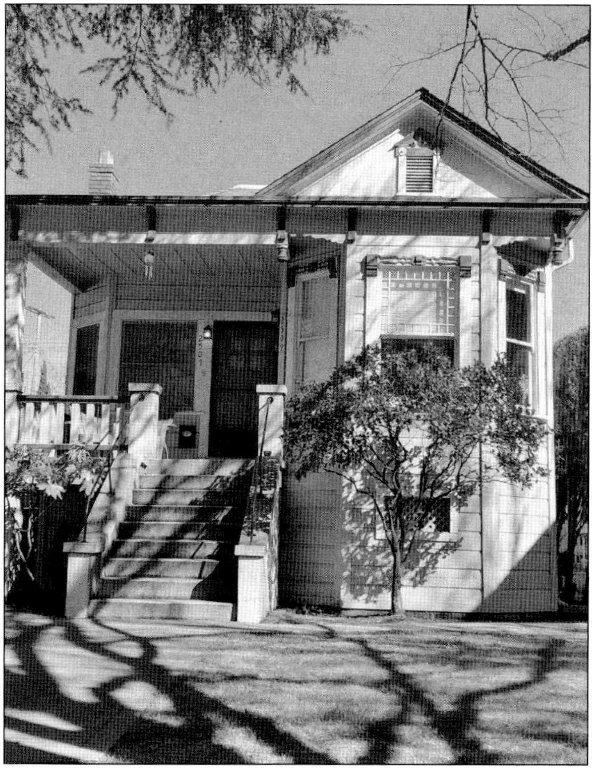

This Queen Anne–style worker's cottage at 2507 W Street was built around 1892 by William and Estelle Uhl. Like many families who operated small farms in the neighborhood in the late 19th century, the Uhls raised poultry for sale on their property. William worked as a blacksmith for the Southern Pacific Railroad and later became a firefighter. All three Uhl children attended the early wooden Newton Booth School. Both Uhl daughters later taught at Newton Booth School. (Author's collection.)

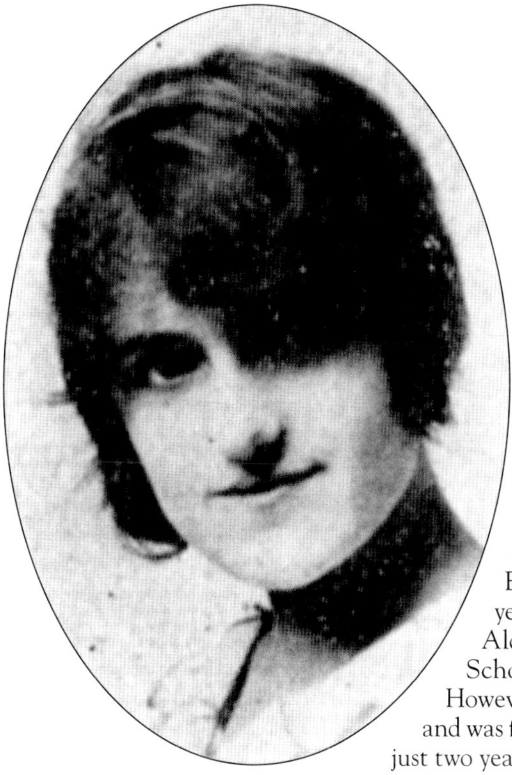

Alda Uhl was the second of William and Estelle's three children. Pictured in her 1914 yearbook photograph at Sacramento High School, Alda later became a teacher at Newton Booth School and continued to live with her parents. However, around 1920, she contracted tuberculosis and was forced to retire from teaching until her passing just two years later. (Courtesy of the Sacramento Room.)

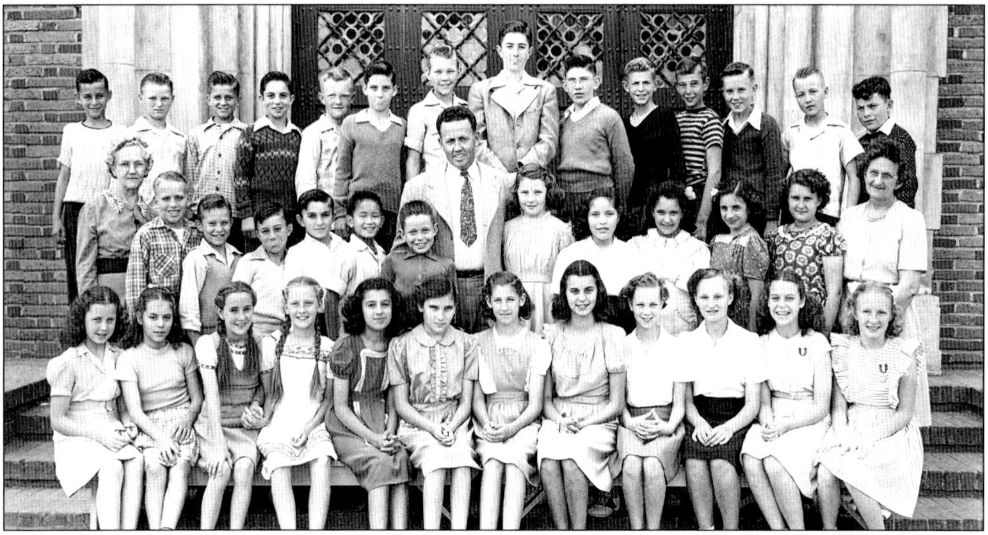

Vivian Uhl Yost is pictured at far right in the second row of this 1946 Newton Booth School class photograph. She was the oldest child of William and Estelle Uhl of 2507 W Street. Like her younger sister Alda, she was also a graduate and a teacher of Newton Booth School. In 1913, Vivian married a young, well-known rancher by the name of Wilfred Yost.

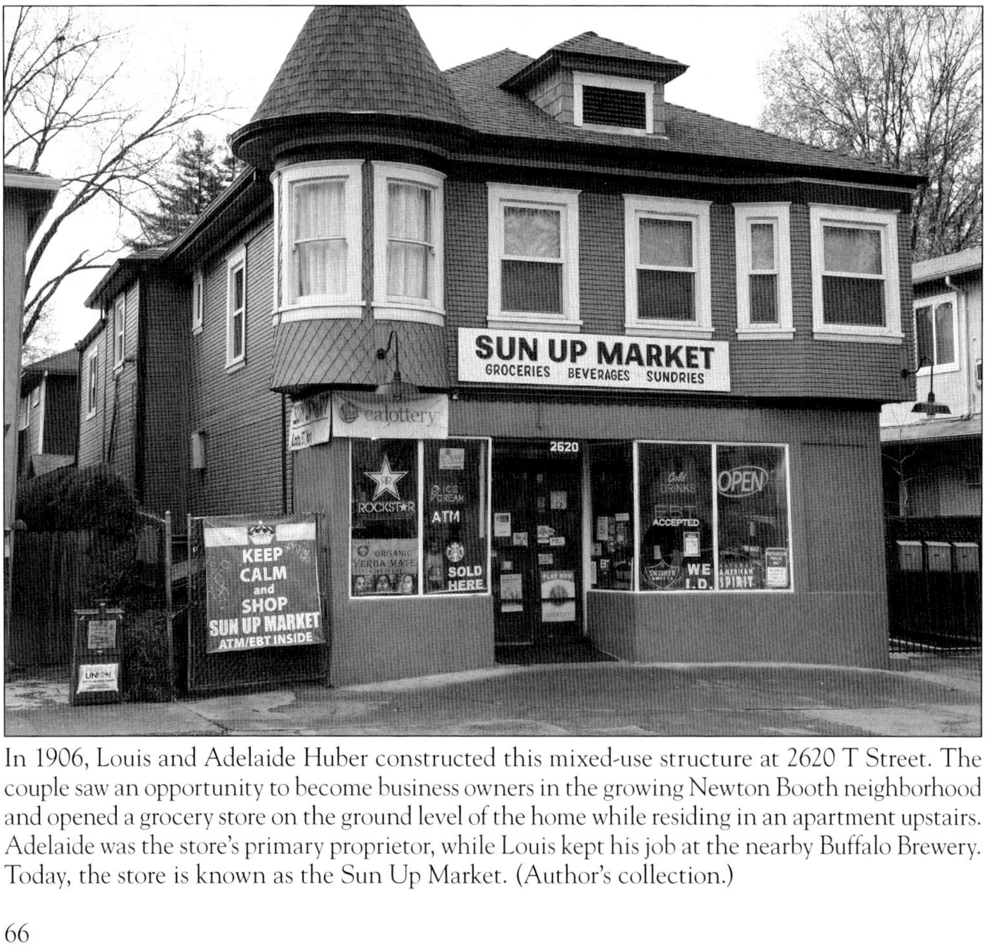

In 1906, Louis and Adelaide Huber constructed this mixed-use structure at 2620 T Street. The couple saw an opportunity to become business owners in the growing Newton Booth neighborhood and opened a grocery store on the ground level of the home while residing in an apartment upstairs. Adelaide was the store's primary proprietor, while Louis kept his job at the nearby Buffalo Brewery. Today, the store is known as the Sun Up Market. (Author's collection.)

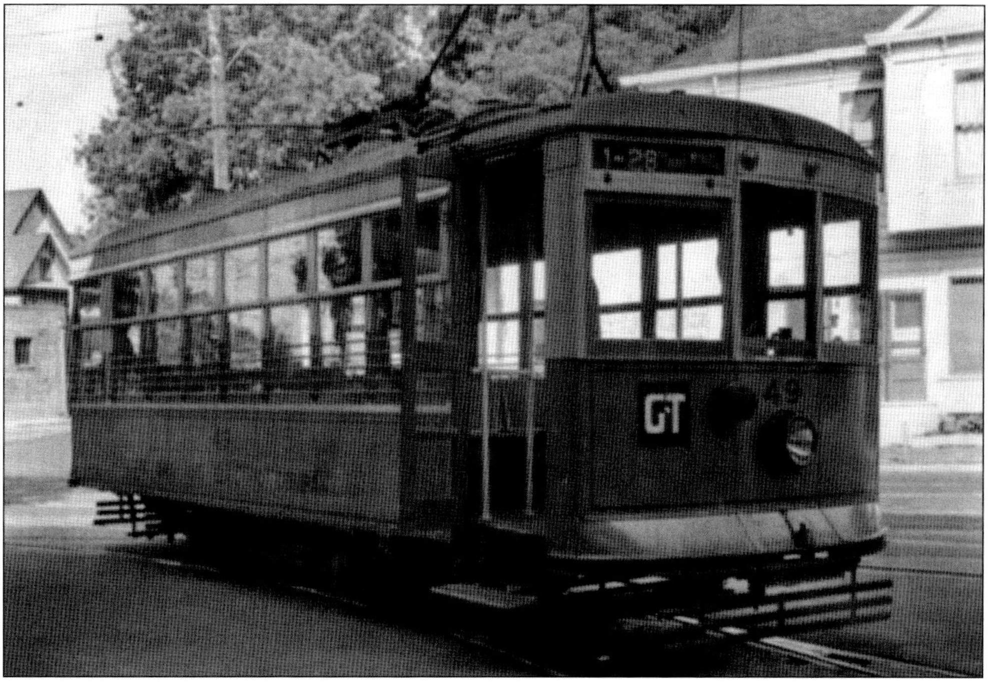

In the 1890s, streetcars arrived in Sacramento, helping to fuel growth in the southeastern portion of the city. In 1906, Pacific Gas & Electric (PG&E) acquired the Sacramento Electric, Gas, and Railway Company, making Sacramento the only city in California to have streetcars owned and operated by PG&E. The neighborhood route ran along Twenty-Eighth Street, the eastern edge of Newton Booth, and Twenty-First Street, through Poverty Ridge. (Courtesy of WRM.)

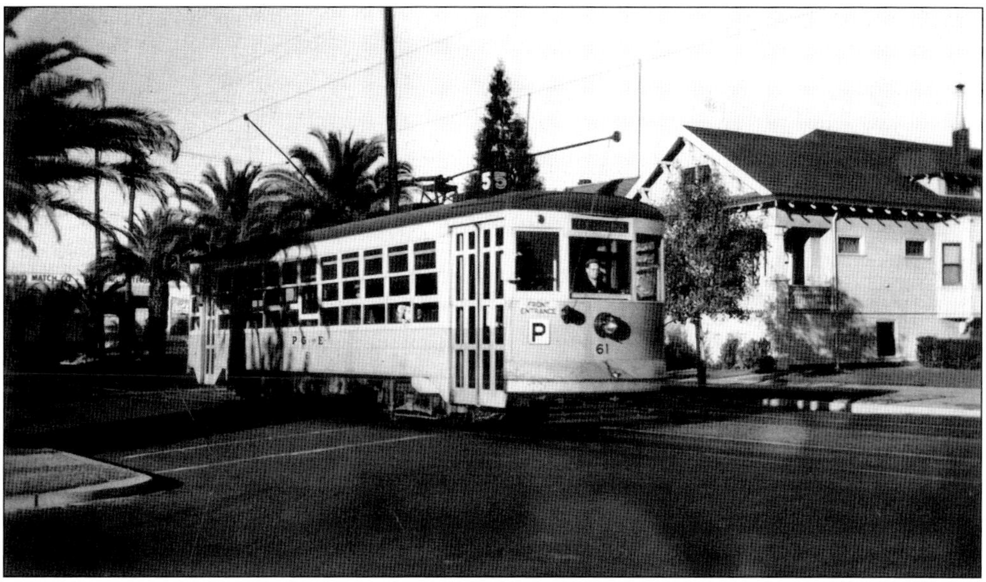

This c. 1937 photograph shows PG&E streetcar No. 61 headed south on Twenty-Eighth Street as it approaches S Street. For the first several decades of the 20th century, streetcars played an integral role in the development of the Newton Booth neighborhood, allowing area residents to more easily commute to their jobs in or near downtown Sacramento. (Courtesy of WRM.)

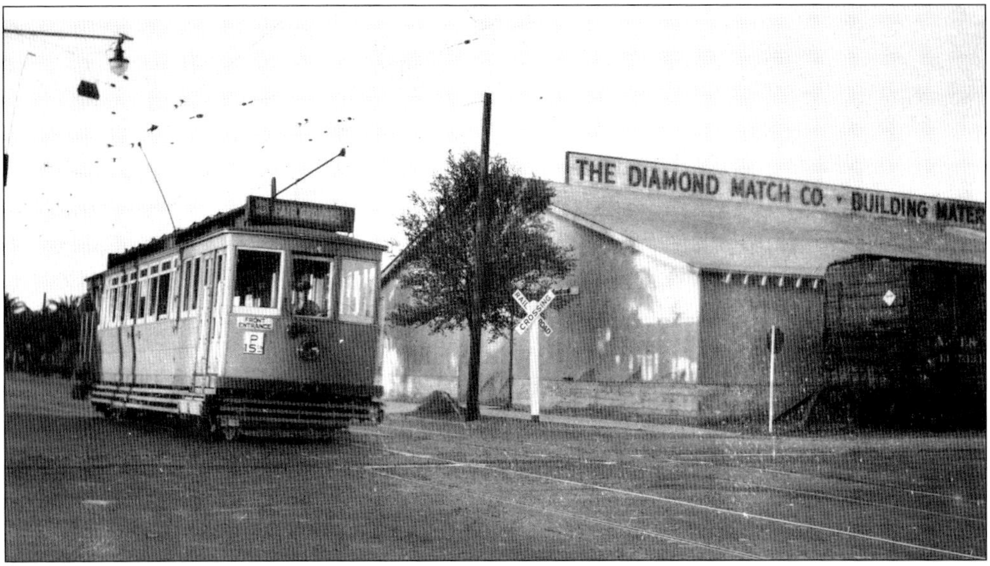

This c. 1943 photograph shows PG&E streetcar No. 20 at Twenty-Eighth and R Streets as it crosses the Southern Pacific mainline. The Diamond Match Company was one of several businesses along the industrial R Street corridor that provided employment to Newton Booth residents. (Courtesy of WRM.)

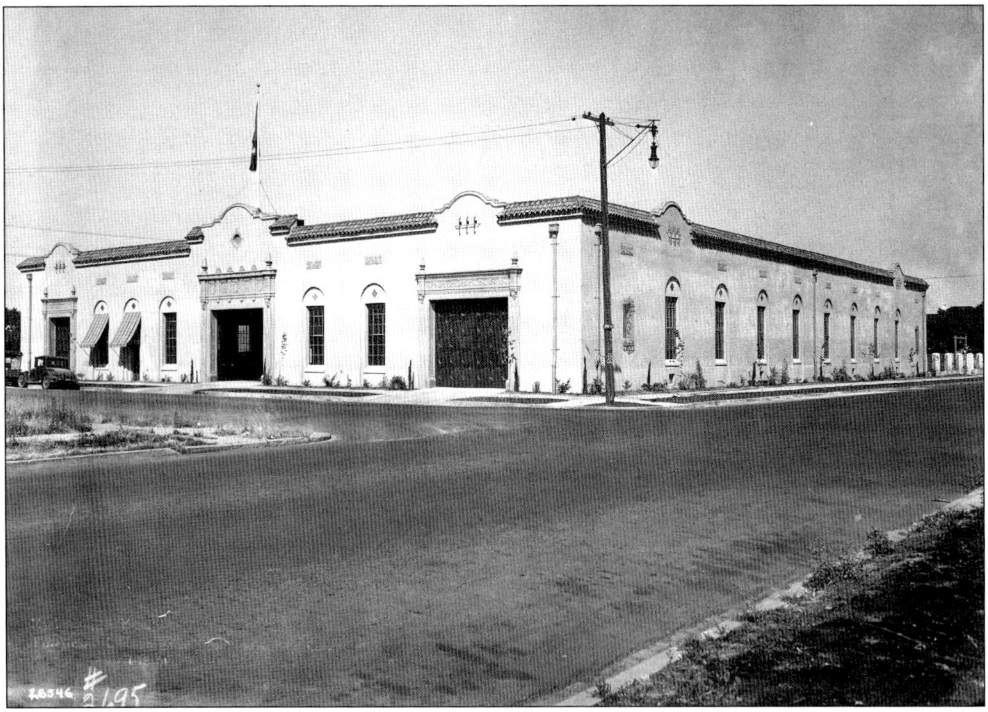

The Pacific Bell Telephone & Telegraph yard at 1821 Twenty-Fourth Street was built during the early 1920s in the Mission Revival style, which was popular during the development of Newton Booth. The building also provided jobs to neighborhood residents and represented the industrial nature of the adjacent R Street corridor. Today, the building serves as the hub for AT&T's Sacramento fleet operations. (Courtesy of CSL.)

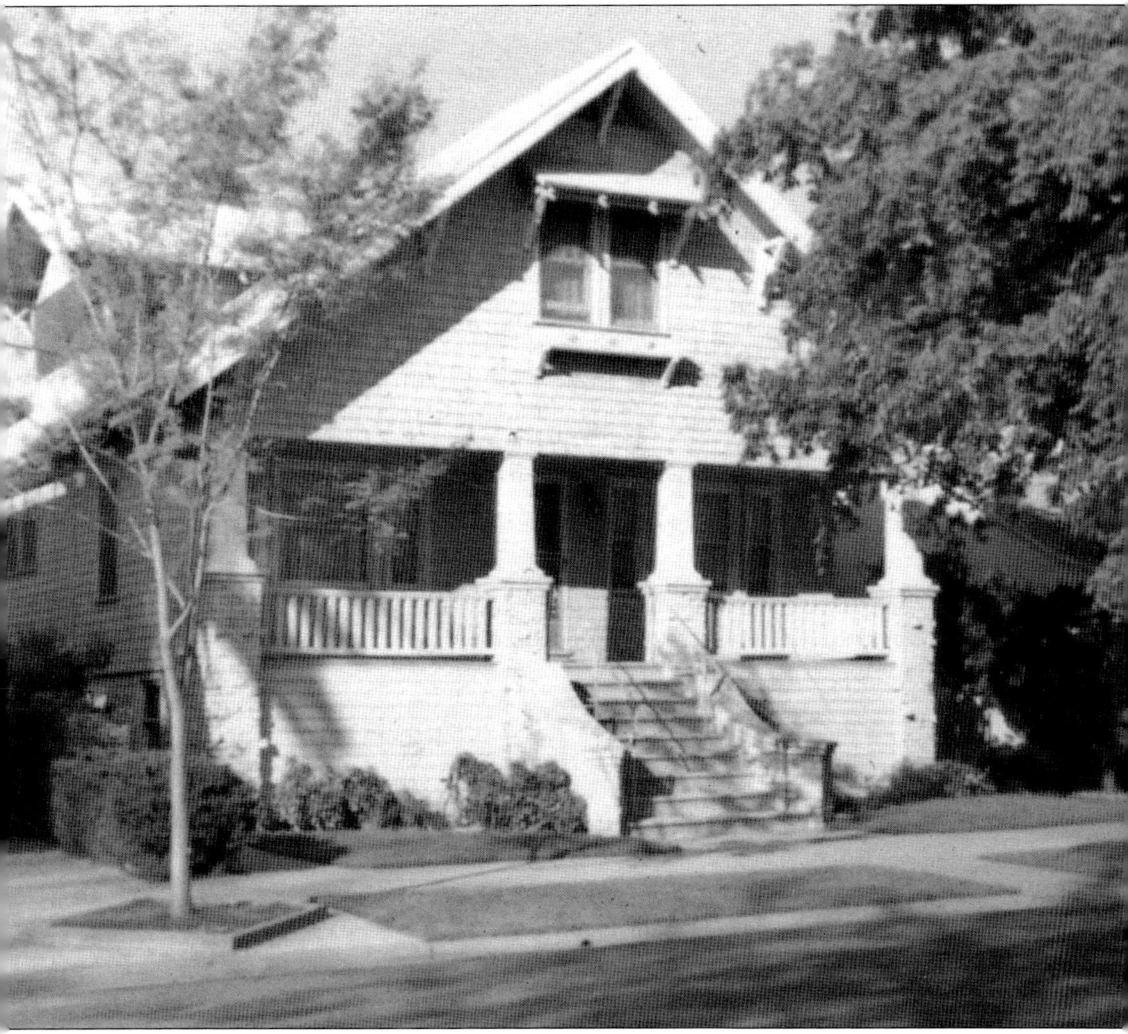

The Arts and Crafts–style home at 2523 U Street was constructed between 1908 and 1912. In 1914, Edgar and Eva Boyles purchased the property and moved in with their two children. Their youngest daughter, Birdie, was born just two years later in an upstairs bedroom. Over the next 90 years, three generations of the Boyles family would occupy the home. (Courtesy of Chris Boyles David.)

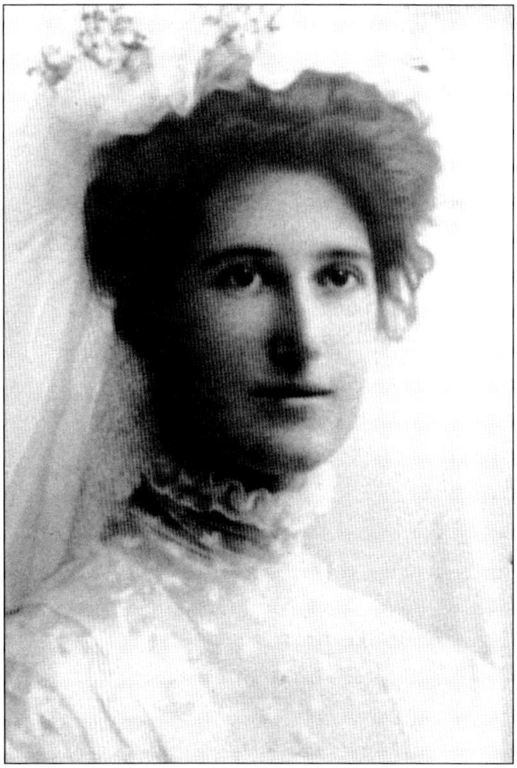

Eva Montfort Boyles came from a family of pioneers who settled in Sacramento in 1849. Pictured in her wedding photograph from 1908, she married Edgar Boyles and settled four years later at 2523 U Street in Newton Booth. They had three children: Edgar Jr., Marian, and Birdie. In 1922, Eva, who had been ill since Birdie was very young, passed away, leaving Edgar Sr. to raise their three children alone. (Courtesy of Chris Boyles David.)

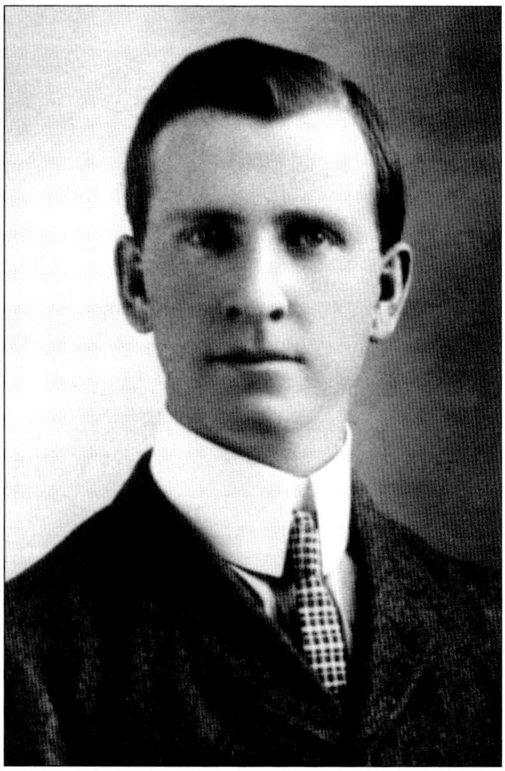

Edgar Amos Boyles, a successful pear grower and manager of the Sacramento River Association (a pear-growing collaborative), was born to a pioneer family in Butte County. After his wife's premature death in 1922, he continued to raise the couple's children in their home at 2523 U Street. All three Boyles children were graduates of the Newton Booth School. Edgar continued to live in the home until his death in 1945. (Courtesy of Chris Boyles David.)

This c. 1918 photograph shows Eva Montfort Boyles holding her two-year-old daughter Birdie on the porch of the family residence at 2523 U Street in Newton Booth. Eva fell ill in the years immediately following Birdie's birth, passing away in 1922. (Courtesy of Chris Boyles David.)

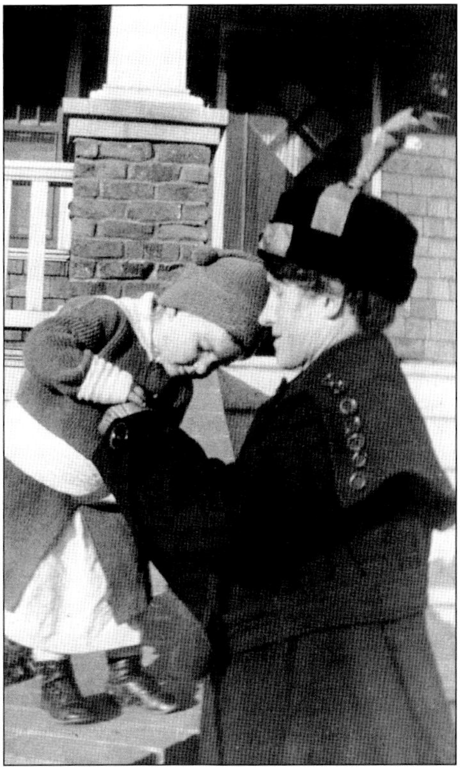

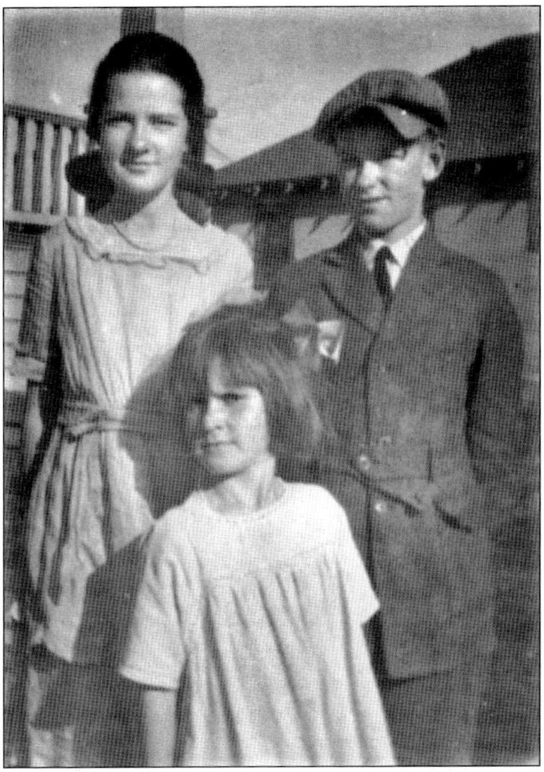

This c. 1921 photograph was taken in front of the Boyles home at Twenty-Sixth and U Streets The three Boyles children are, from left to right, Marian, Birdie, and Edgar Jr. (Courtesy of Chris Boyles David.)

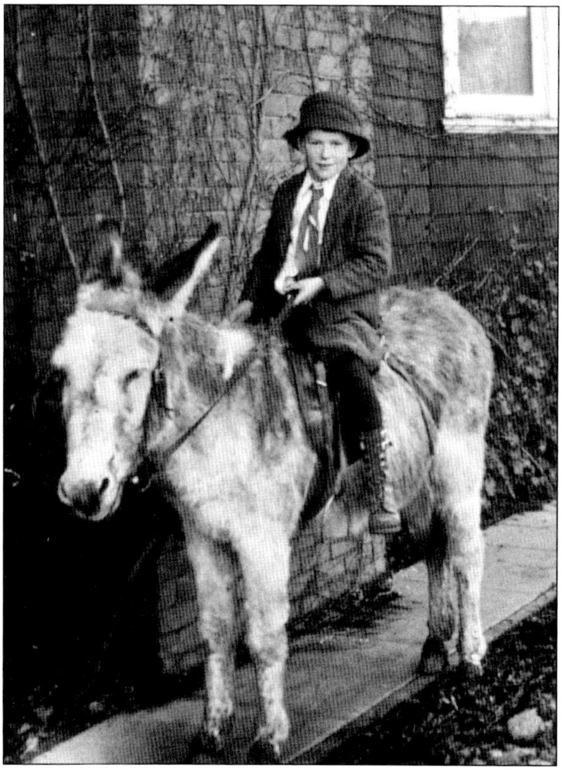

These c. 1920 photographs show Edgar Boyles Jr. (left) and Marian Boyles (below) in the side yard of their Newton Booth home. It was not uncommon for enterprising photographers to go door-to-door and solicit neighborhood residents for photo sessions featuring their children mounted on donkeys or riding in carts hitched to a goat. (Both, courtesy of Chris Boyles David.)

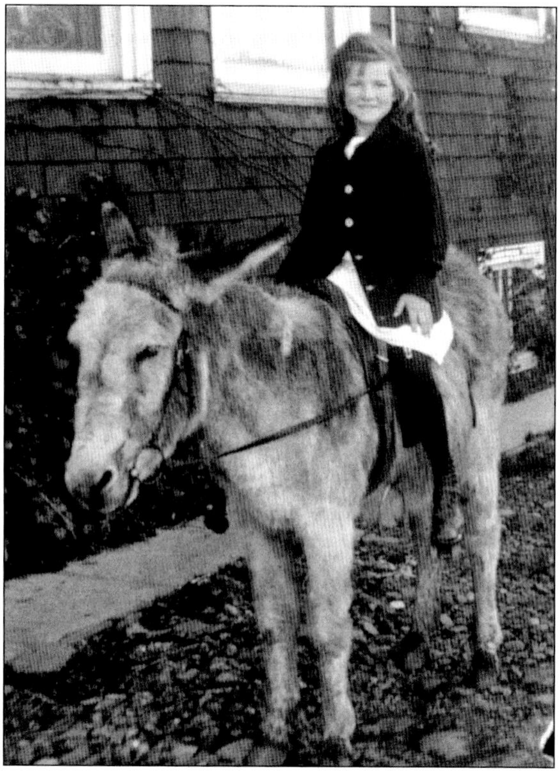

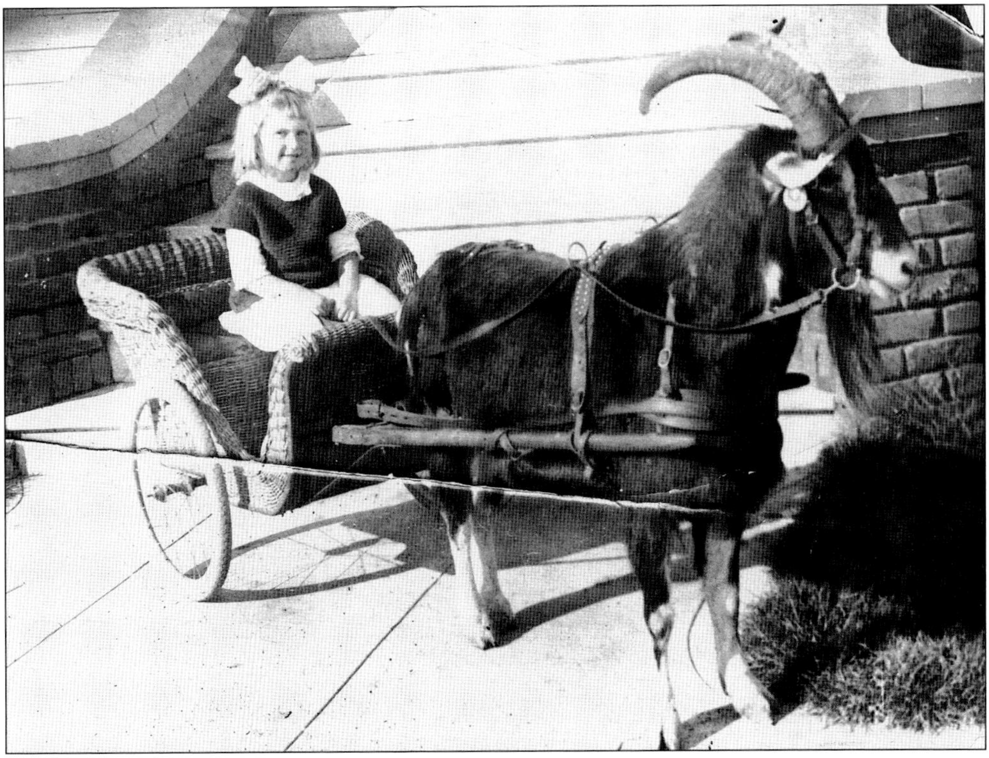

This c. 1920 photograph shows five-year-old Birdie Boyles in a goat cart before the front porch steps of her family home at 2523 U Street in Newton Booth. (Courtesy of Chris Boyles David.)

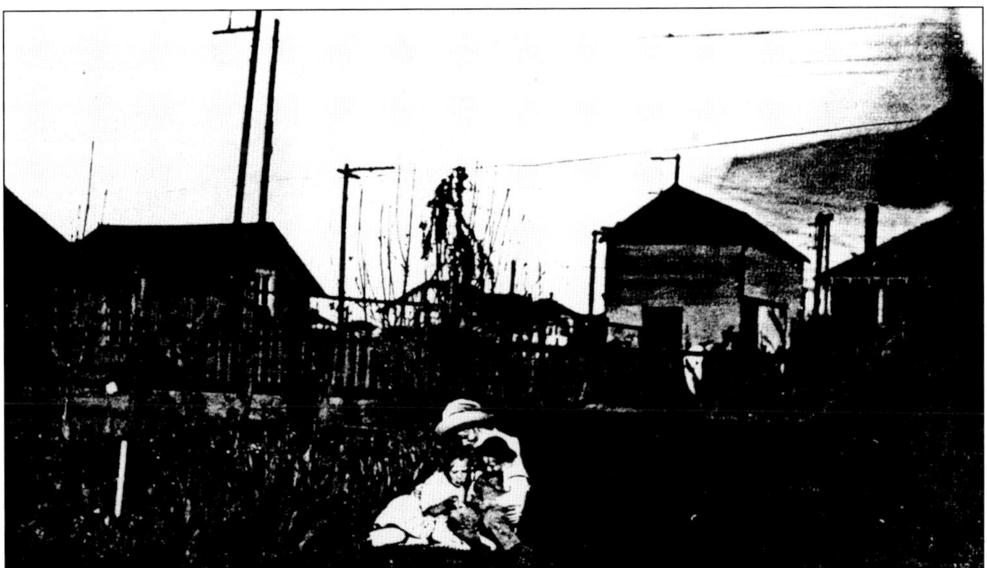

This undated image, likely taken before 1920, shows the Boyles family barn before it burned down. Many early Newton Booth residents raised chickens or cultivated small farms or orchards, even after the neighborhood began to develop rapidly in the early 20th century. (Courtesy of Chris Boyles David.)

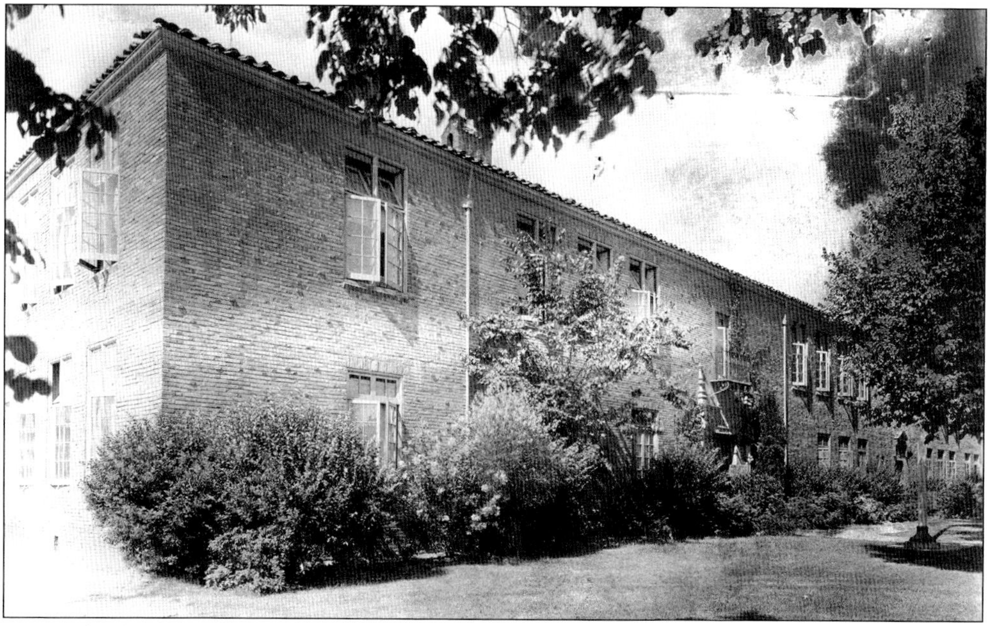

As families built homes in Newton Booth and Poverty Ridge during the first two decades of the 20th century, the need for a larger neighborhood school became urgent. By 1918, the school's two classrooms were insufficient for the growing population. Between 1920 and 1921, the old schoolhouse was razed and replaced with a much larger concrete-and-brick Spanish eclectic–style campus. The new school featured 13 classrooms, four special rooms, a principal's office, and a teachers' area. (Courtesy of CSL.)

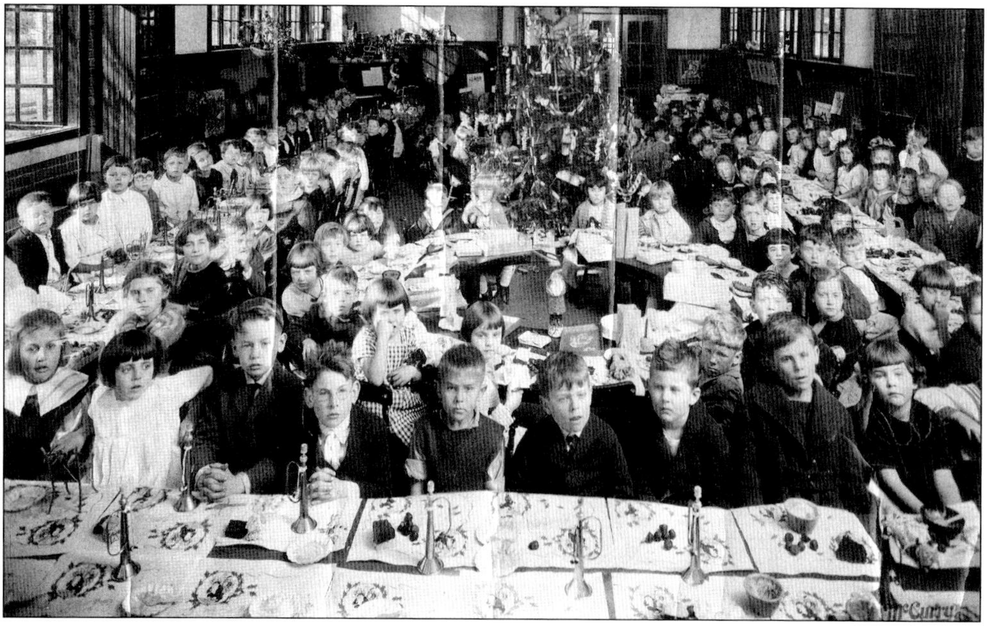

This c. 1925 photograph shows a school Christmas party in the newly rebuilt—and much larger—Newton Booth School. Notice the cake, candies, and horns placed before each student forced to outlast the photo session for their reward. Birdie Boyles of 2523 U Street is seated at the far left, on the right side of the table, in the second seat down. (Courtesy of Chris Boyles David.)

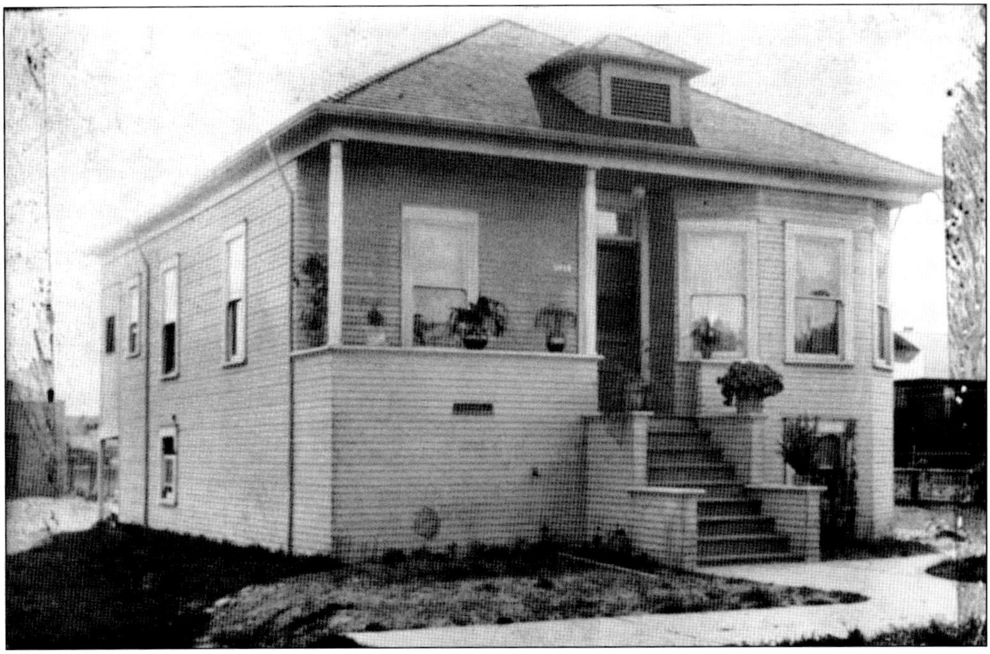

Pictured around 1915 is a handsome Craftsman bungalow at 2618 S Street. The home was built in 1913 for Fannie Ray Grubbs. In addition to its two bedrooms, the residence featured an unfinished eight-foot basement, which was designed with the potential for a rental flat. After the property left the Grubbs family, the basement was enlarged and the top floor slightly raised to make the lower level more spacious.

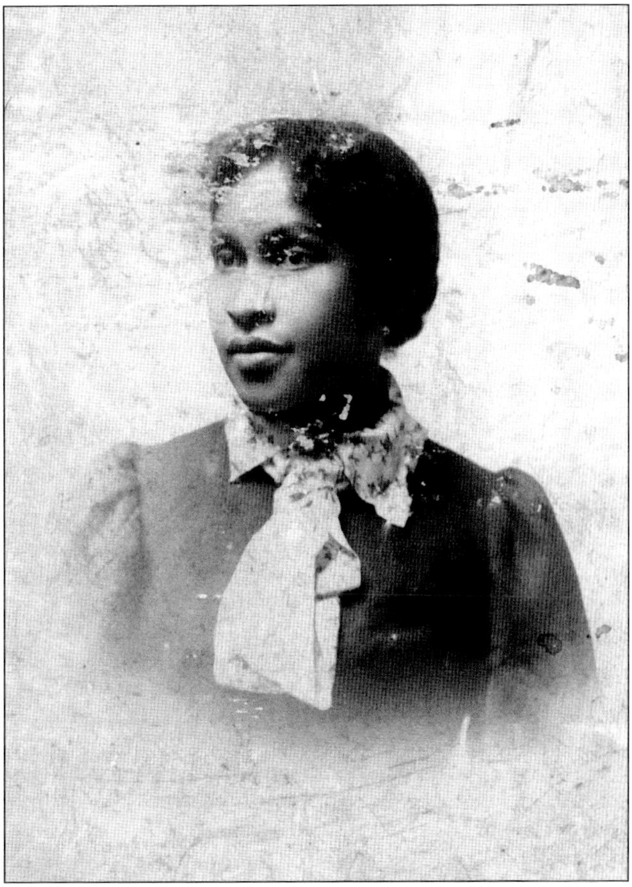

Fannie Elizabeth Ray Grubbs was a native of Texas and the daughter of a former slave. In 1886, she married Eugene Grubbs. The couple had three daughters, Alma, Isabelle Clarissa, and Grace Evelyn. Originally settling in Oak Park, the Grubbs family later moved to the central city. Fanny Grubbs acquired 2618 S Street shortly after it was built in 1913 and passed away in 1920.

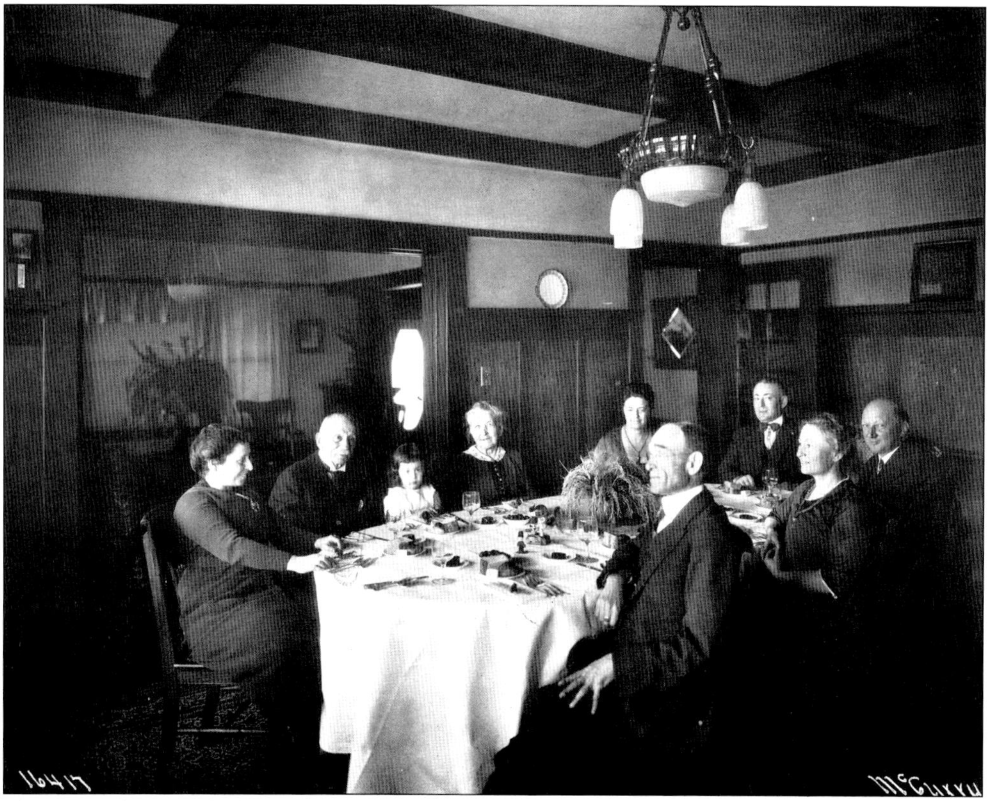

This 1921 photograph shows the golden wedding anniversary celebration inside the home of Julius (second from left) and Joanna Asher (fourth from left). The Ashers lived in the Craftsman-style bungalow at 1916 Twenty-Sixth Street. Julius was a photographer who operated portrait studios out of San Francisco and Sacramento from the 1870s through the early 20th century. His Sacramento studio was at 244 J Street.

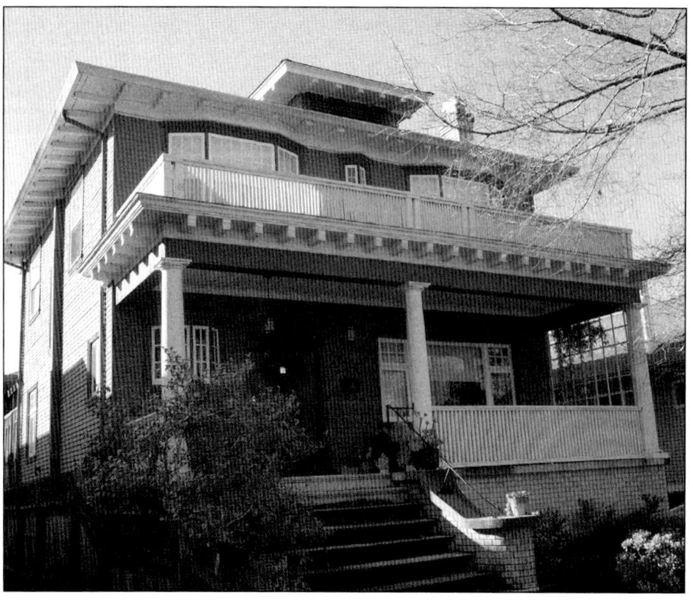

The cube-like Colonial Revival–style home at 2514 U Street was built in 1915 for Benjamin and Elizabeth Colton. Benjamin Colton was a successful rancher who had owned and operated a 263-acre farm in Elk Grove. At the age of 62, he decided to retire from ranching. The following year, the Coltons bought land on the 25th block of U Street and built an impressive two-story home. (Author's collection.)

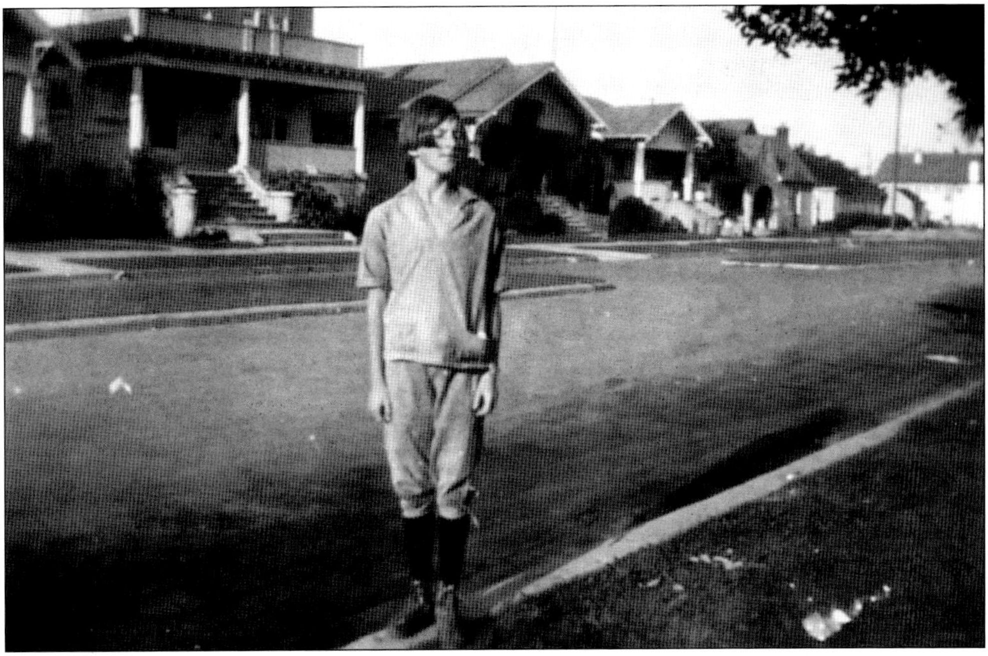

The residence at 2514 U Street—pictured over the left shoulder of a young Birdie Boyles—was built in 1915 by Benjamin and Elizabeth Colton. Elizabeth Colton became a powerful force for good in Sacramento's charitable and philanthropic circles. For over two decades, she served as the president of the board of the Sacramento Orphanage, raising funds needed to expand and improve services at the orphanage. (Courtesy of Chris Boyles David.)

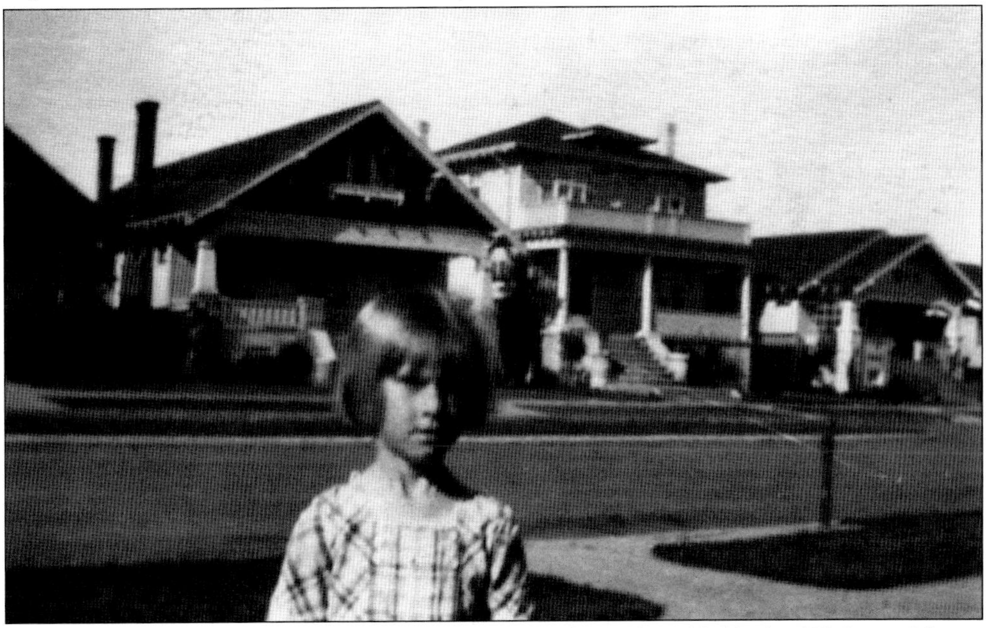

This c. 1920 photograph shows a young girl facing north on the 25th block of U Street. Notice the grass medians that used to be in the center of the street, as well as the hitching post. The home of Benjamin and Elizabeth Colton can be seen over the girl's right shoulder. (Courtesy of Chris Boyles David.)

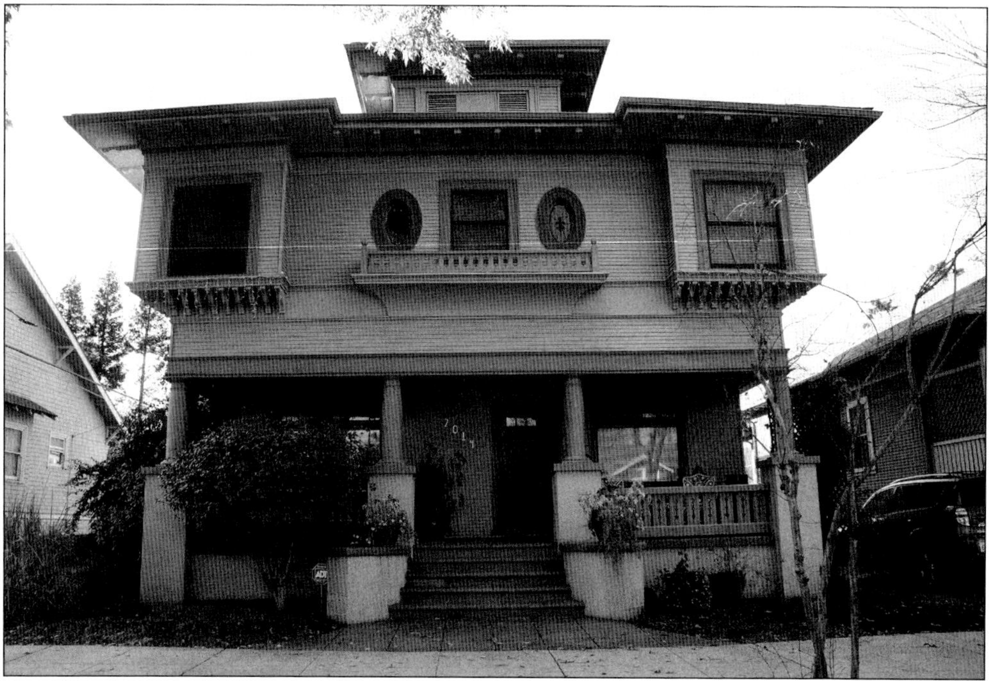

Located at 2014 Twenty-Fifth Street, this beautiful Prairie-style residence was constructed in 1910. In 1915, newlyweds Augusta and Adolph Teichert Jr. purchased the home. Over the next several years, the Teicherts raised four children at their Newton Booth residence. Augusta Teichert was the maternal granddaughter of renowned Sacramento pioneer Adolph Heilbron. As a young adult, she studied music in Dresden, Germany. (Author's collection.)

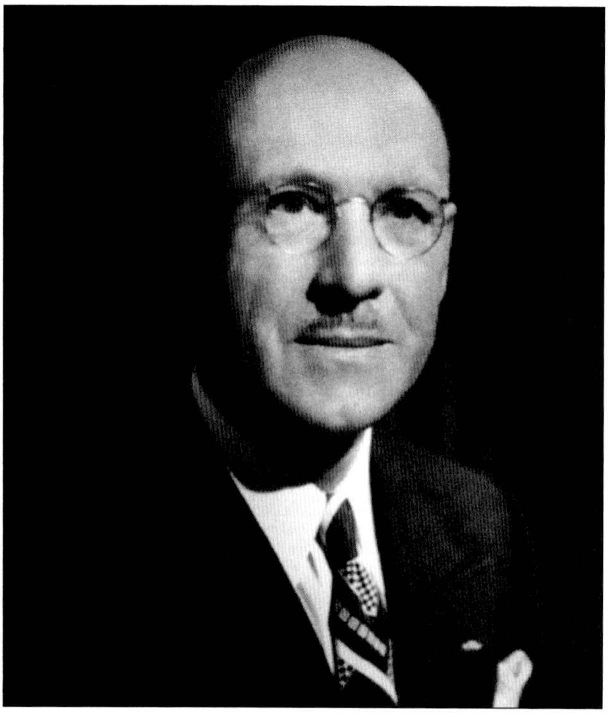

Adolph Teichert Jr. lived with his wife, Augusta, and four children at 2014 Twenty-Fifth Street. Adolph Jr. served alongside his father in the capacity of vice president of A. Teichert & Son until his father's retirement, at which point Adolph Jr. was elected president of the company. Teichert Construction holds California state contractor's license No. 8, the oldest active contractor's license in California. (Courtesy of Teichert family.)

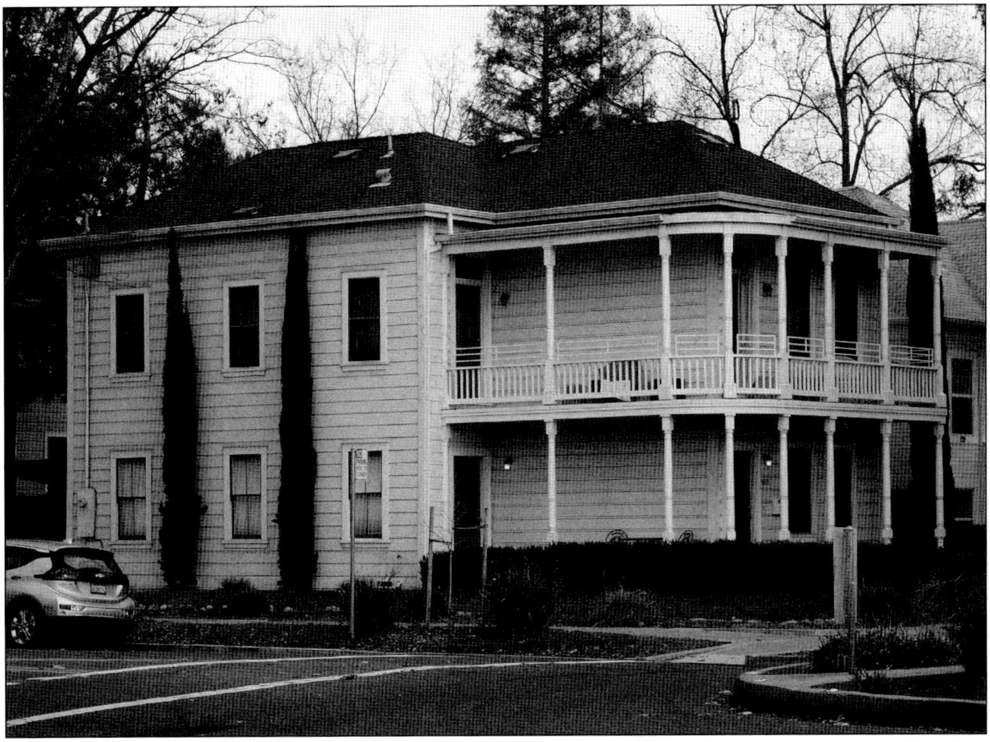

The Italianate vernacular home pictured here was likely built around 1880 in another part of the city. It was moved in the 1920s to its current location at 2601 S Street. Several homes built in the 1880s and 1890s were moved to the Newton Booth neighborhood in the early 20th century, as this was sometimes cheaper than building a home from scratch. (Author's collection.)

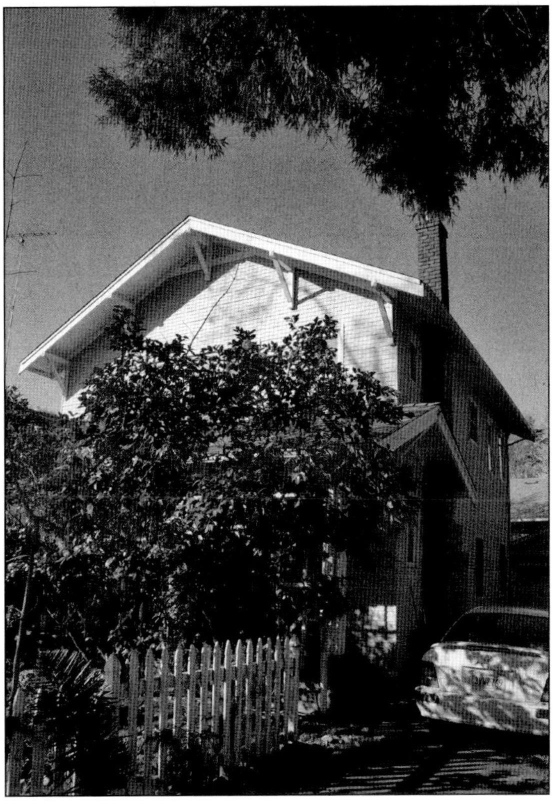

Built around 1915, this Craftsman-style home at 2006 Twenty-Fourth Street was constructed by prolific Sacramento developer and vice president of the Farmers and Mechanics Bank Phillip Wolf. The home was purchased in 1917 by George Engelhardt, a purser for steamships operating along the Sacramento River. (Author's collection.)

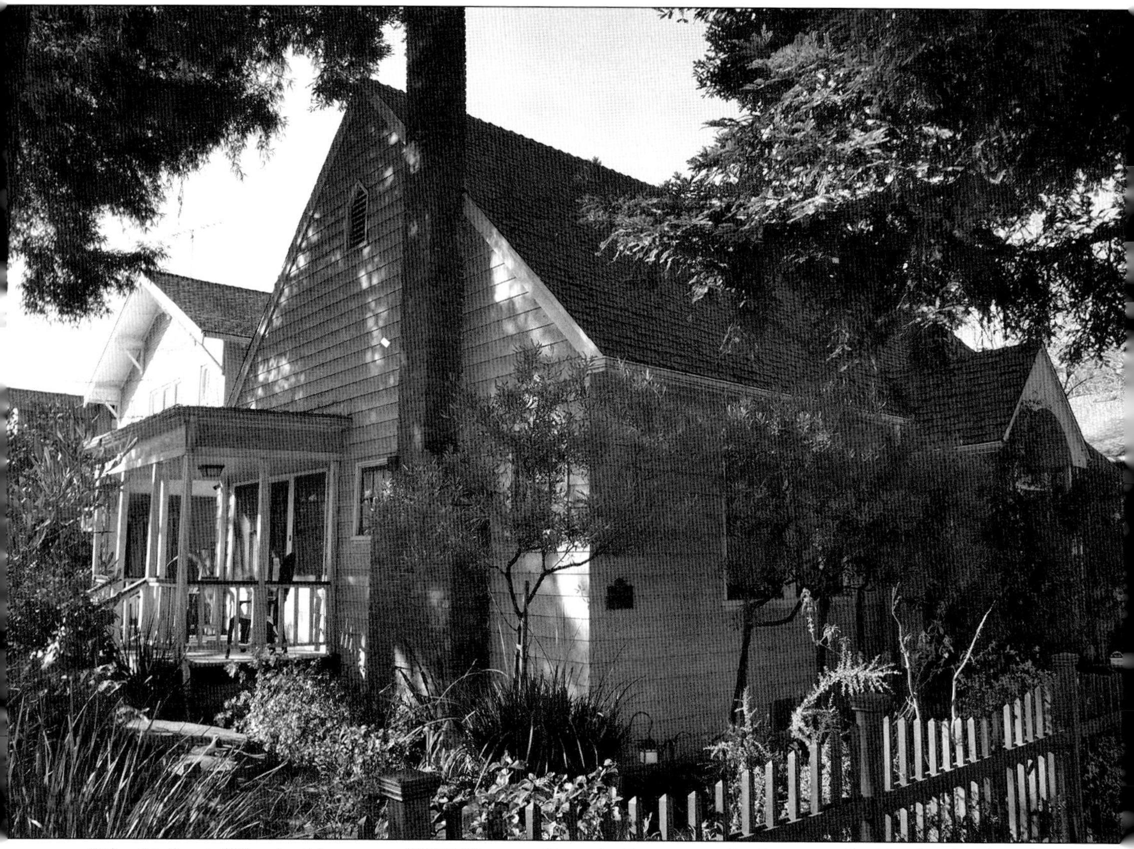

The Colonial Revival home at 2000 Twenty-Fourth Street was built around 1922 for the family of *Sacramento Bee* managing editor J. Earl Langdon. The original address was 2330 T Street. Today, the home retains front entrances representing both addresses, with the original door facing T Street and the new entrance facing Twenty-Fourth Street. (Author's collection.)

Five

Boom Times before and after World War II

As the Great Depression of the early 1930s ravaged Sacramento's industrial economy, many former household breadwinners found themselves unemployed for prolonged periods of time. Neighborhood families adapted when and how they could, often renting out rooms to boarders and living with extended family members. The Depression era also substantially shifted the roles of women in the workforce. Many wives, mothers, and daughters entered the workforce as sales assistants, office clerks, and secretaries, even as their husbands and fathers lost employment at the railroad yards, canneries, and plants along the R Street corridor and beyond.

Notwithstanding the Depression, the Newton Booth and Poverty Ridge neighborhoods continued to grow, albeit at a constrained pace. Although homes were constructed even during the Depression, they were less elaborate and more reflective of the practicality and frugality observed during hard times and war. The revival architectural styles were in full swing, with minimal traditional and simple Tudor, Spanish, and Colonial Revival style homes constructed, including cottage communities and large apartment complexes.

Throughout the 1940s and during the Second World War, employment opportunities in the defense sector, paired with a rise in state and local government employment, ushered in a new era of growth for the neighborhoods of Sacramento. Apartments were in high demand, and several multifamily units were added to the local housing inventory. Newton Booth and Poverty Ridge demographics trended increasingly transient, including military families, young couples, and unmarried female workers living alongside opportunistic investors, generous philanthropists, and dream-chasing hustlers. In short, it was the most dense, fluid, and diverse demographic seen in the neighborhoods prior to the 21st century.

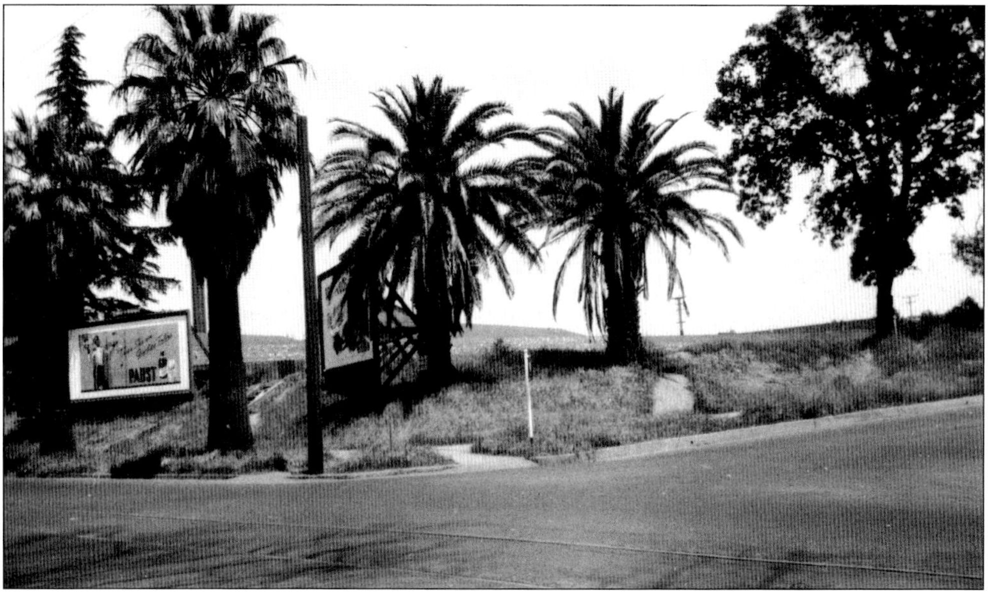

This 1938 image of the northeast corner of Twenty-First and S Streets in Poverty Ridge shows a billboard for Pabst beer, which stands alongside a set of old steps leading up the terraced hill to where another structure once stood. Growth in the neighborhoods slowed during the Depression, but the 1940s brought new development and growth to vacant lots such as this one near the R Street corridor.

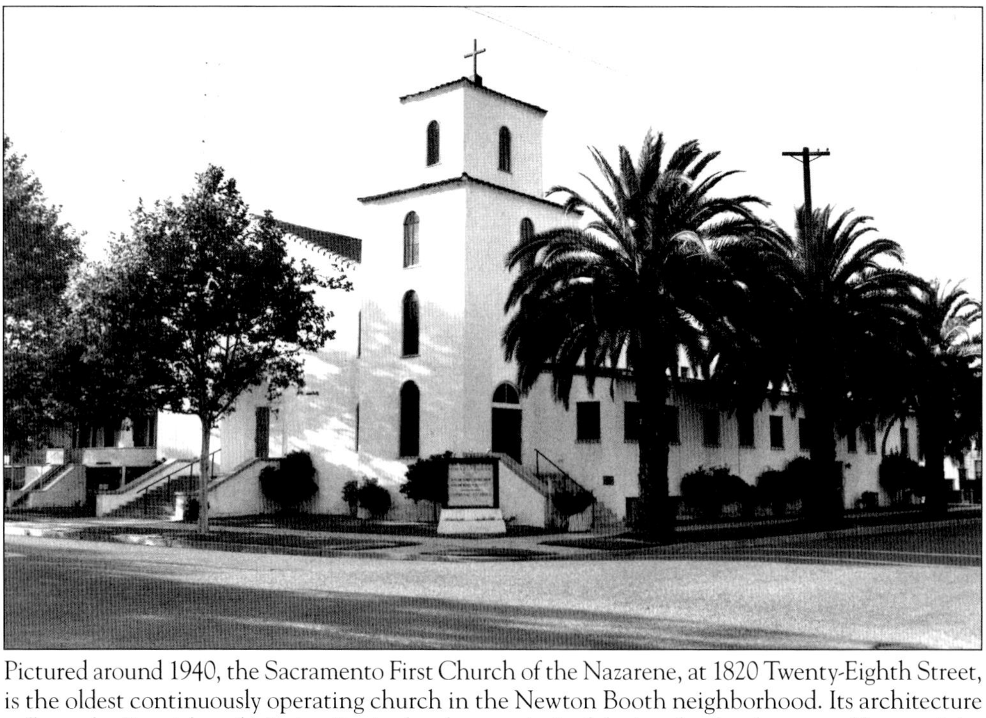

Pictured around 1940, the Sacramento First Church of the Nazarene, at 1820 Twenty-Eighth Street, is the oldest continuously operating church in the Newton Booth neighborhood. Its architecture reflects the Spanish and Mission Revival styles popularized during the developmental boom of the neighborhood in the 1920s. The "Gospel Tabernacle" was erected at the corner of Twenty-Eighth and S Streets in the fall of 1922. (Courtesy of the Sacramento First Church of the Nazarene.)

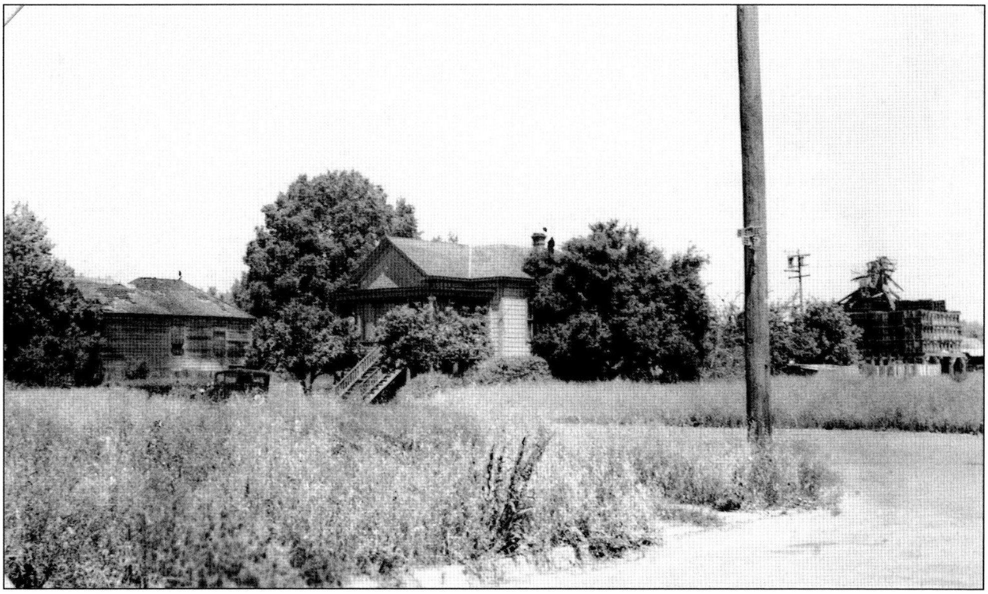

This c. 1940 image shows the intersection of Twenty-Sixth and S Streets. A small Victorian-era worker's cottage can still be seen in the time before new construction began to accelerate following World War II. The postwar building boom resulted in the construction of large apartment communities where small farms and 1890s workers' cottages once stood. Today, two large apartment complexes from the postwar years stand at the western edge of this intersection.

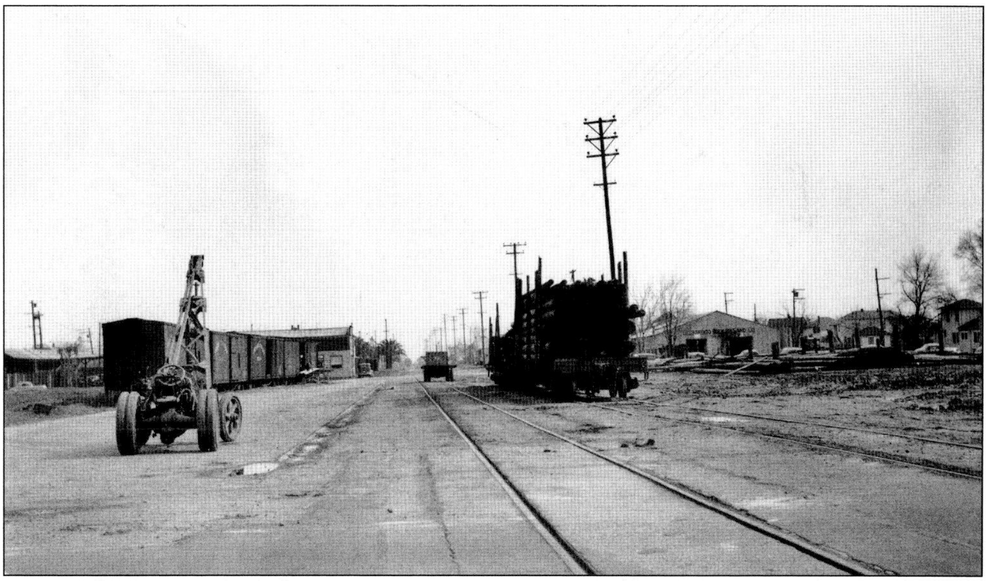

This c. 1940 image shows the railroad tracks facing east at Twenty-Fourth and R Streets. The Sacramento Rock and Gravel Company can be seen to the right at Twenty-Fifth Street. In the late 1930s and 1940s, there were still plenty of vacant lots available for development, especially the blocks adjacent to the R Street industrial corridor. The demand for apartment buildings and cottage communities increased significantly after World War II.

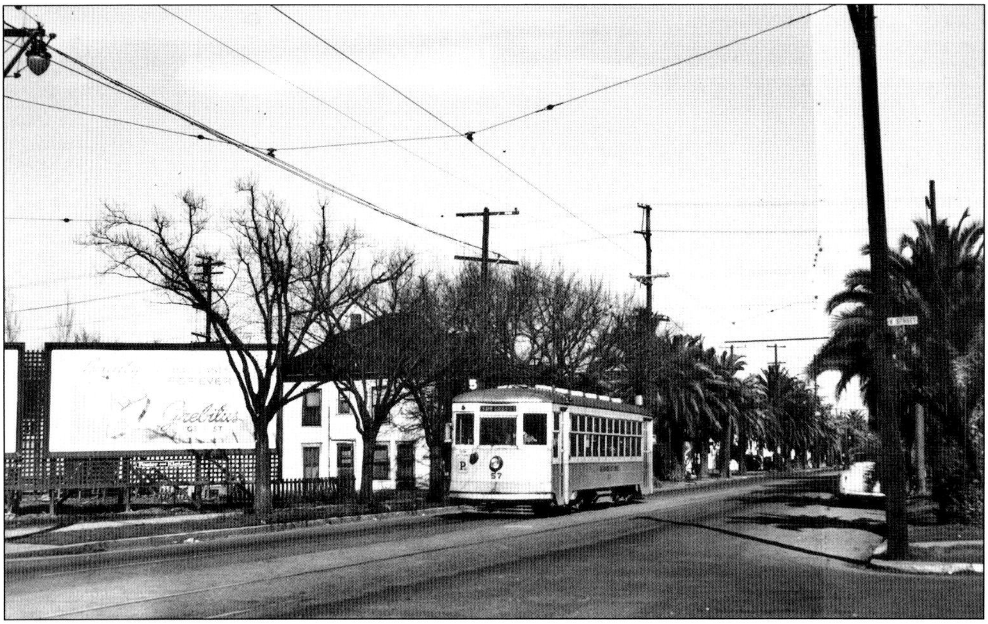

This c. 1940s image shows streetcar No. 57 on Twenty-Eighth Street near V Street in Newton Booth. The mobility offered by streetcar lines running through Newton Booth and Poverty Ridge helped further growth and development in the neighborhoods during the 1930s and 1940s. (Courtesy of WRM.)

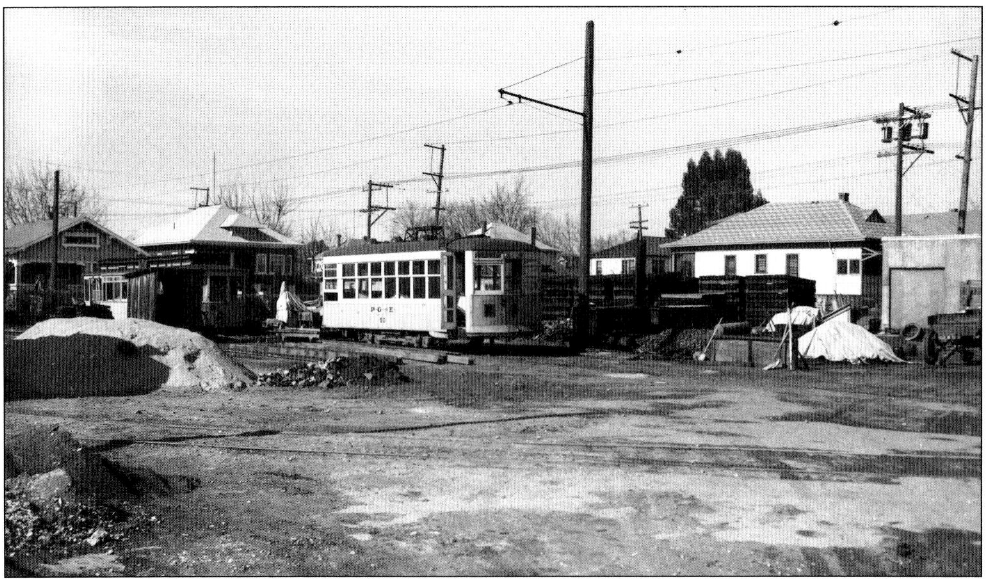

This c. 1939 photograph shows a northwest view of streetcar No. 50 at the PG&E supply yard at Twenty-Eighth and R Streets. A Birney car, which is partially dismantled, can be seen farther to the left. As seen in the picture, on certain blocks, the neighborhood continued to develop right up to the edge of the busy R Street corridor. (Courtesy of WRM.)

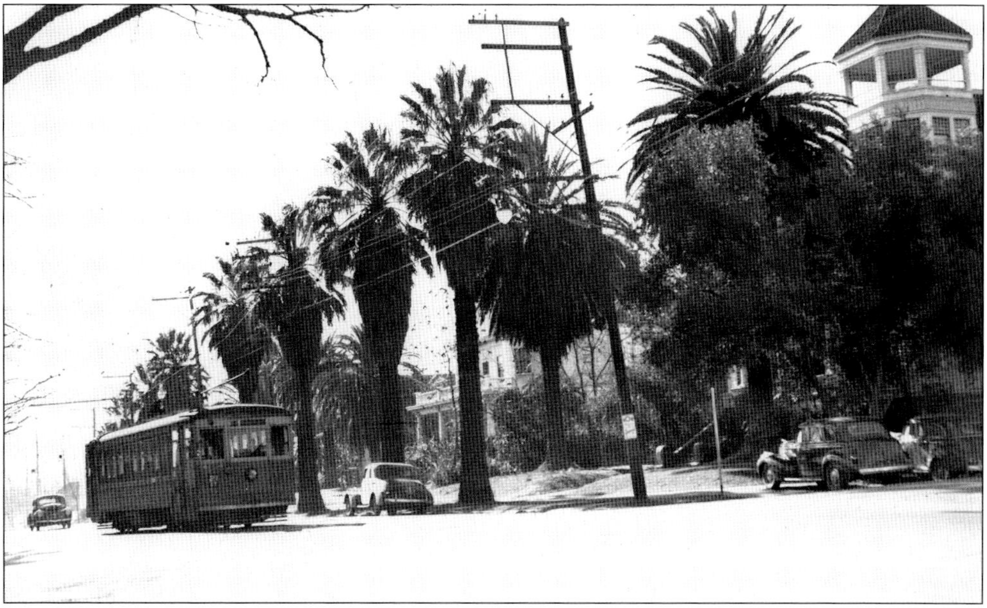

Pictured around 1940, streetcar route No. 6 entered Poverty Ridge at Twenty-First and W Streets and continued north into midtown and on to downtown. The old Anna E. Clark and Herman H. Grau homes can be seen in the background at Twenty-First and V Streets. (Courtesy of WRM.)

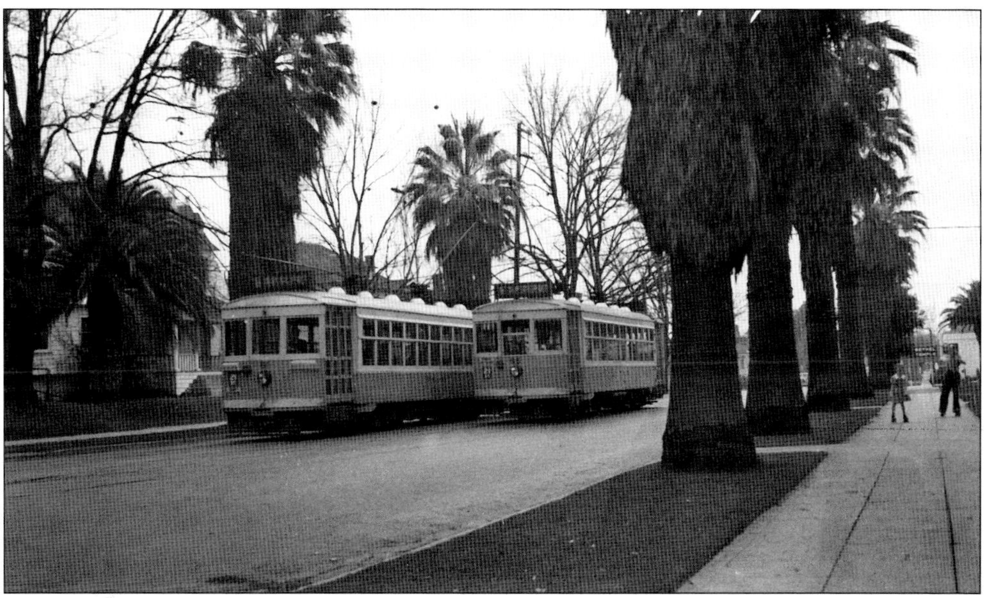

In this c. 1940 image, two route No. 6 PG&E streetcars are seen heading north at Twenty-First and V Streets. The E.P. Howe Jr. residence can be seen to the east. (Courtesy of WRM.)

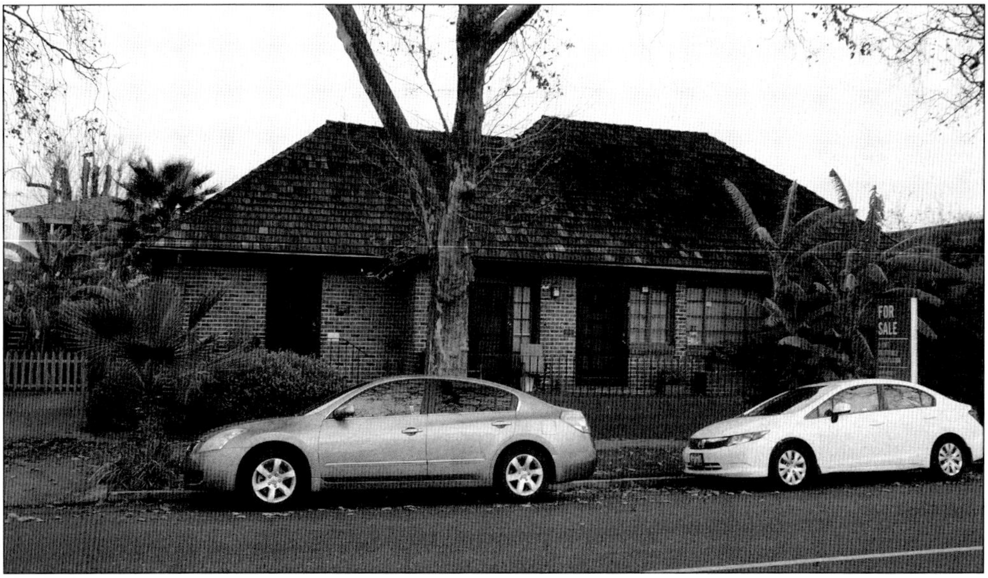

Gladys Kipp Powell, a working mother employed by the Department of Agriculture, developed the nine-unit properties pictured above at 2121 and 2323 S Street around 1935. From the late 1930s into the early 1940s, she developed several Tudor Revival, minimal traditional, and cottage-style properties along the 23rd and 24th blocks of S Street. (Author's collection.)

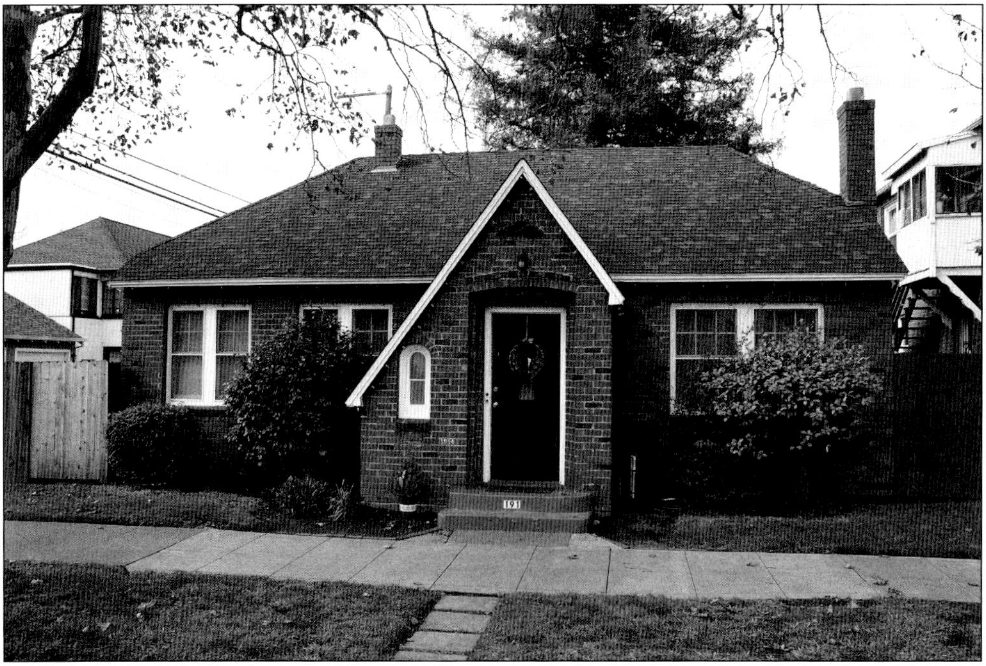

This c. 1935 brick Tudor Revival cottage at 1914 Twenty-Fourth Street was built by neighborhood resident Gladys Powell. One of her sons, Maurice, later lived in the cottage for a brief time while starting a family of his own. Gladys also built the neighboring brick triplex at 1908 Twenty-Fourth Street. As was common with many families in the neighborhoods at the time, relatives occupied several of Gladys's cottages and apartments during the late Depression through World War II. (Author's collection.)

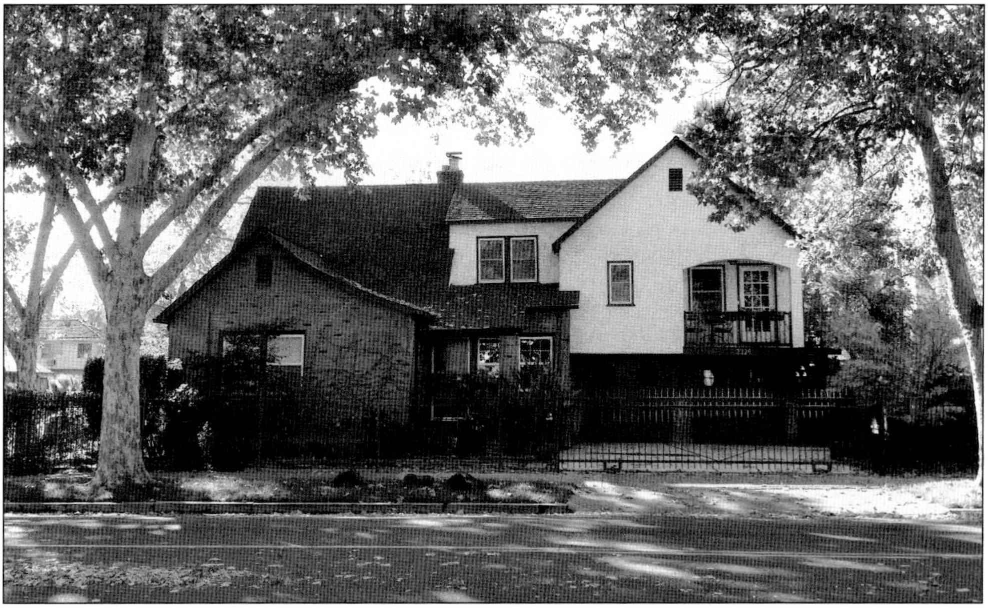

Gladys Powell built another Tudor Revival–style duplex at 2330–2328 S Street in addition to the minimal traditional home next door at 2320 S Street. As cash flow from the rental properties increased, she was able to build a 14-unit cottage community at Twenty-Sixth and O Streets in midtown. The Powell family continues to operate several family-built or -acquired cottage and apartment communities across Sacramento today. (Author's collection.)

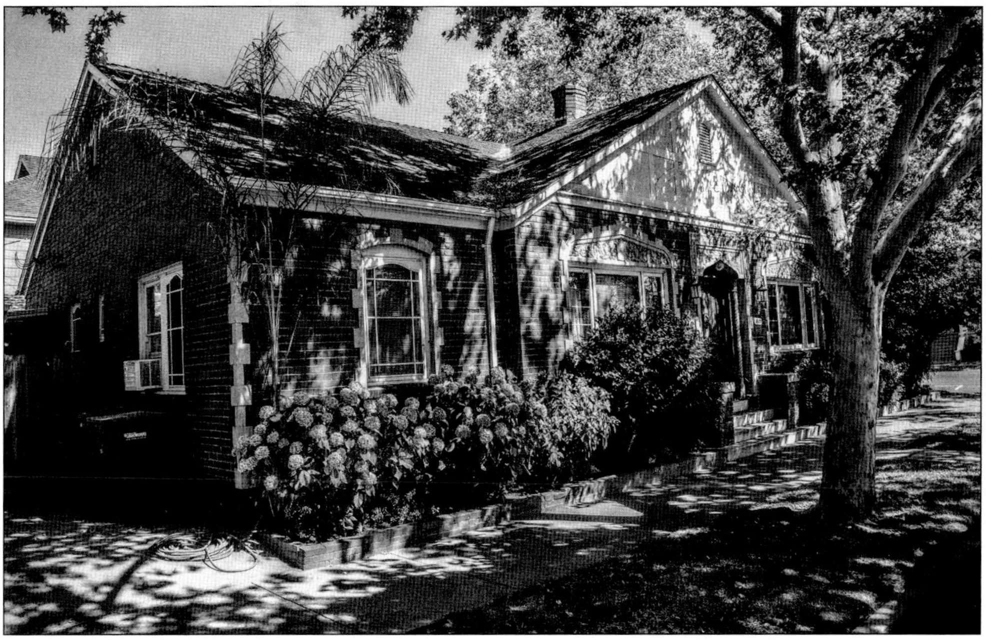

The brick Tudor Revival duplex at 1827 and 1829 Twenty-Seventh Street was constructed around 1929 as an investment property for prominent Sacramento physician Halleck H. Look. The structure, which featured an ornately carved main door as well as intricate exterior trim work, was consistently leased to middle-class tenants such as machinists, mechanics, nurses, plumbers, and clerics throughout the 1930s and 1940s. (Author's collection.)

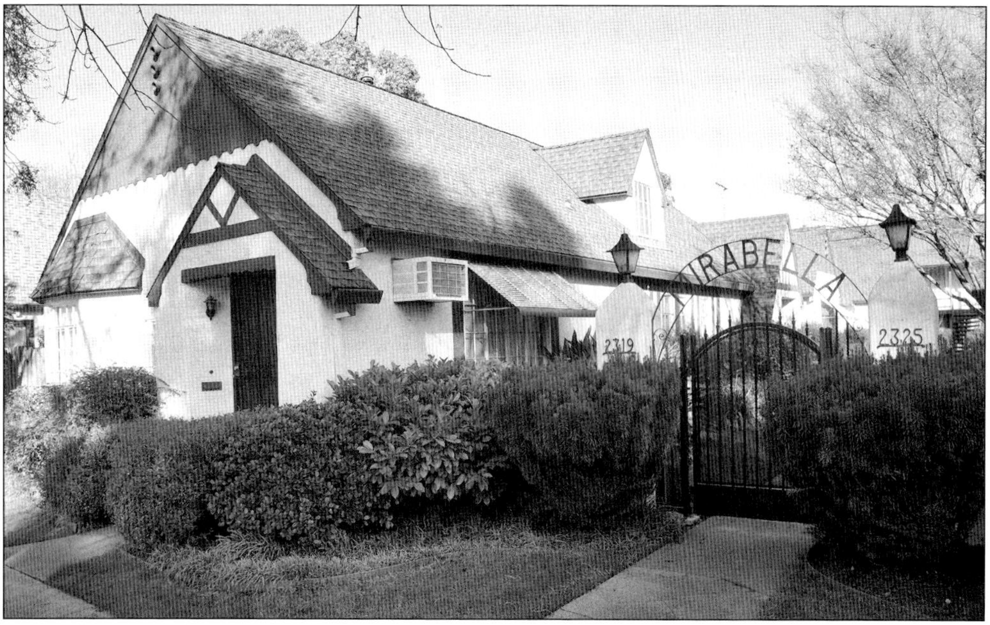

Mirabella Court, located at 2319–2325 T Street, was constructed in 1936 by William Reddy, who hired local contractor Paul Opdyke to build the eight-unit cottages comprised of four duplexes with garages in a U shape that encompassed two landscaped courts. Bungalow courts became popular in the central city—and many other growing cities—during the first half of the 20th century. Bungalows offered renters more autonomy and cost efficiency relative to traditional flats. (Author's collection.)

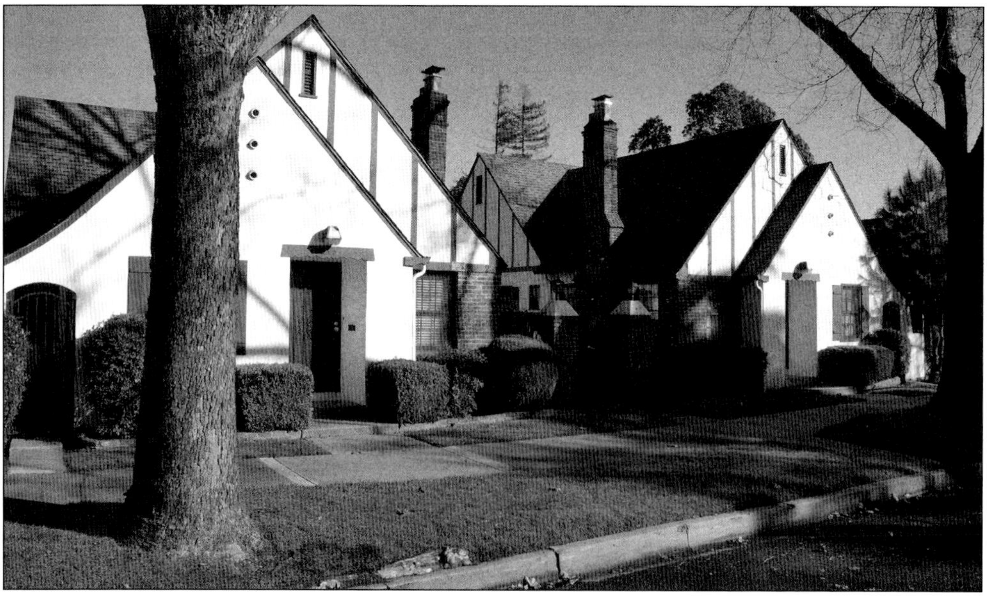

In 1937, H. Wacker constructed the Tudor Revival bungalows pictured here at 2313–2315 T Street, next door to Mirabella Court. Additional bungalows were added to the rear in 1950. Many single professional women such as teachers, nurses, and stenographers leased bungalows along T Street. Court communities were promoted nationwide as being safe and respectable living arrangements for single women. (Author's collection.)

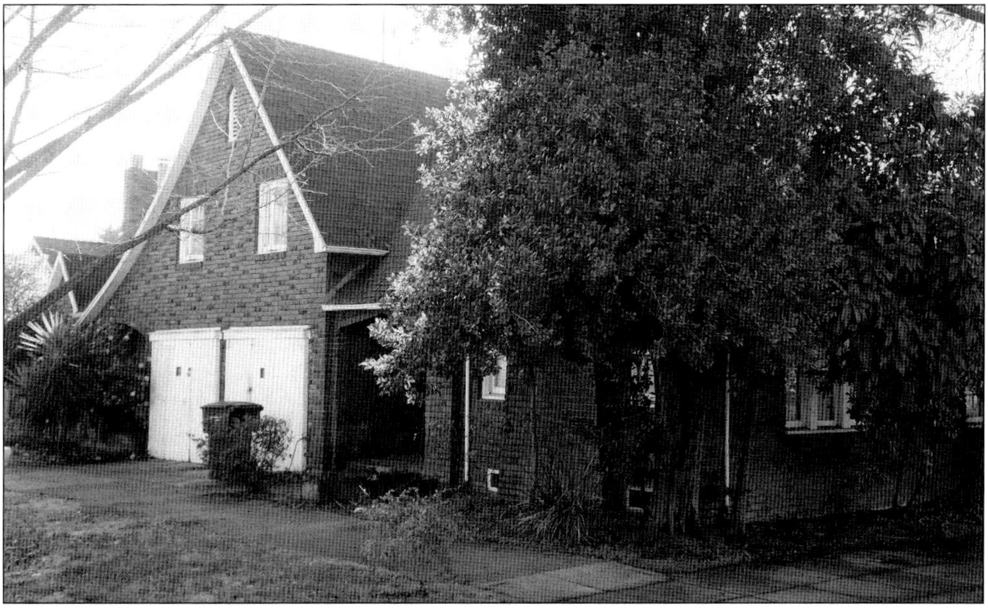

Built around 1932 by Eugene F. Herman at a cost of $6,000, the brick Tudor Revival duplex at 2300–2302 U Street was constructed with central adjacent garages separating the two units. Unlike many families during the Depression, the Hermans were able to finance the construction of an income property during uncertain and unstable economic times. Their newlywed daughter and son-in-law occupied one of the units shortly thereafter. (Author's collection.)

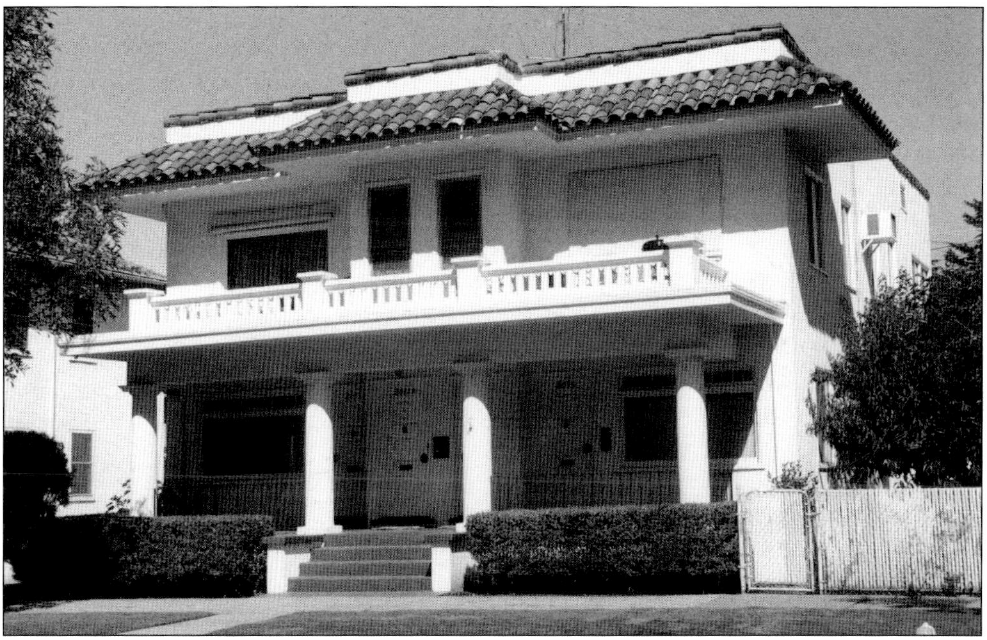

This c. 1922 four-flat building, located at 2011–2015 Twenty-Second Street, was constructed in the Spanish eclectic and Colonial Revival architectural styles by contractor George E. Harvie at a cost of $12,000. The average monthly rents were about $35 at the time, and throughout the 1920s and 1930s, the units were primarily rented by single working women as well as young couples, many of whom welcomed a first child while living at the property. (Author's collection.)

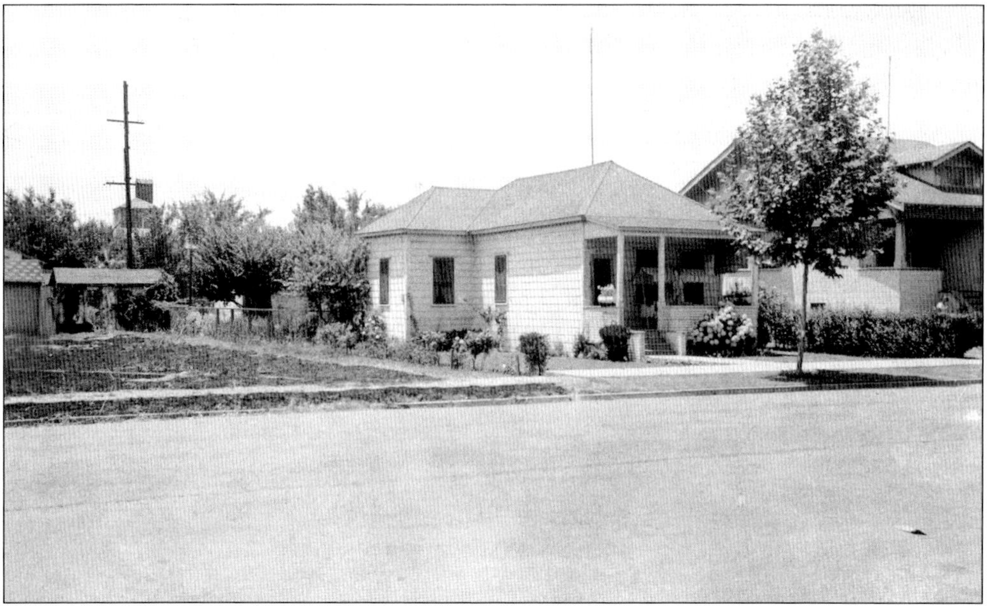

This 1935 view of 2622 U Street shows the c. 1900 home of Sacramento police officer John Duhaine. Notice the orchards in the backyard, a throwback to the time when Newton Booth was sprinkled with small farms. The tower of the Newton Booth School can be seen above the tree line. By the 1940s, a minimal traditional bungalow community and adjacent apartment building covered the land previously occupied by Duhaine's home and its small orchard.

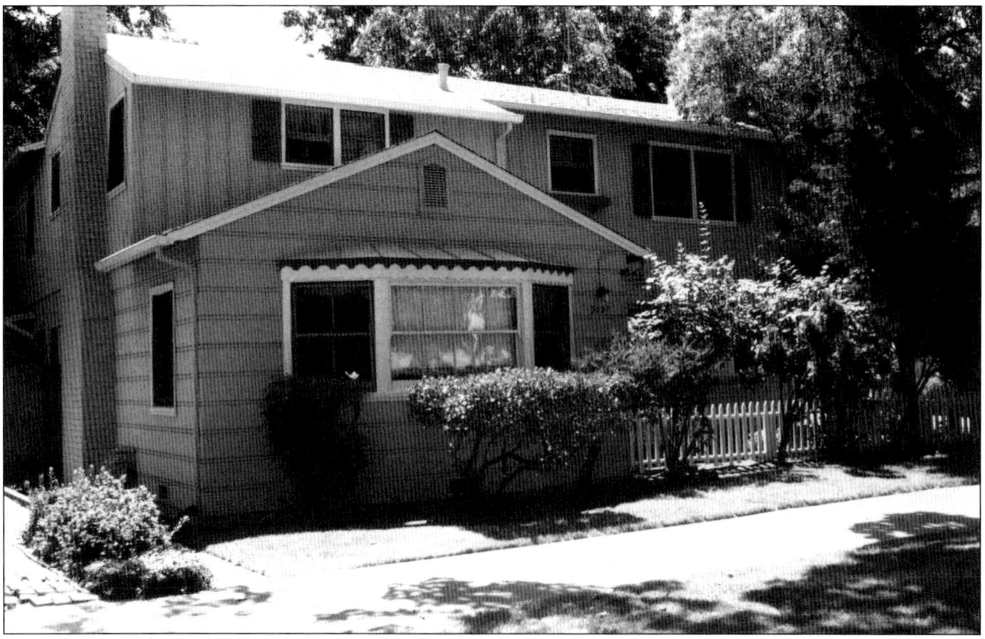

This duplex at 2021–2023 Twenty-Third Street was constructed around 1938 in the popular minimalist style using Colonial Revival elements. The first two couples to occupy the units were Warren and Ethel Reed and Dr. Gustave and Helen Wilson. Ethel Reed was the daughter of Sacramento pioneer T.B. Hall, founder of the Hall-Luhrs Company, a prominent Sacramento wholesale grocer. Both the Reeds and the Wilsons were active in civic and philanthropic matters.

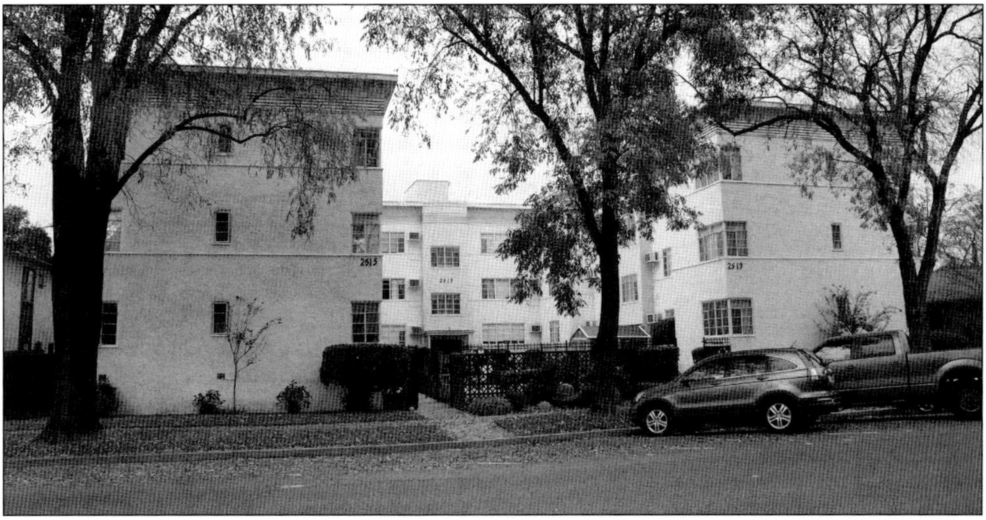

The c. 1940s eighteen-unit art modern–style apartment building at 2513–2519 S Street was constructed by cement contractor Louis Jansen. The building was the largest apartment complex in the neighborhoods and one of the only representations of this particular architectural style. The complex was popular with young, single working tradespeople and professionals during the transition from mostly single-family residential neighborhoods to a mixed primary and transient community in the 1940s. (Author's collection.)

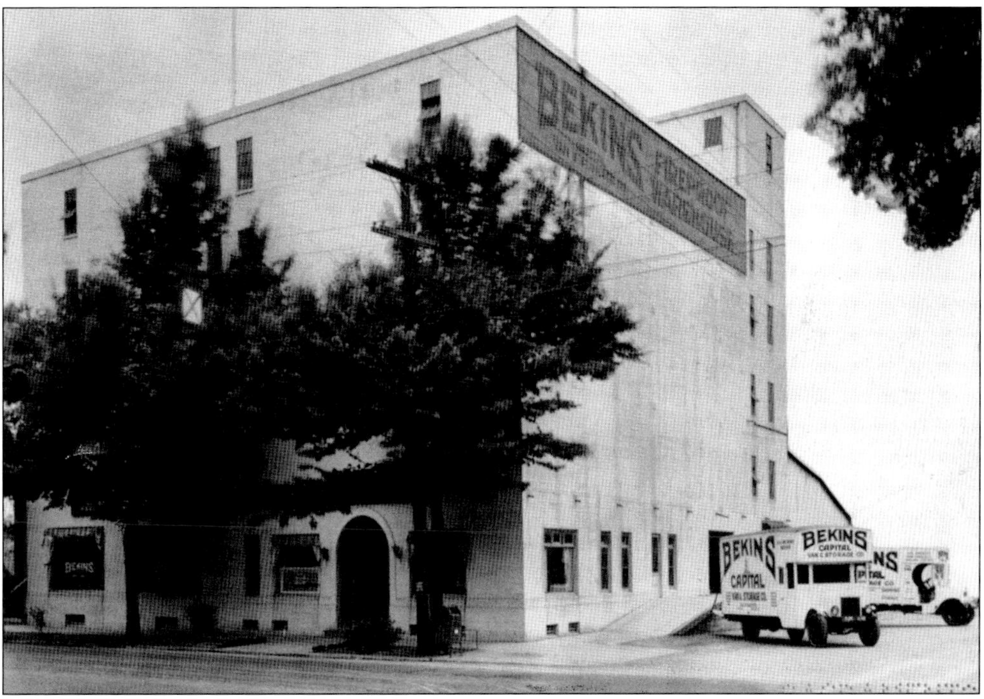

This c. 1940 photograph shows the new warehouse and trucks of the Bekins Capital Van and Storage Company at 1800 Twenty-First Street. The building, which was situated along the Southern Pacific Railroad tracks on R Street, was considered to be state-of-the-art at the time and assured clients that the allegedly fireproof brick warehouse was the safest place to temporarily store belongings. (Courtesy of the Sacramento Room.)

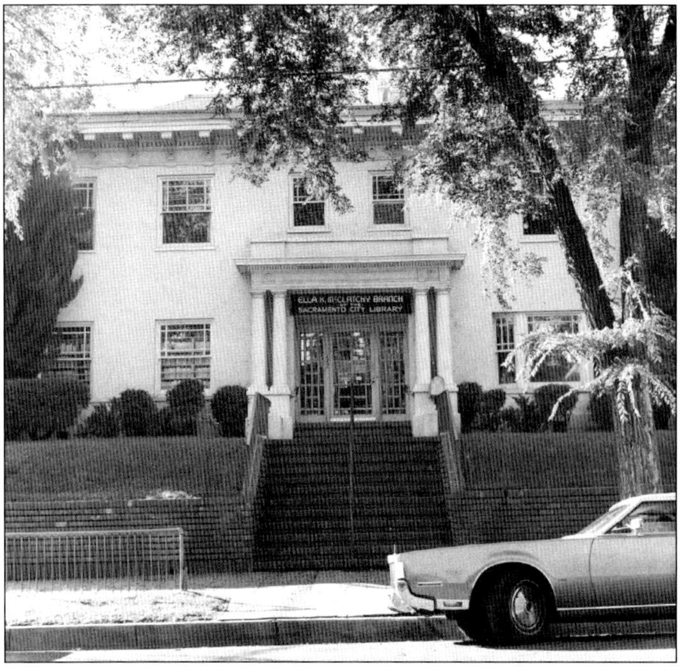

Following Ella McClatchy's death in 1939, her two surviving children, Eleanor and Charlotte, presented the home to the City of Sacramento for use as a youth library in memory of their mother. Ella McClatchy had always been an avid supporter of young people and education. The McClatchy daughters also wanted to have a public library closer to the recently constructed C.K. McClatchy High School, named in honor of their father.

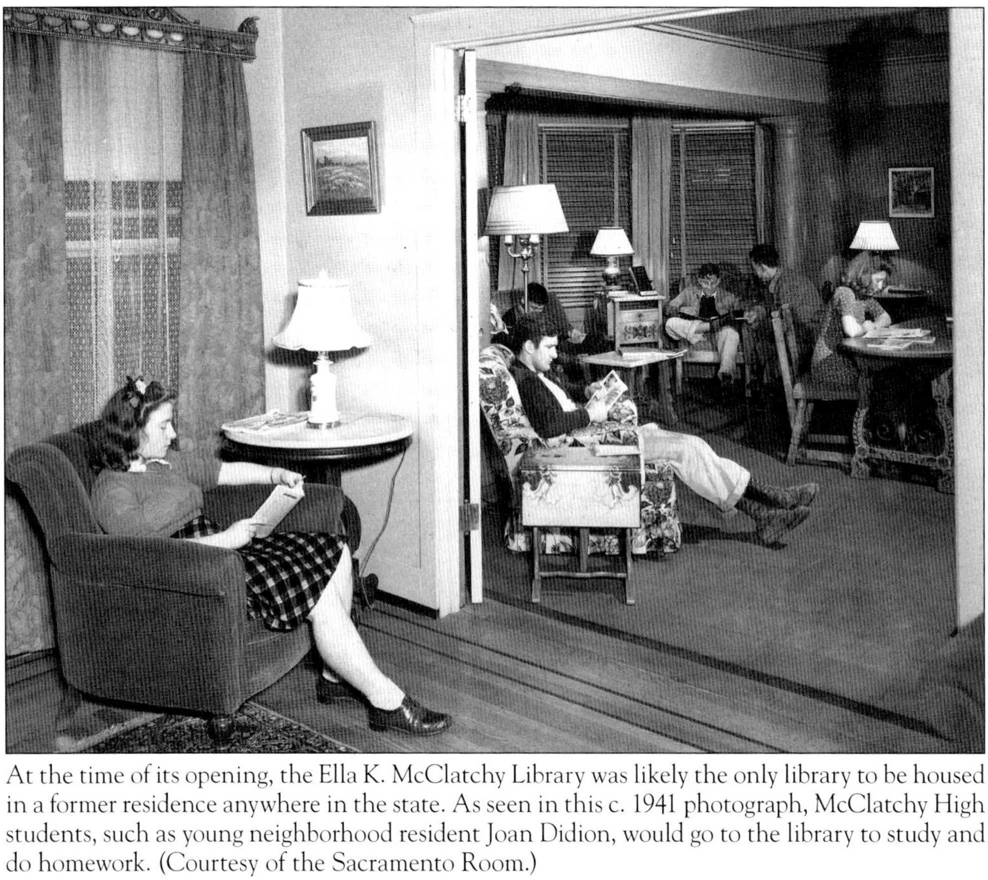

At the time of its opening, the Ella K. McClatchy Library was likely the only library to be housed in a former residence anywhere in the state. As seen in this c. 1941 photograph, McClatchy High students, such as young neighborhood resident Joan Didion, would go to the library to study and do homework. (Courtesy of the Sacramento Room.)

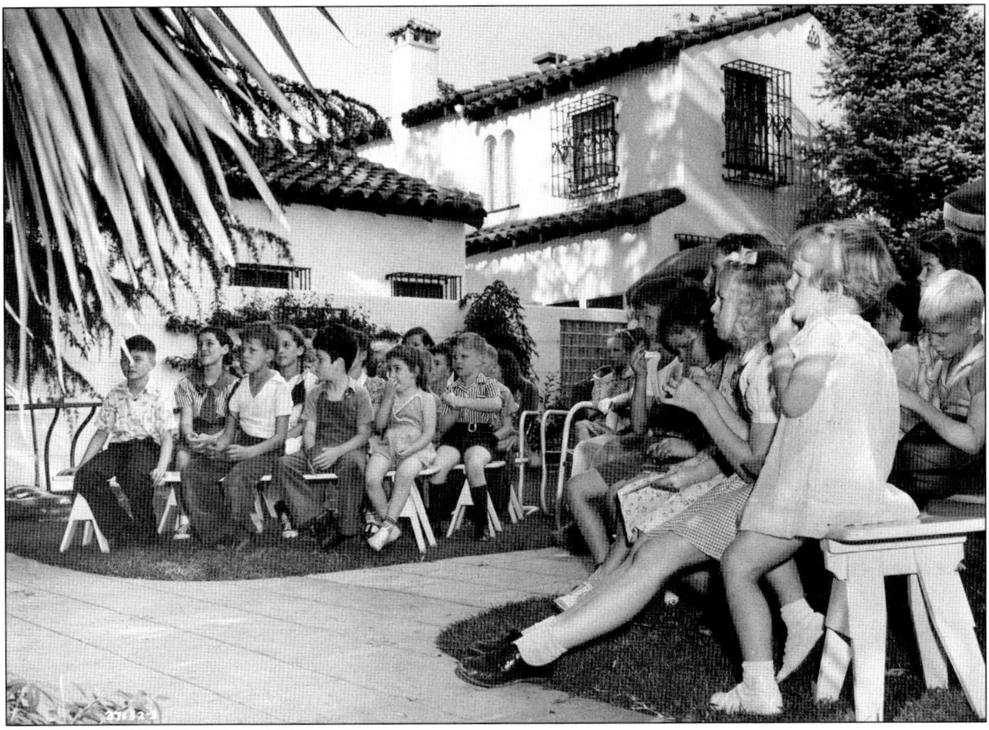

These c. 1941 photographs show a group of young children enjoying story time (above) and reading (below) on the back patio of the new Ella K. McClatchy Library for Young People. Notice the Spanish Revival home of *Sacramento Bee* publisher Eleanor McClatchy in the background. She eventually annexed her mother's gardens and built a wall between her private residence and the back patio of her childhood home, which was now a public library. (Both, courtesy of the Sacramento Room.)

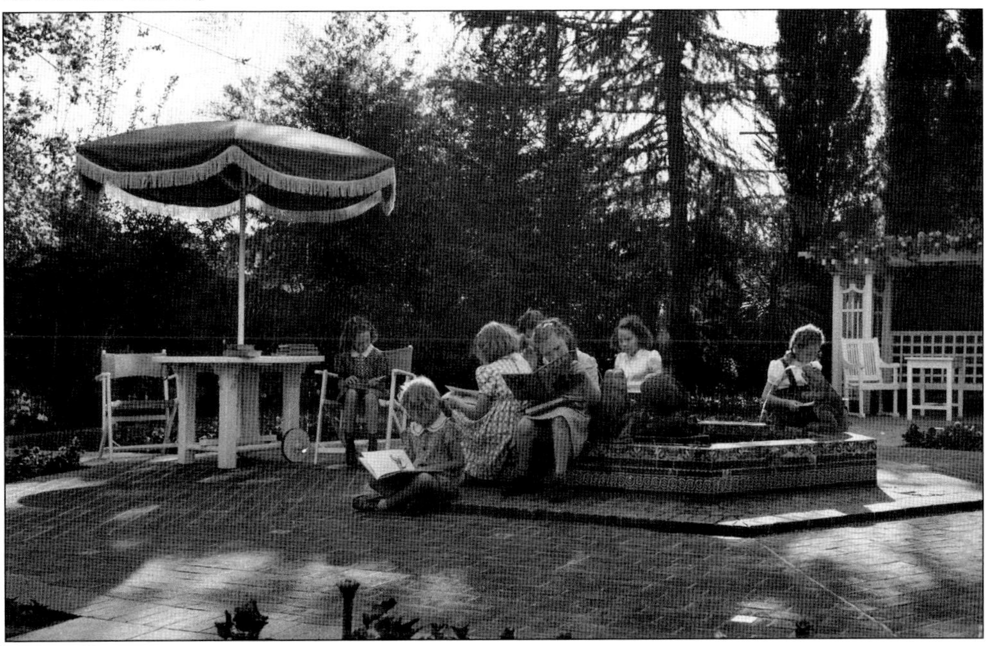

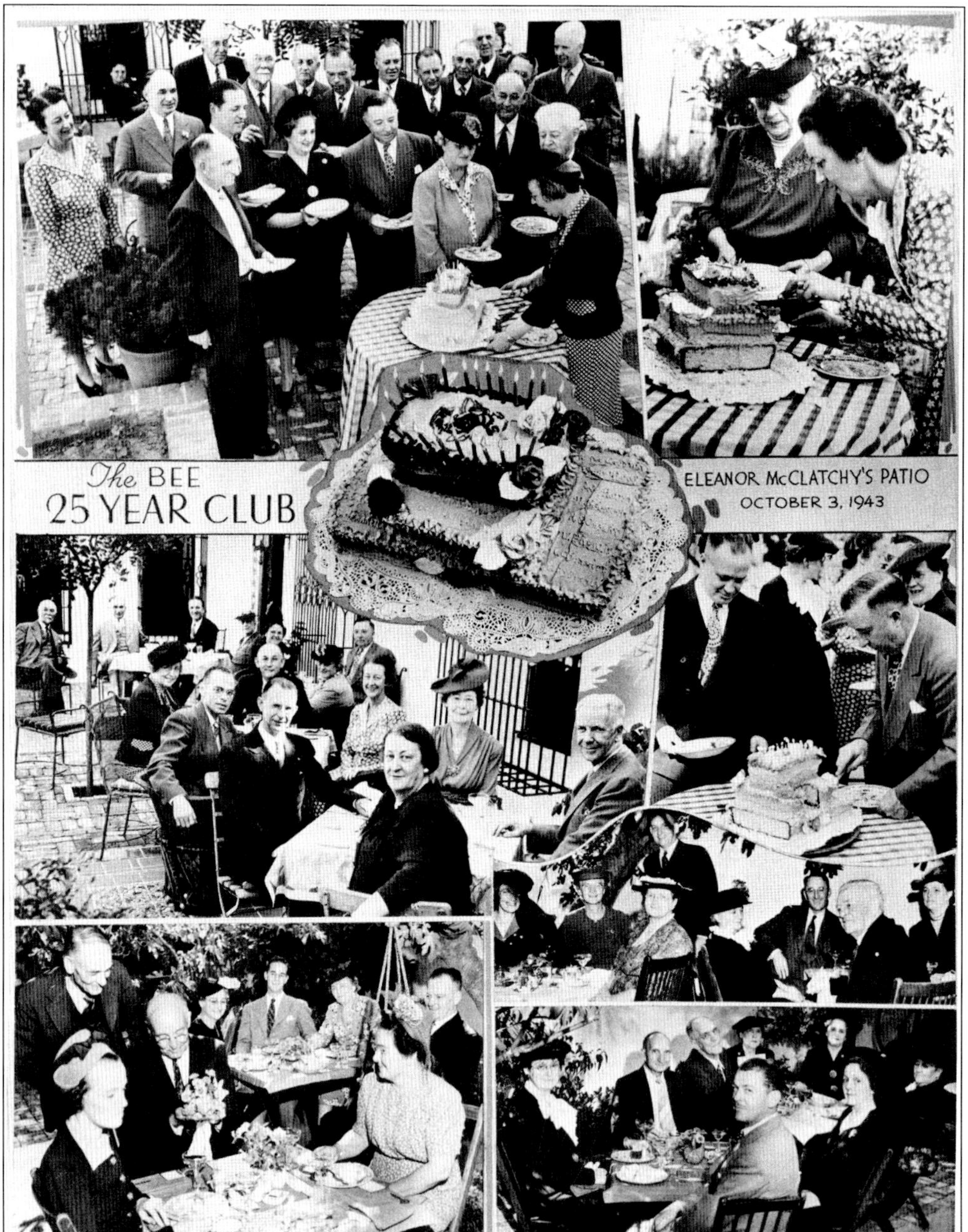

Eleanor McClatchy served as president and editor of the *Sacramento Bee* from the time of her father C.K. McClatchy's death in 1936 into the 1970s. She took great pride in Sacramento, her longtime neighborhood Poverty Ridge, and the family newspaper, which was headquartered along the R Street corridor. This c. 1943 collage shows longtime *Sacramento Bee* staff gathered at one of McClatchy's annual 25-Year Club events, which were held on her patio at 2124 U Street to celebrate the service of long-tenured employees of the *Sacramento Bee*. McClatchy is seen cutting cake for attendees at top right.

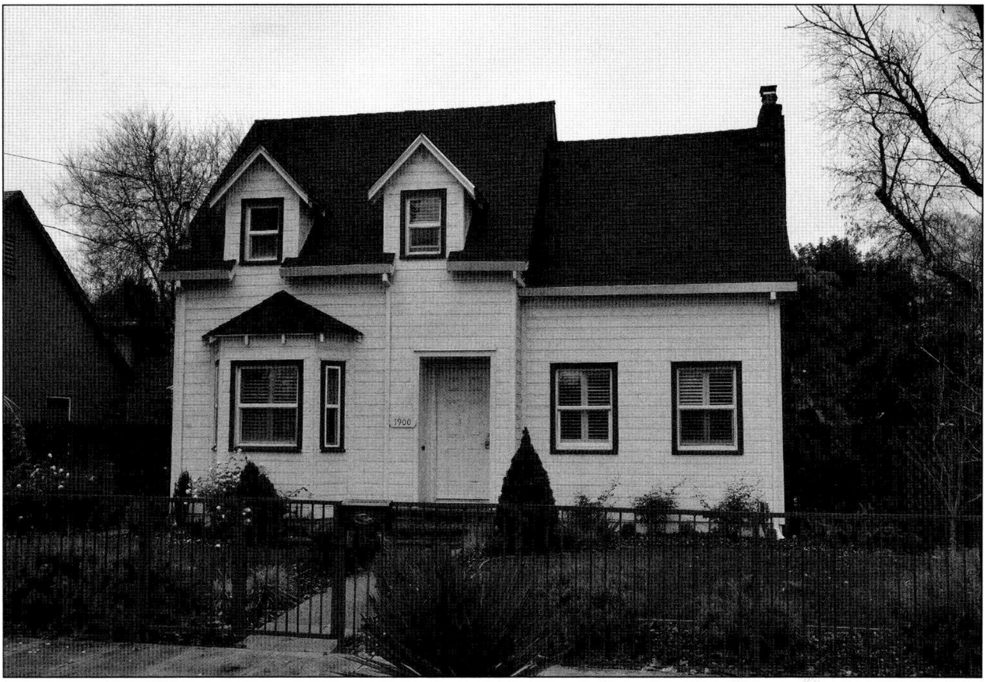

The Colonial Craftsman home at 1900 Twenty-Third Street was built in 1941 for Henry and Sally Taketa. The day after the Taketas occupied their new home, panic swept the nation as the Japanese attacked Pearl Harbor. The Taketa family managed to sell their home just before being unconstitutionally forced by the US government to relocate to the Tule Lake Japanese Internment Camp. (Author's collection.)

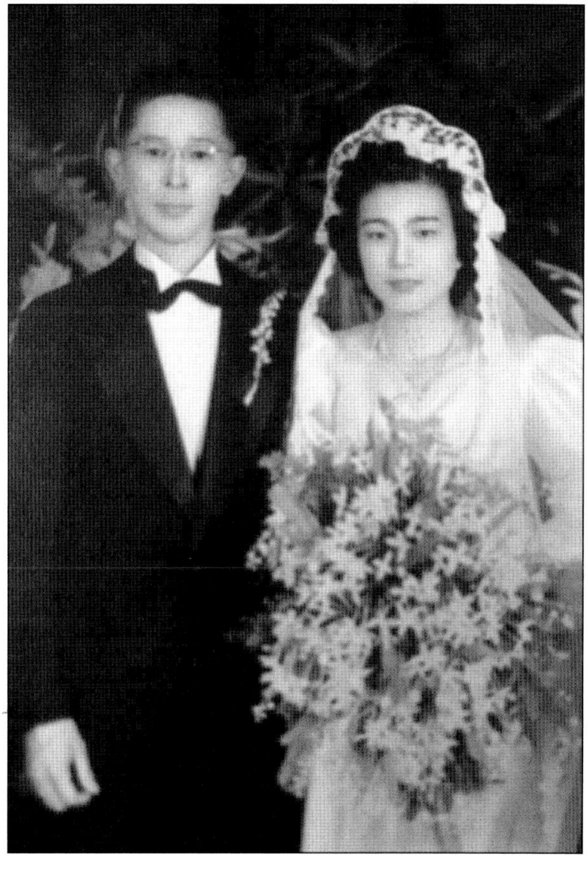

In 1941, Henry and Sally Taketa of 1900 Twenty-Third Street were sent to Tule Lake. Henry volunteered for the draft, and after the war, the Taketas returned to Sacramento, where they became active in addressing the postwar issues that confronted Sacramento's Japanese American community. Henry's tireless efforts to document and share Japanese American history in the region led to the creation of California State Historic Landmark No. 934. (Courtesy of the Taketa family.)

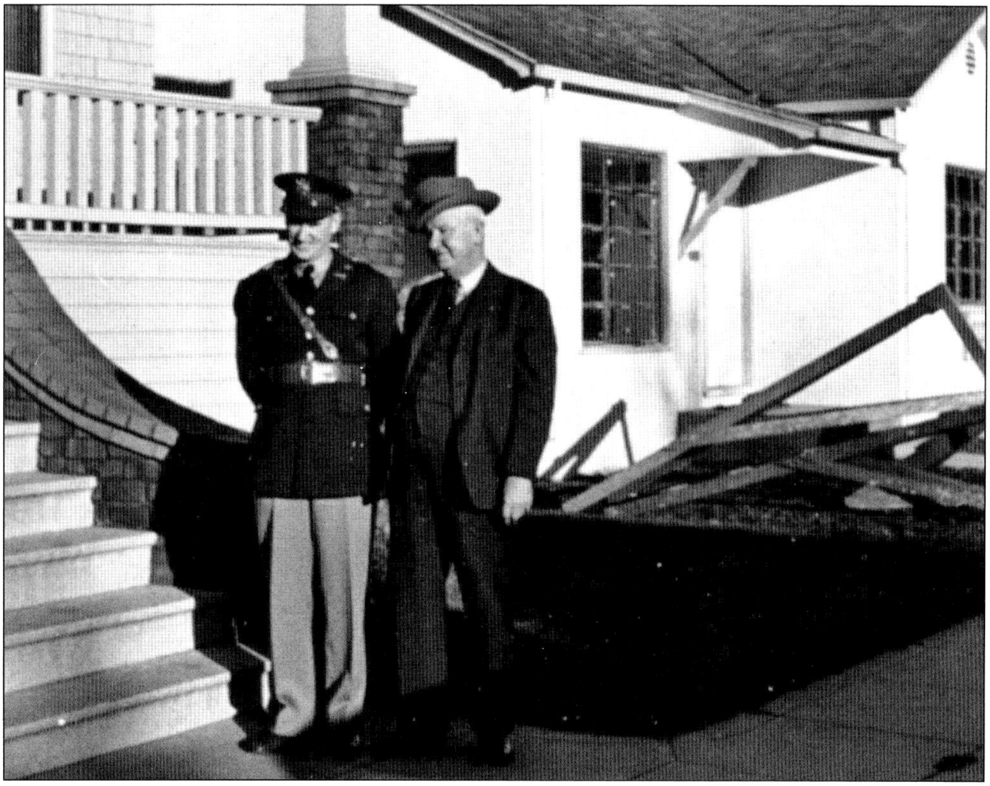

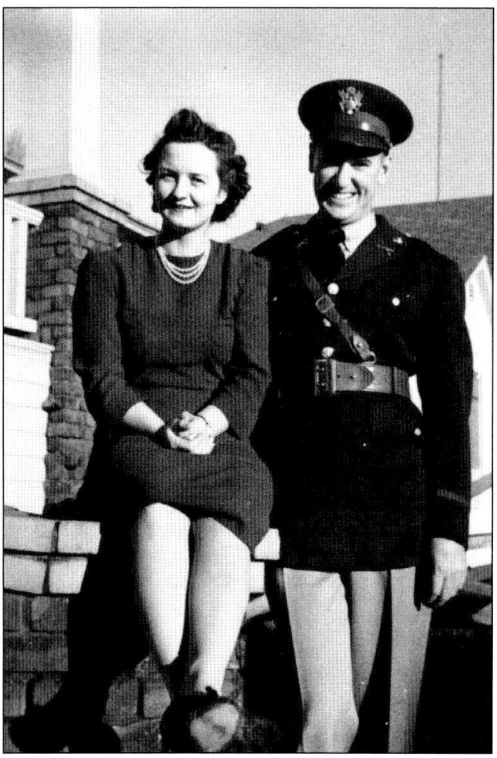

This c. 1942 photograph shows Edgar Boyles Jr. (left) and Edgar Boyles Sr. standing in front of their home at 2523 U Street shortly before Edgar Jr. was deployed to the South Pacific. Like many families in the neighborhood at the time, the Boyles family had multiple members serving in the war effort. Notice the minimal traditional Jurach home at 2525 U Street under construction in the background. (Courtesy of Chris Boyles David.)

Edgar Boyles Jr. and his young wife, Phyllis Roberts Boyles, are pictured in front of the Boyles family home at 2523 U Street in January 1942, shortly before Edgar Jr. was deployed. Edgar Jr. had been in the Reserve Officers Training Corps during his college years and later earned the rank of captain while serving in the South Pacific. (Courtesy of Chris Boyles David.)

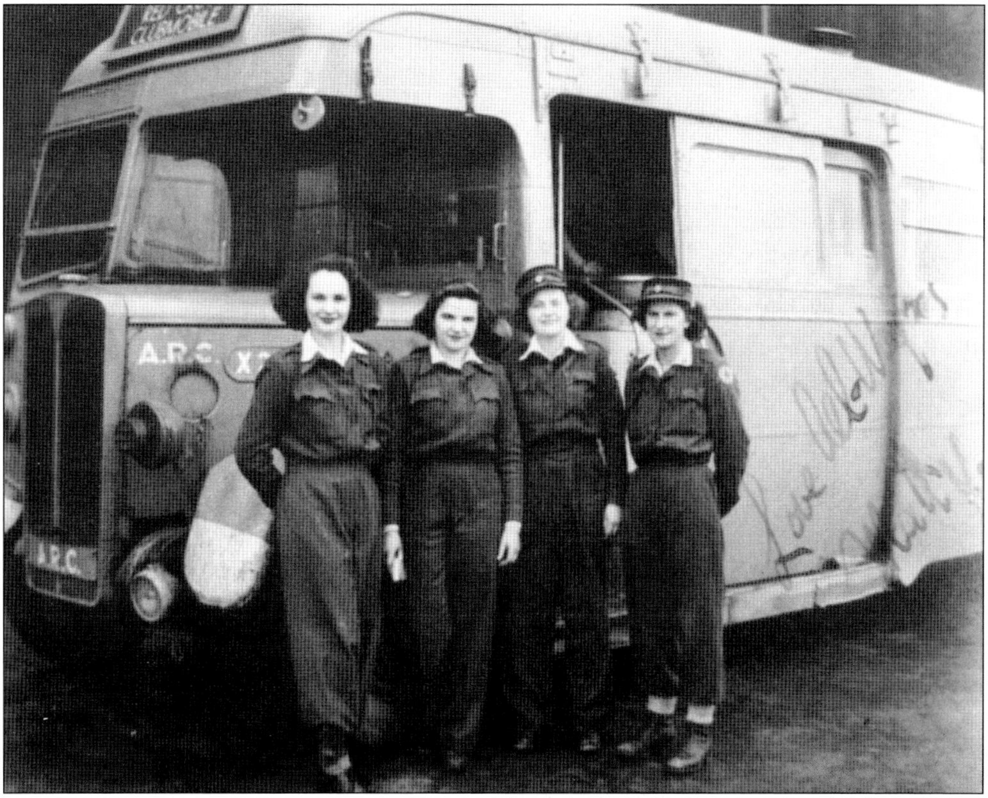

This c. 1944 photograph shows recent Stanford graduate Birdie Boyles (far right) of 2523 U Street with fellow members of the American Red Cross Mobile Canteen Service, a morale-boosting mission where women college graduates brought coffee and donuts to soldiers and airmen along the front lines. Birdie was later awarded the Bronze Star for courageously maneuvering her Clubmobile close to intensive fighting in Germany. (Courtesy of Chris Boyles David.)

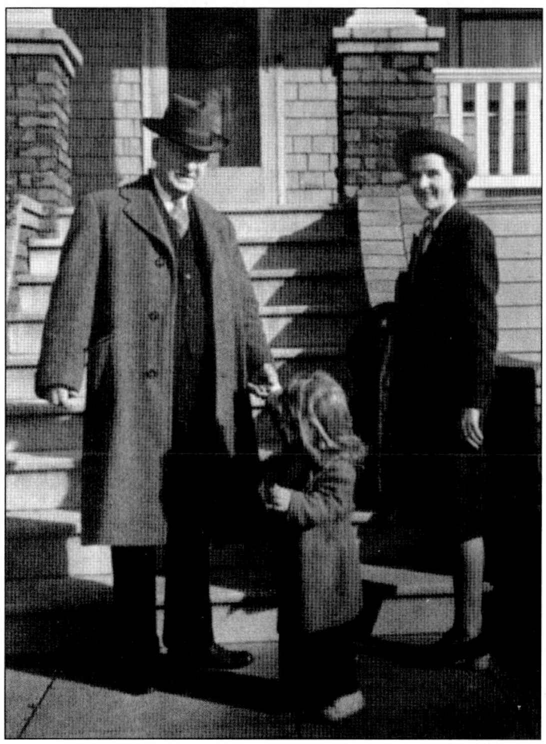

Marian Boyles Sprinkel is pictured around 1940 with her father, Edgar Boyles Sr., and her young daughter, Kay, in front of 2523 U Street. During World War II, Marian's husband, Capt. Robert Sprinkel, served in Europe. Meanwhile, her sister Birdie was serving as a Red Cross volunteer in Germany, and her brother Capt. Edgar Boyles Jr. was serving in the South Pacific. In May 1945, Edgar Sr. suddenly passed away. (Courtesy of Kay Sprinkel Grace.)

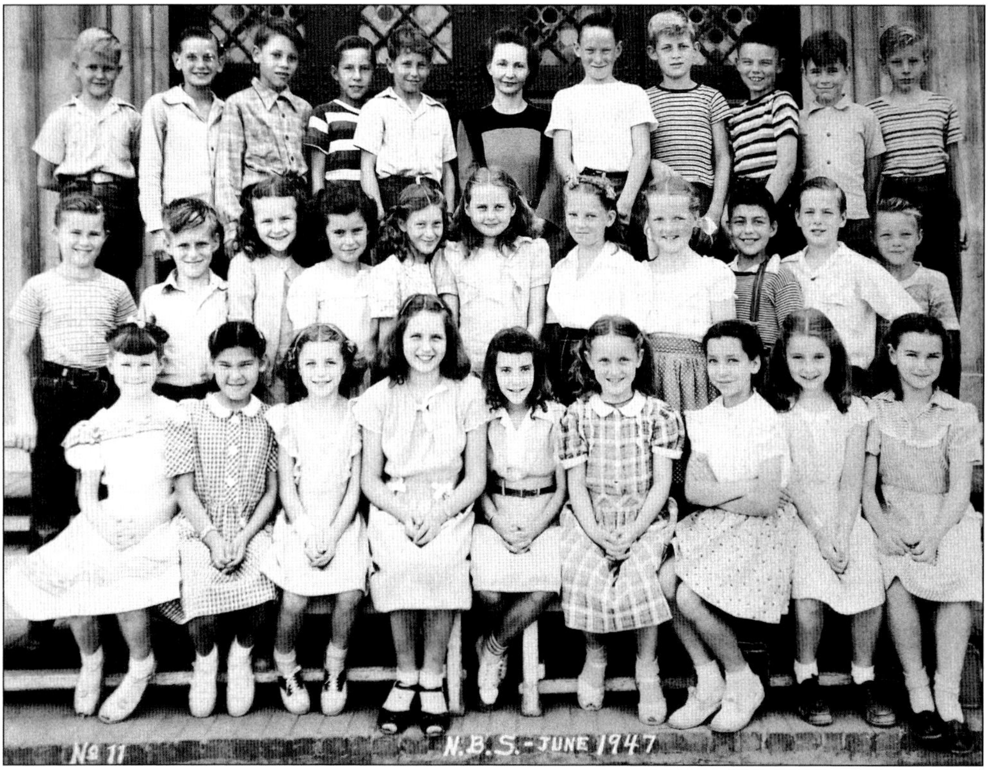

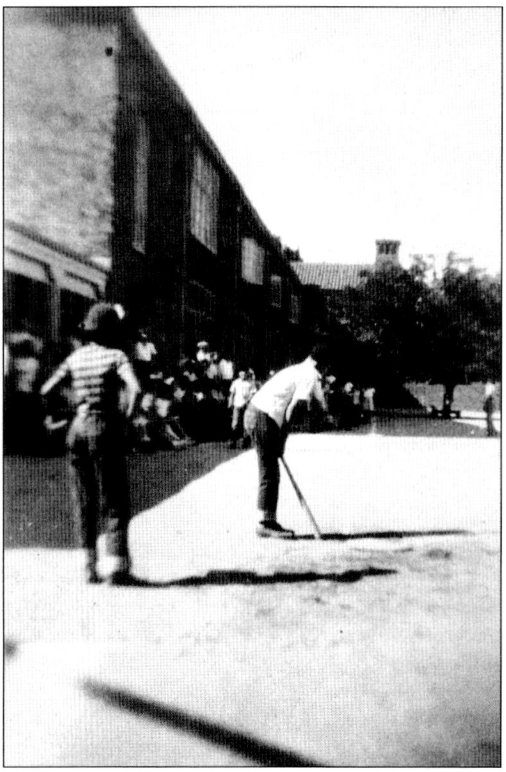

This 1947 Newton Booth School portrait shows Mrs. Green's fourth-grade class. Kay Sprinkel, standing fourth from the right in the second row, was the second generation of her family to attend Newton Booth School. She was the daughter of Robert and Marian Boyles Sprinkel. Marian attended Newton Booth School while growing up at 2523 U Street. (Courtesy of Kay Sprinkel Grace.)

Newton Booth School student Glenn Busbee is at bat in a schoolyard ball game with students and school principal Mr. Spencer. (Courtesy of Kay Sprinkel Grace.)

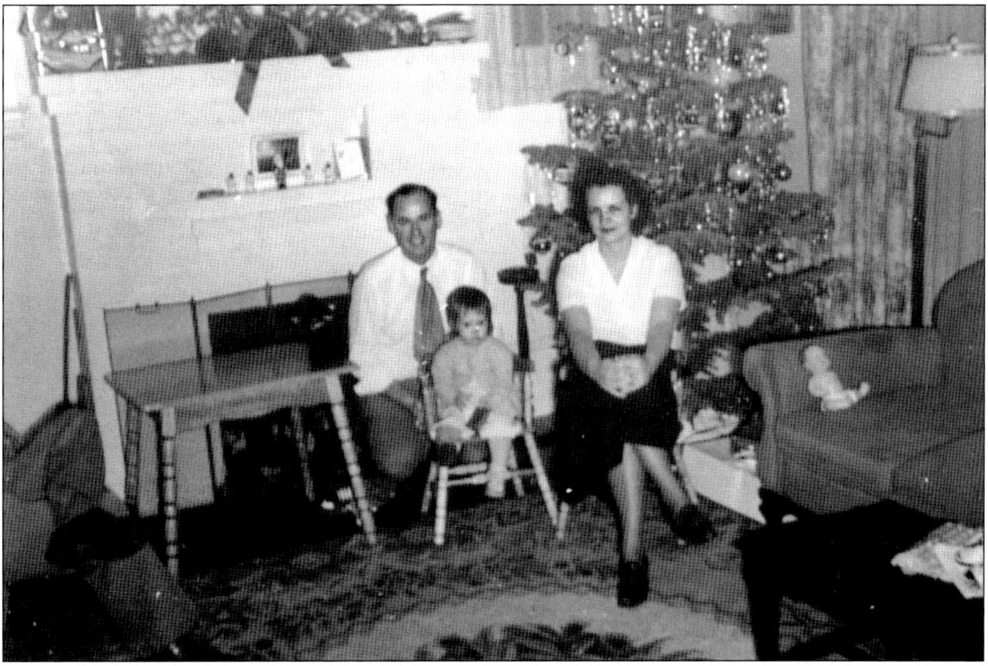

This 1948 Christmas photograph shows Edgar and Phyllis Boyles with their young daughter Christine in the living room of the family home at Twenty-Fifth and U Streets. Like many longtime owners of single-family homes in Newton Booth, multiple generations of the Boyles family lived in the residence and attended Newton Booth School. (Courtesy of Chris Boyles David.)

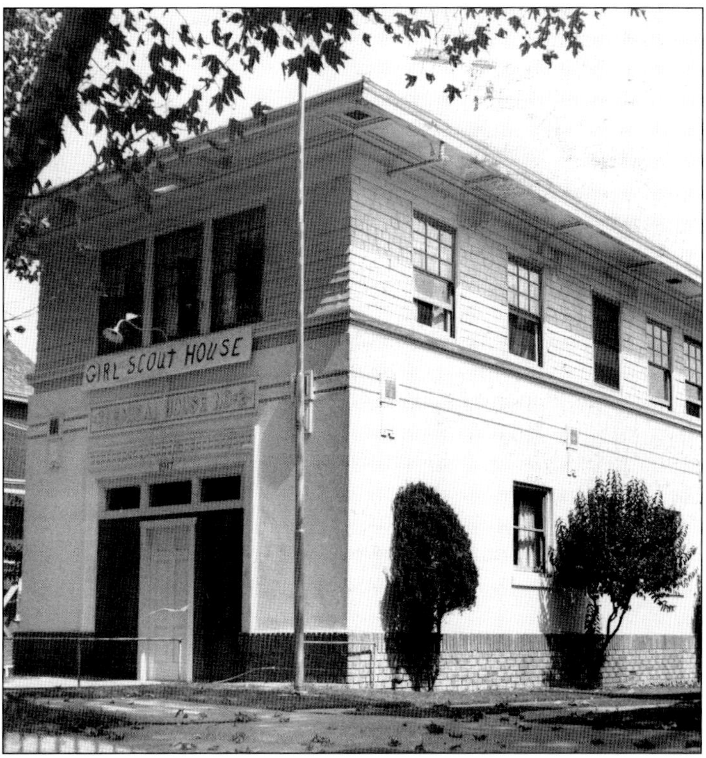

This 1951 photograph shows the old Chemical House No. 2 building at Twenty-Second and T Streets with a banner reading "Girl Scout House." Once firefighting technologies rendered the need for chemical houses obsolete, many of the buildings were sold and repurposed. A Girl Scout troop was likely permitted to use this property until it was sold and converted into office space for an engineering firm.

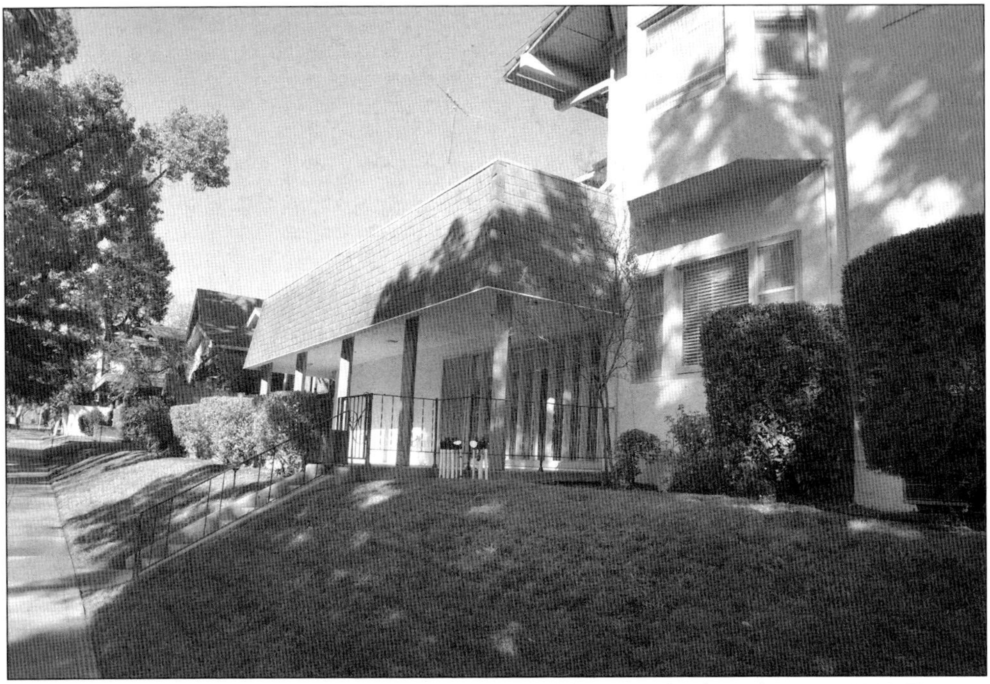

In 1957, Dr. Oscar Johnson converted the former Robb-Carmichael residence at 2030 Twenty-Third Street into the Lutheran Home for the Aged. In 1965, the Lutheran Development Society added a six-unit annex to the rear of the home. As of 2020, the facility is known as the Ivy Ridge Assisted Care Facility. (Author's collection.)

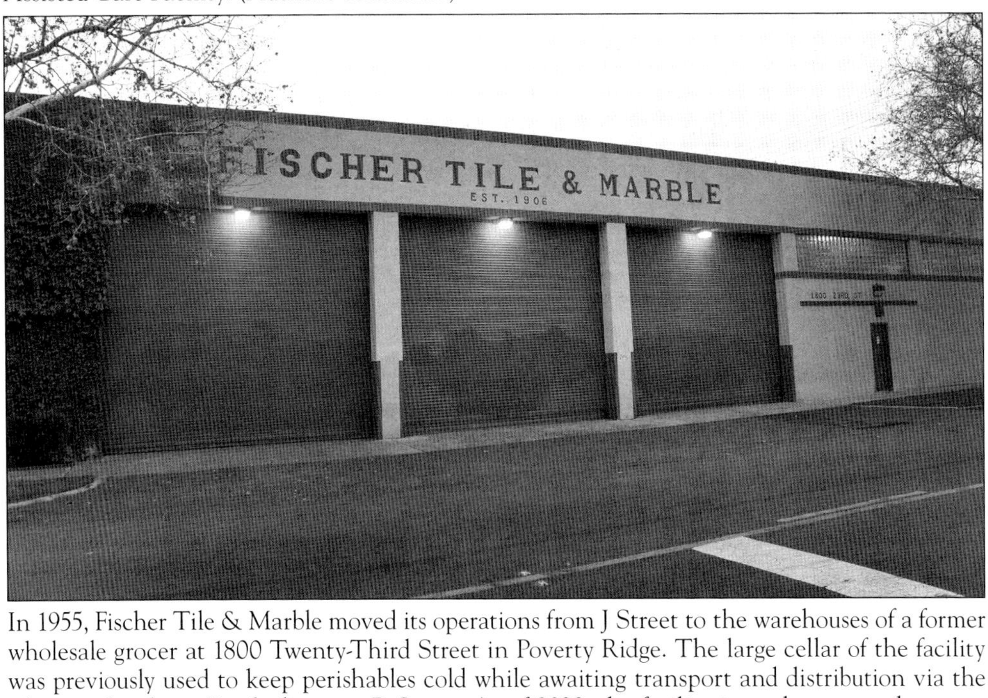

In 1955, Fischer Tile & Marble moved its operations from J Street to the warehouses of a former wholesale grocer at 1800 Twenty-Third Street in Poverty Ridge. The large cellar of the facility was previously used to keep perishables cold while awaiting transport and distribution via the adjacent Southern Pacific lines on R Street. As of 2020, the facility is used to cut and prepare tile and stone orders before installation. (Author's collection.)

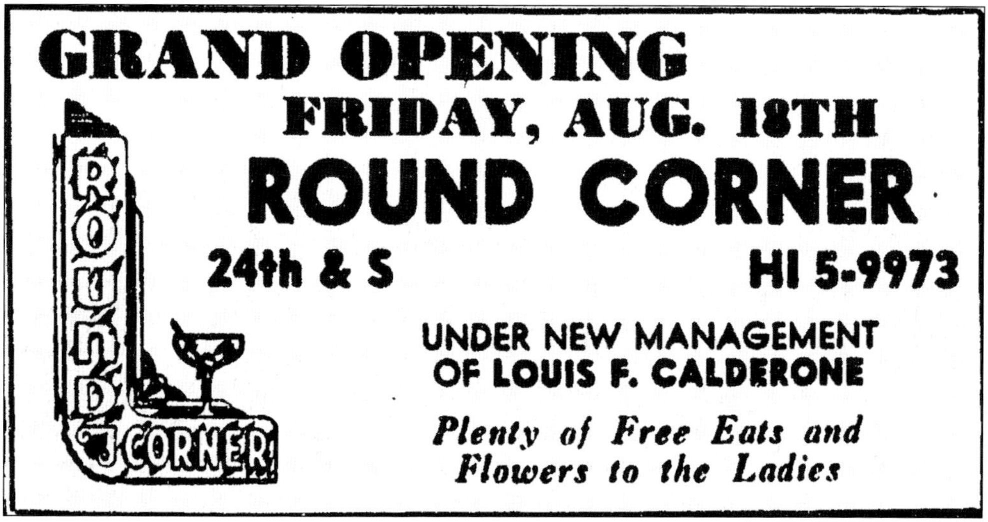

The Round Corner Tavern was built at 2333 S Street around 1945 and displays a rounded corner at its front entrance that is reminiscent of the rounded corner of a pool table. Around the time of this c. 1951 advertisement, the establishment was managed by Louis Calderone. Nestled along the R Street industrial corridor, it served as a local watering hole for many of the workmen from neighborhood businesses, such as Fischer Tile & Marble. The Round Corner even used to cash payday checks for area workers, a portion of which would often cover their bar tabs. (Courtesy of the Sacramento Library.)

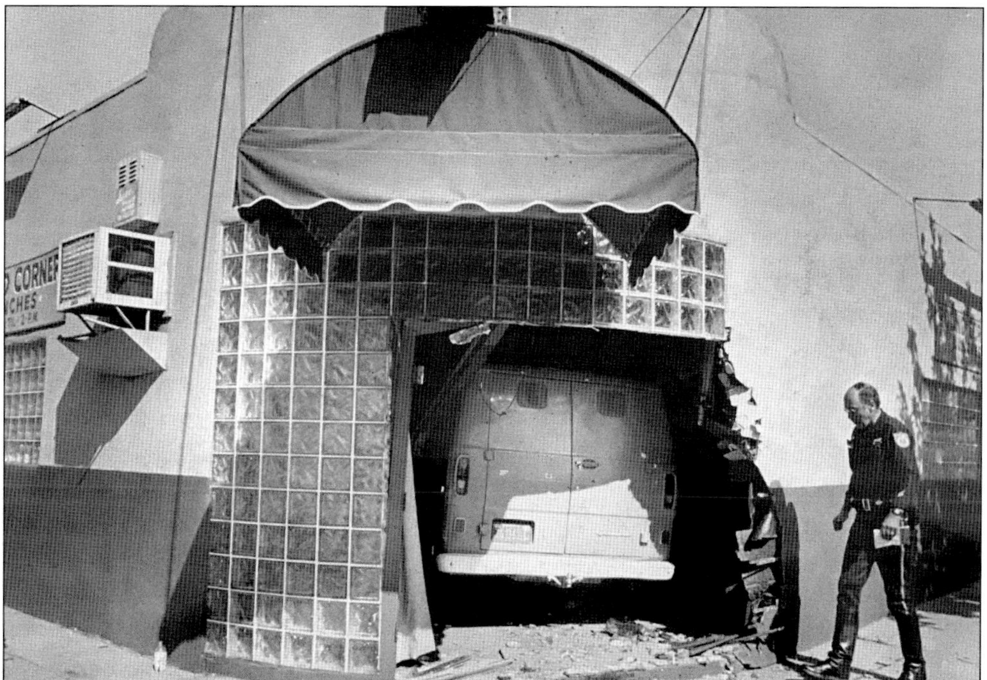

This c. 1986 photograph shows one of two instances when someone plowed a vehicle through the main entrance to the Round Corner Tavern. Fortunately, this incident occurred early in the day when only staff were present, and no one was injured. (Courtesy of the Round Corner Tavern.)

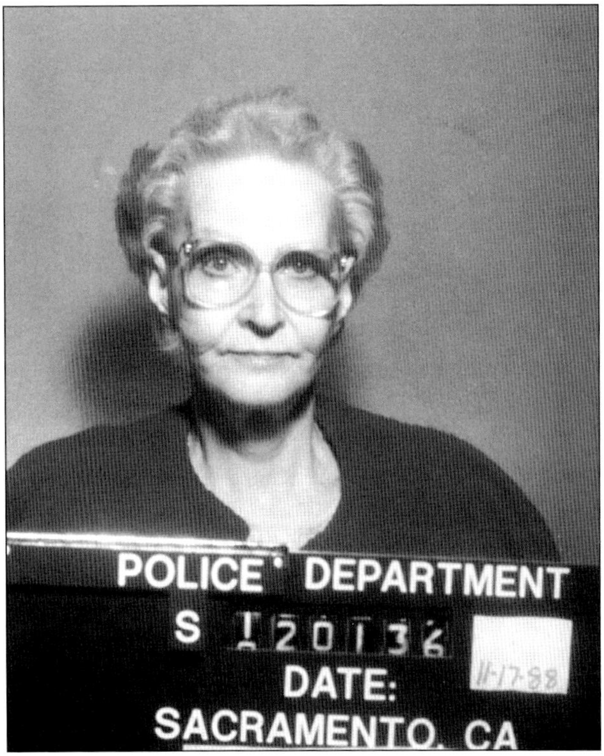

Pictured in her 1988 mugshot is Sacramento's most notorious serial killer, Dorothea Puente. In 1981, Puente and a business partner leased the kitchen at the Round Corner Tavern. Puente was arrested soon after and is believed responsible for the murders of at least eight people, seven of whom were found buried under the rose garden of her boardinghouse at Fourteenth and F Streets. Well known for her exceptional culinary skills, Dorothea's dishes were well regarded by hungry patrons at the Round Corner. (Courtesy of the Sacramento Police Department.)

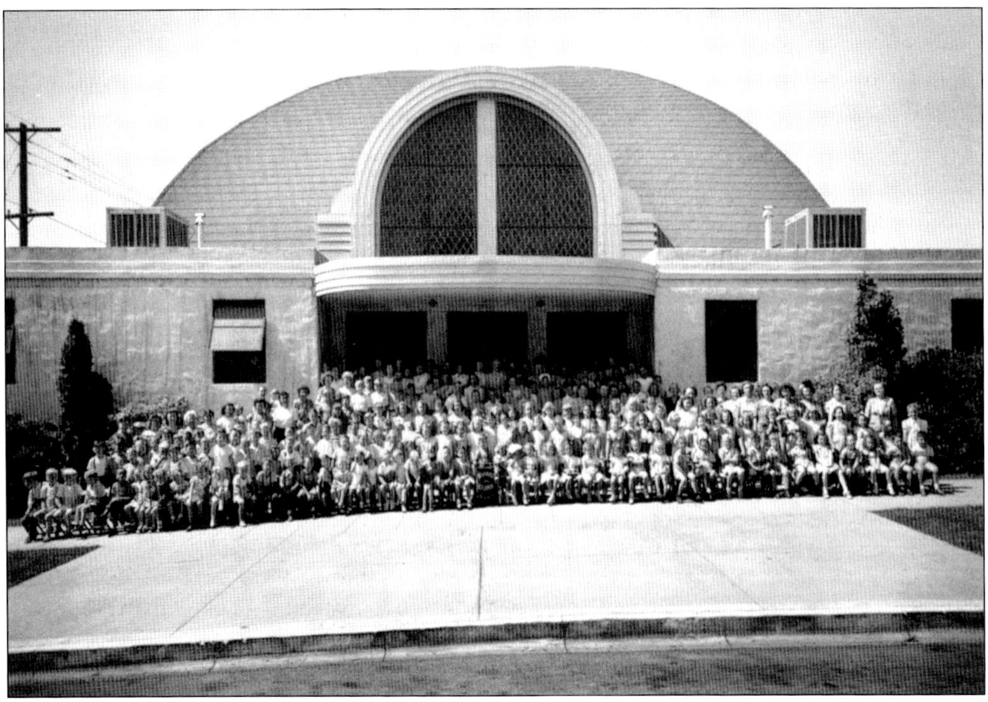

This c. 1942 image shows the Bethel Temple Full Gospel Church at 2030 W Street. The church was built around 1940 and often hosted large regional retreats and conferences. In 1964, construction of the W-X Street freeway forced the temple to relocate. (Courtesy of the Sacramento Room.)

Six

Urban Decay, Freeways, and Redevelopment

As Sacramento entered the mid-20th century, the pre-1950s urban density was replaced by a new national vision of suburbia, commuter living, and larger properties. Once-beautiful stately homes on relatively small plots began to show their age. With the advent of new transportation technologies and ever-present economic pressures, younger generations migrated outwards from city centers, and commerce quickly followed. Economically and legislatively, investment shifted from urban cores to suburban growth centers, driving new class segregations and creating new economic haves and have-nots.

Those who could do so tended to relocate to new tract homes and suburban developments farther from the original urban core. These efforts were supported by the construction and expansion of freeways throughout the region. In the 1960s, the long-anticipated Capital City Freeway project was underway and resulted in the complete leveling of one contiguous city block along the four-mile southeastern flank of the old central city.

When the southern leg of the project was completed, every house and business and public space from the 19th to the 28th blocks of W and X Streets had been razed to make room for freeways supporting automobiles, new commuters, and new commerce in the ever-growing Sacramento footprint, now exponentially grown from its origins at Sutter's Fort.

The new proximity to a loud and busy freeway took a hard toll on central city property values—including the neighborhoods of Newton Booth and Poverty Ridge—while whetting the appetites of land speculators who built parking lots and entry-level apartment buildings where older Victorian and Edwardian architecture had fallen into disrepair, decay, and public disfavor.

Some vintage and historic buildings were saved by generous and preservation-minded longtime neighborhood residents who had the financial means to do so. Others were protected by entrepreneurs who opted to use them as places of business rather than tear them down for new construction. Nevertheless, as previously optimistic investment in the maintenance of late-19th- and early-20th-century structures gave way to a new era of enthusiasm for sleek mid-century modern design, many of the historic homes of Poverty Ridge and Newton Booth fell victim to blight, urban decay, and eventually the wrecking ball.

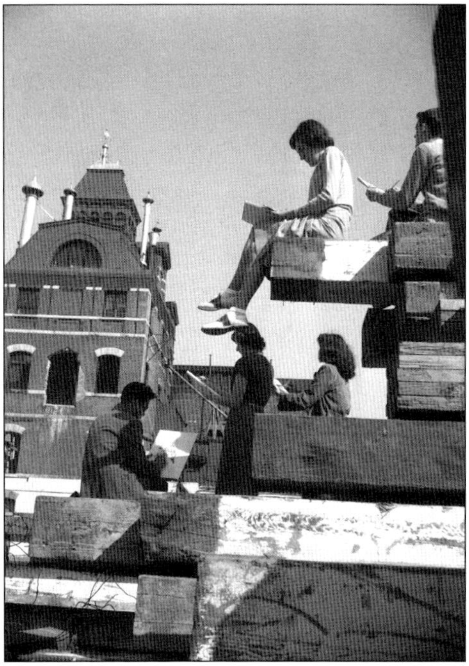

In this 1950 image from a *Sacramento Bee* piece, "Buffalo Brewery, Sketching a Vanishing Landmark," members of a Sacramento Junior College art class sketch the Buffalo Brewery shortly before it was demolished to make way for the new *Sacramento Bee* building. Upon closing in 1945, the complex quickly fell into a blighted state.

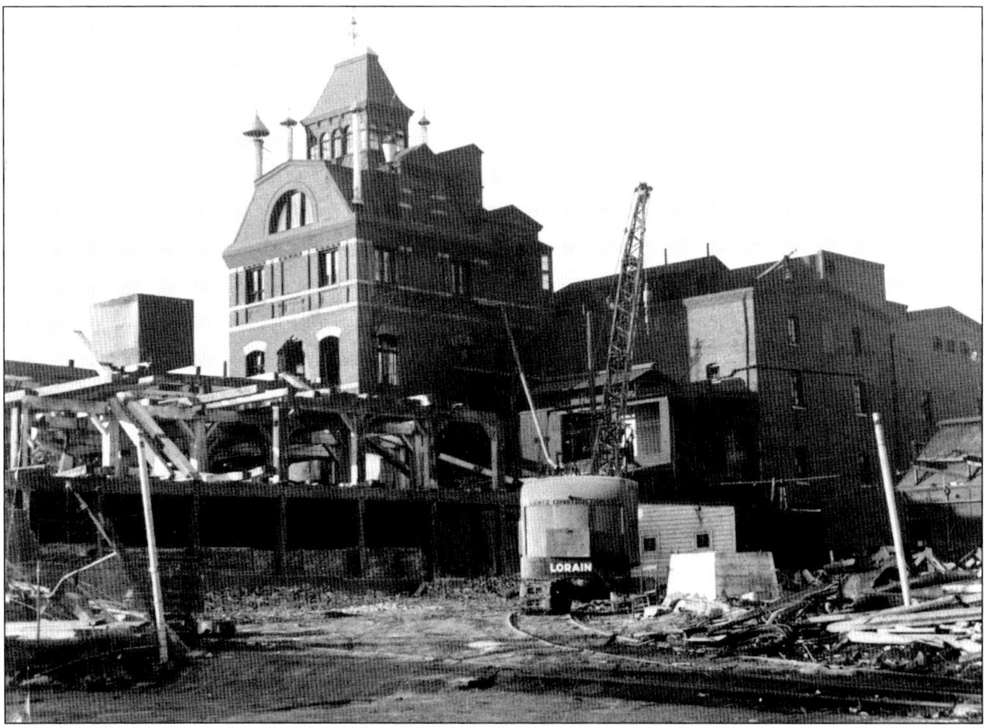

This c. 1950 image shows the demolition of the Buffalo Brewery at Twenty-First and R Streets. For over 60 years, the brewery was a regional source of pride and a major driver of economic growth along the R Street corridor. Notwithstanding the loss of the historic brewery, the new *Bee* headquarters substantially revitalized the blocks previously inhabited by the brewery and significantly contributed to the evolving local economy.

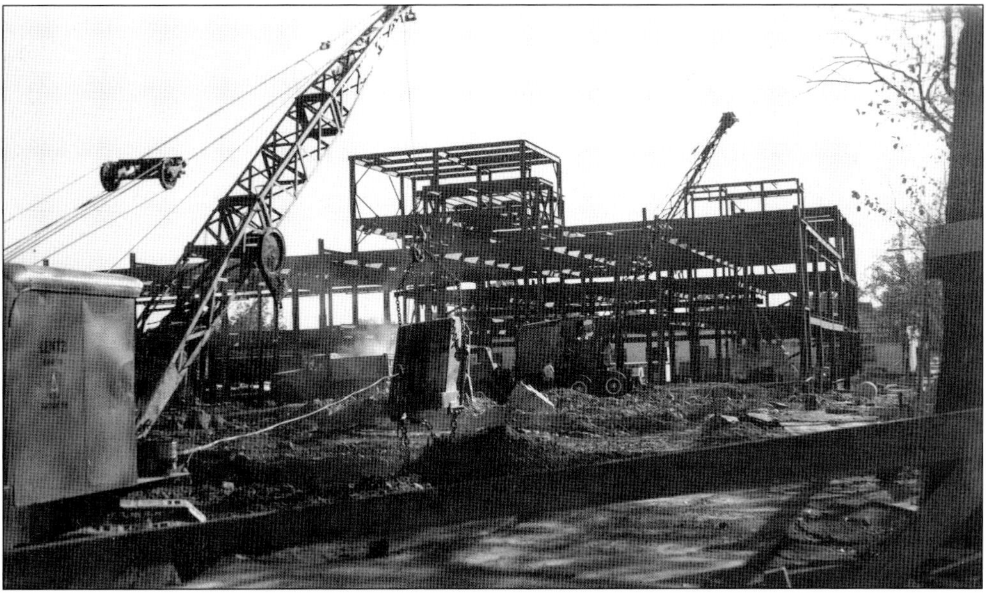

This c. 1951 photograph shows the new *Sacramento Bee* building under construction. After outgrowing its old building at 911 Seventh Street, the company opted to build a modern complex on the site of the recently shuttered Buffalo Brewery. The new location would also be adjacent to the R Street rail lines, which would help to facilitate content distribution. Not coincidentally, *Bee* publisher Eleanor McClatchy also shortened her commute to just three short blocks from her home in Poverty Ridge.

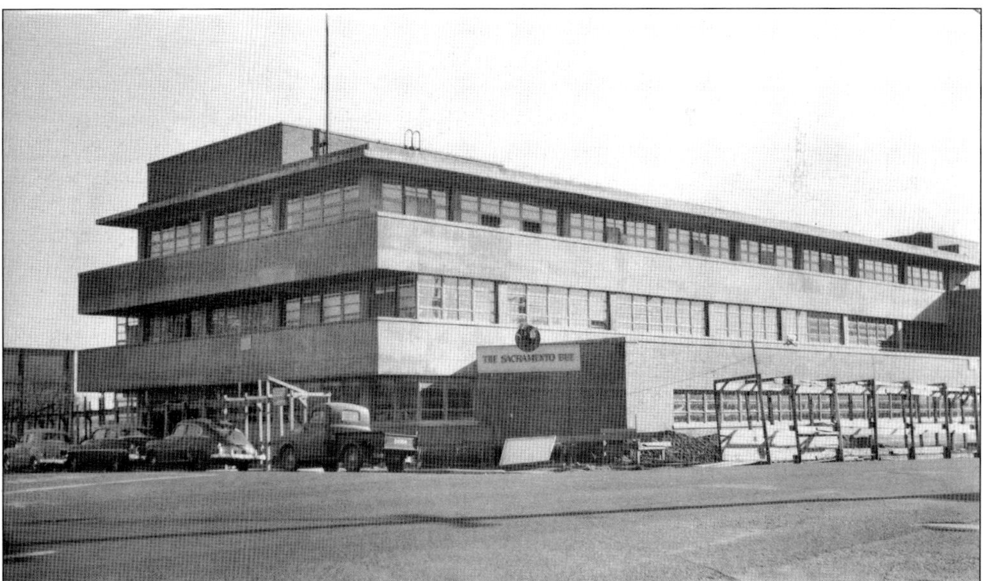

The new *Sacramento Bee* building was finished around 1952. The massive complex covered land previously occupied by the Buffalo Brewery and the original Sisters of Mercy Hospital (Mater Misericordiae). (Courtesy of the Sacramento Room.)

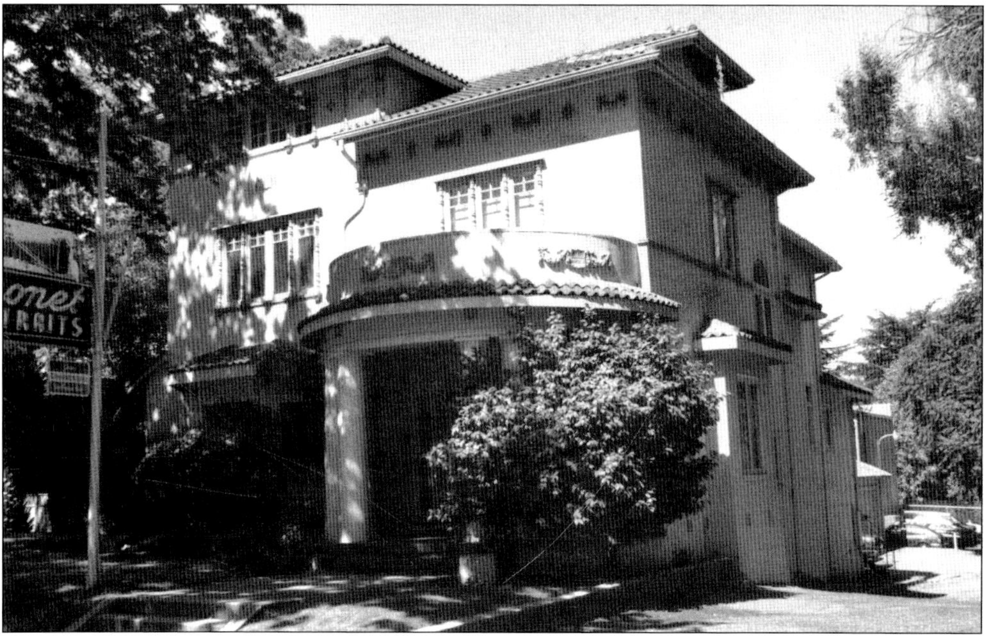

The Coronet Portrait Studio opened its doors in the former home of winegrower J.C. Coffing at 2116 Twenty-First Street. The exterior architectural details of the c. 1910 Mission and Colonial Revival home remained well preserved. The portrait studio was one of several businesses that took up residence in the old mansions of Poverty Ridge as old family homes gave way to commercial, multiuse, and multifamily purposes.

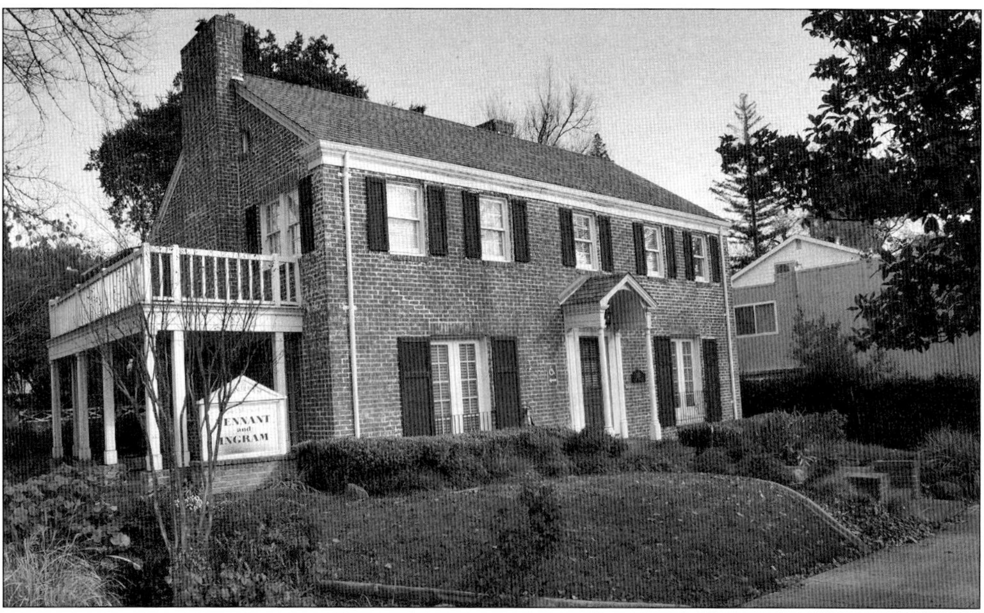

The 1927 brick Colonial Revival home at 2101 W Street was built for Albert and Jessie Chrisler, who occupied the property until the 1970s. The residence was later converted to law offices. Many older homes in the Newton Booth and Poverty Ridge neighborhoods survived demolition, in part because they were repurposed at a time when many families and individuals had moved out of the neighborhoods. (Author's collection.)

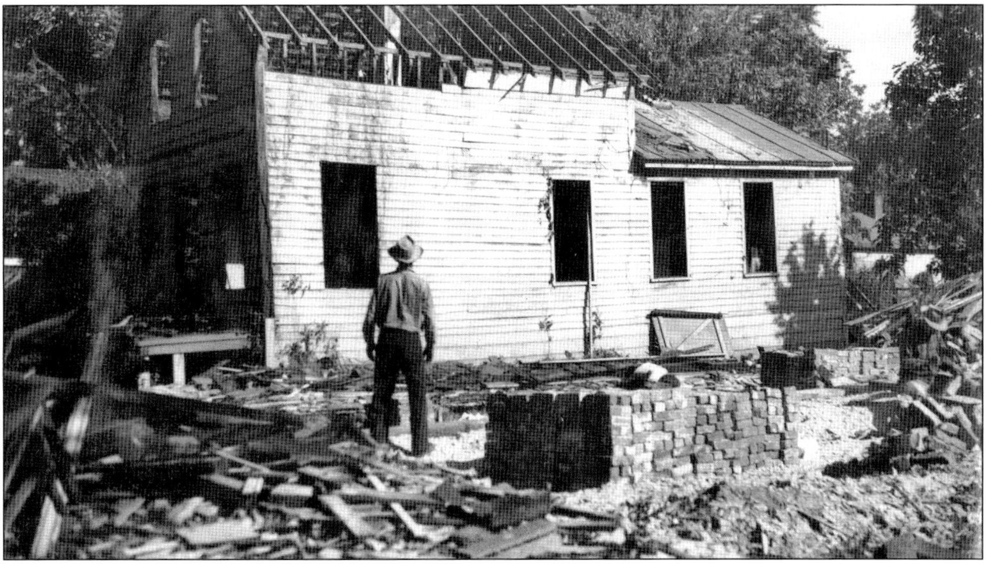

This c. 1950s photograph shows the old John Moloney home at 2031 Twenty-First Street being demolished. As Sacramento entered the mid-century, single-family homes in the old city became less desirable for parents of baby boomers, who sought new, modern tract homes in the suburbs outside the original urban core. Over the 1950s, 1960s, and early 1970s, many of Sacramento's 19th- and early-20th-century homes fell victim to demolition.

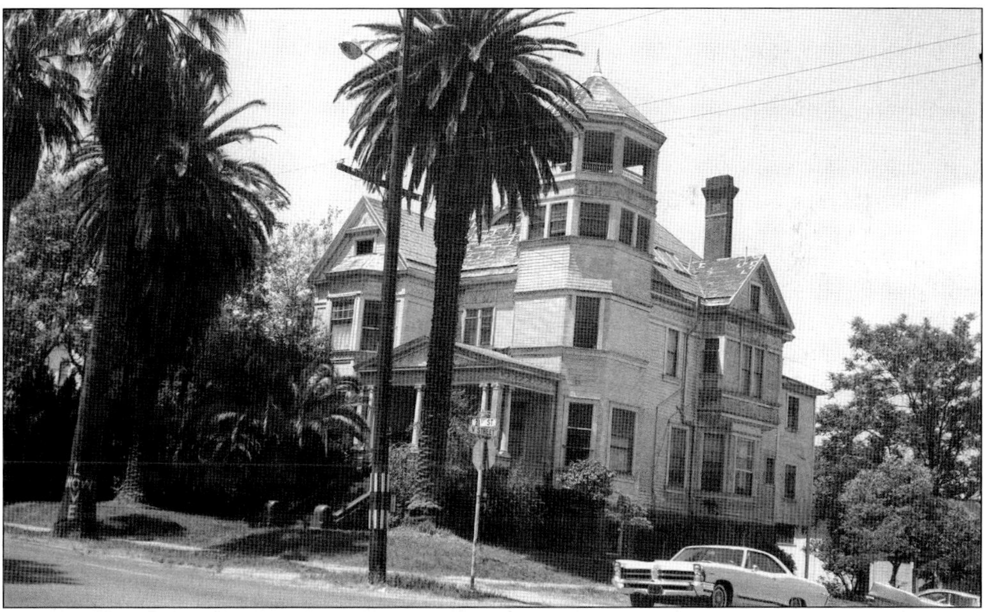

This 1967 image shows the blighted shell of the once-grand Herman H. Grau mansion at Twenty-First and V Streets. Without a generous benefactor such as Eleanor McClatchy or an adaptive-minded business such as Coronet Portrait Studio, the future of several of the neighborhood homes seemed bleak. The former Grau family home at 2200 Twenty-First Street was demolished and, in 1972, replaced with a mid-century office building.

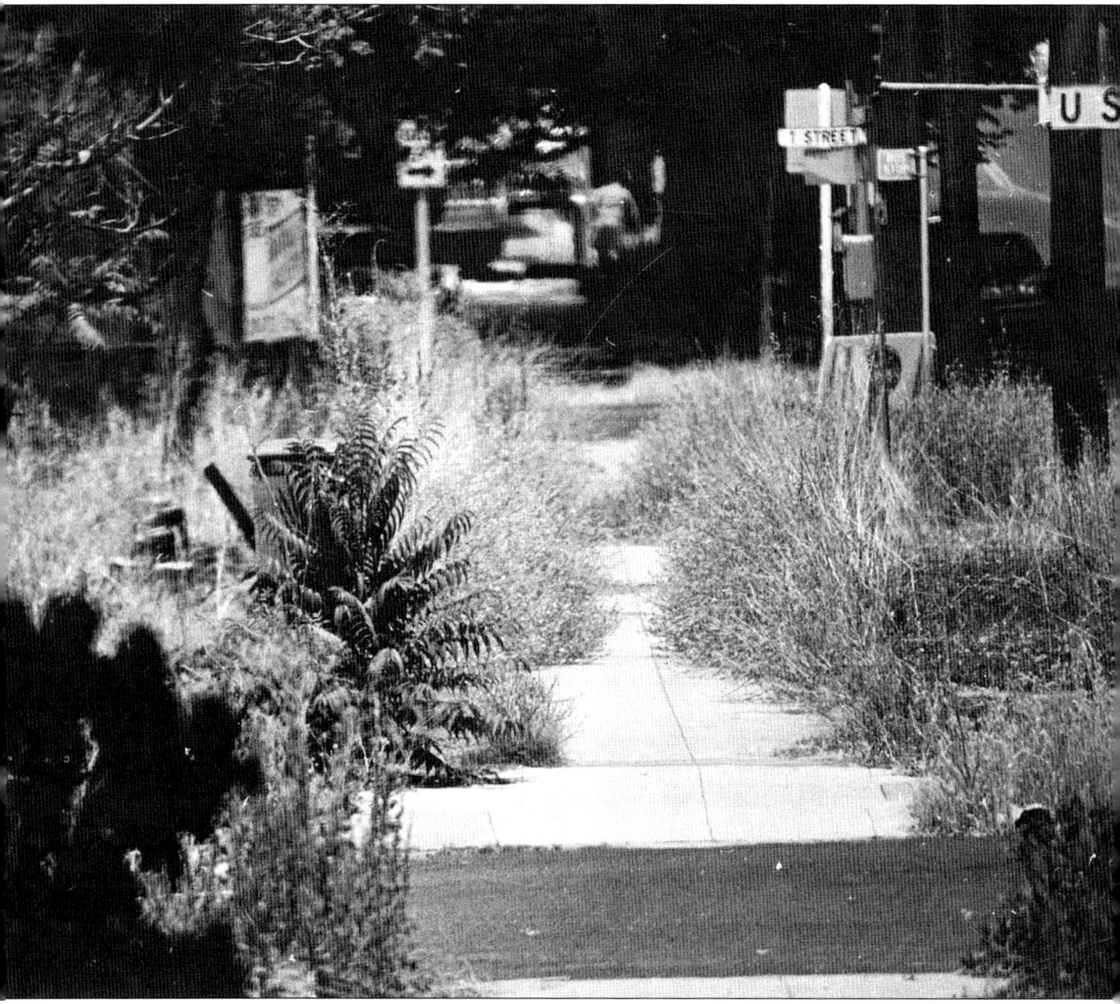

This 1968 photograph shows an area overgrown with thick weeds where a property's yard met the sidewalk on the west side of Twenty-First Street between T and U Streets. An article in the *Bee* at the time stated that the absentee landlord of the property had already been fined by the city for neglect. Nevertheless, the issue persisted. Absentee landlords and land speculators were a common issue during the redevelopment phase of the 1950s through the 1970s.

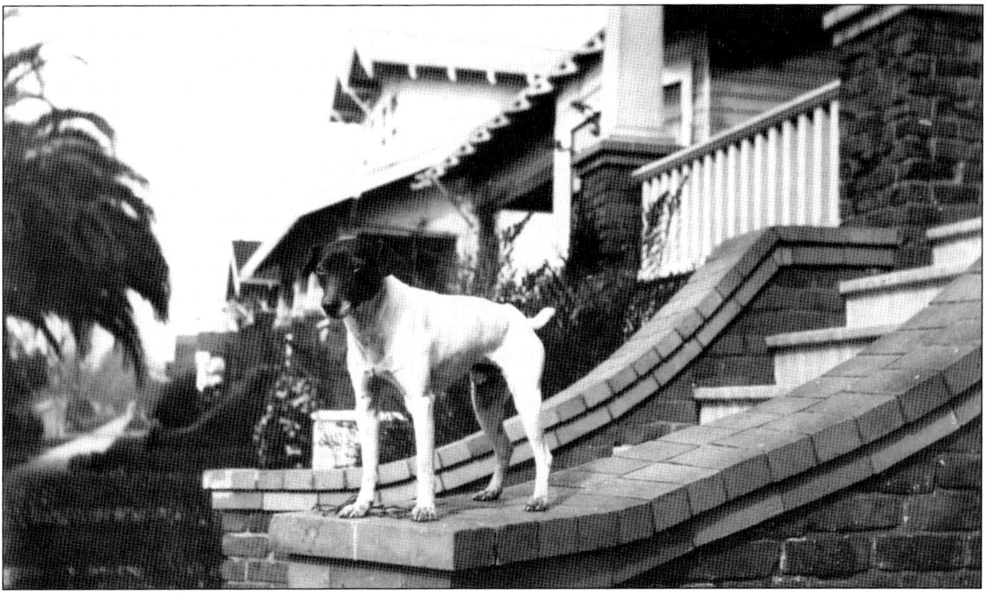

The Boyles family dog, Jiggs, stares up U Street around 1925. Behind Jiggs, the small 1912 Craftsman-style Smith-Fulmer home at 2517 U Street can be seen. The home was sold and demolished in the late 1950s to make way for a new apartment building. (Courtesy of Chris Boyles David.)

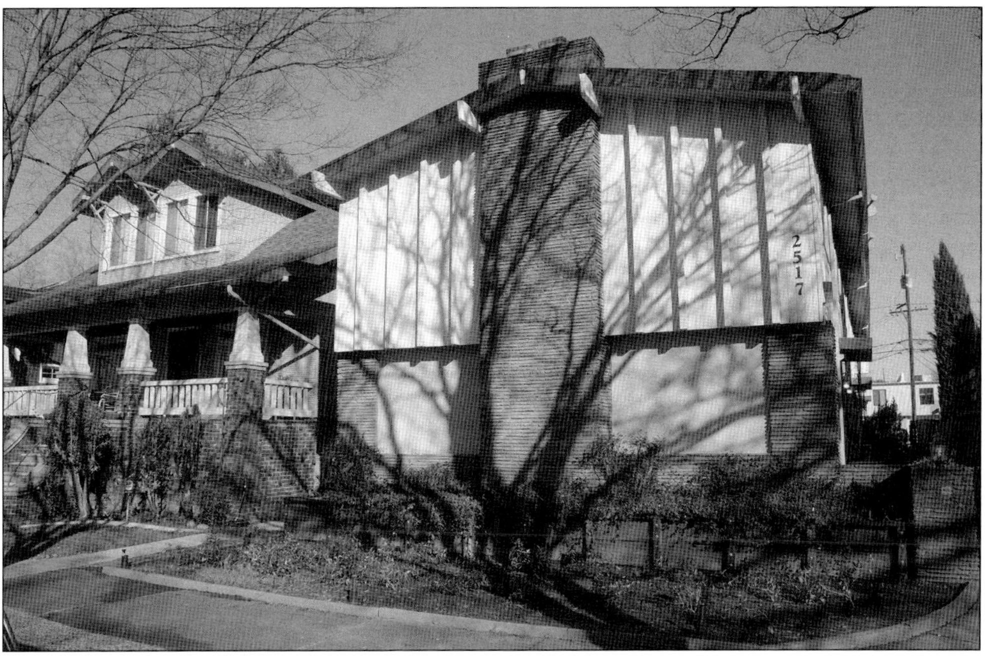

This 1960s apartment building at 2517 U Street was built in place of the 1912 Craftsman home. Many early-20th-century properties were lost in Newton Booth from the 1950s to the 1970s as state and city redevelopment programs created incentives to demolish old single-family homes. Many of the neighborhood's working-class families, particularly ethnic minorities, were systematically and institutionally denied credit and loans even as developers were given preferential subsidies to build entry-level housing. (Author's collection.)

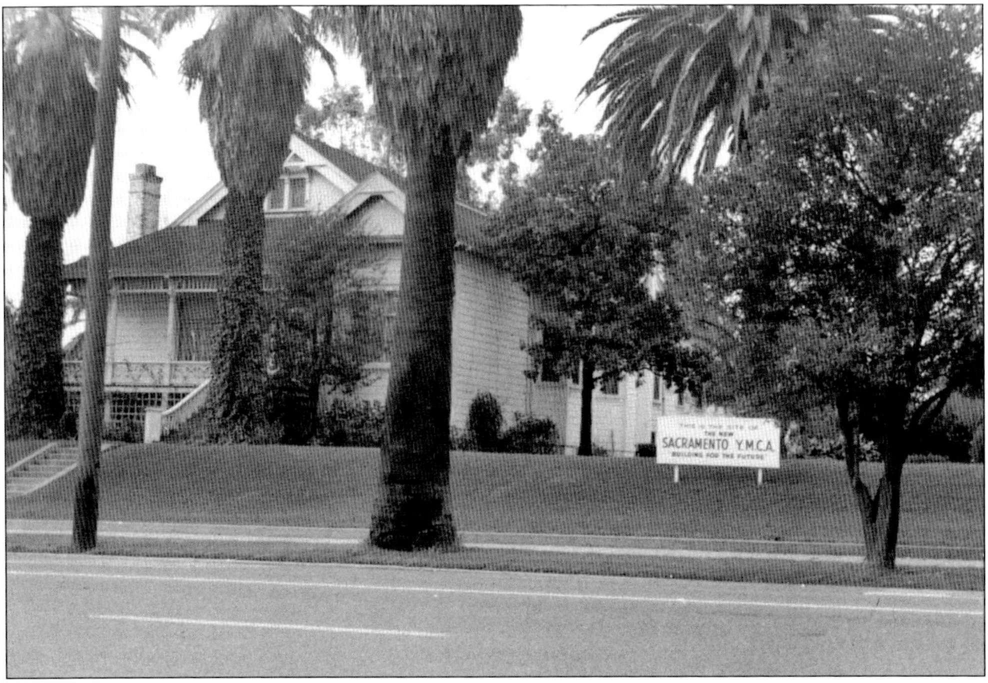

This c. 1950 image shows a sign in the yard of the former Peltier home at 2228 Twenty-First Street identifying it as the future location of the Sacramento YMCA. After George Peltier's passing, the home was inherited by the Peltiers' only daughter, Jeanette, and her husband, Byron Vandenberg. Around 1950, the Vandenberg family, who had long been supporters of the YMCA, sold their home and land to the organization at a discounted price.

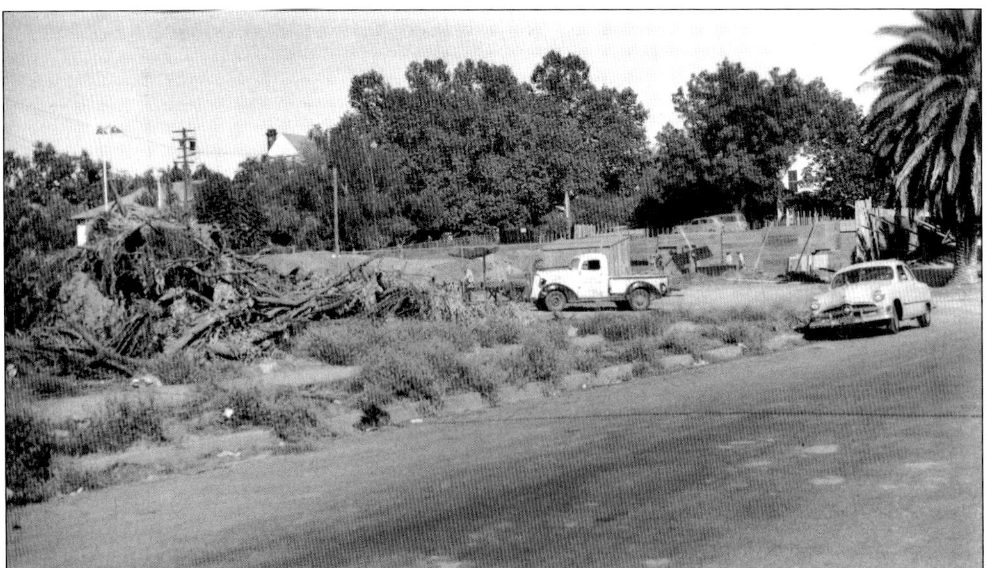

As seen in this image from 1951, the YMCA broke ground on a new Sacramento facility at the site of the former Vandenberg home at 2228 Twenty-First Street. A parking lot stands today at the former location of the home.

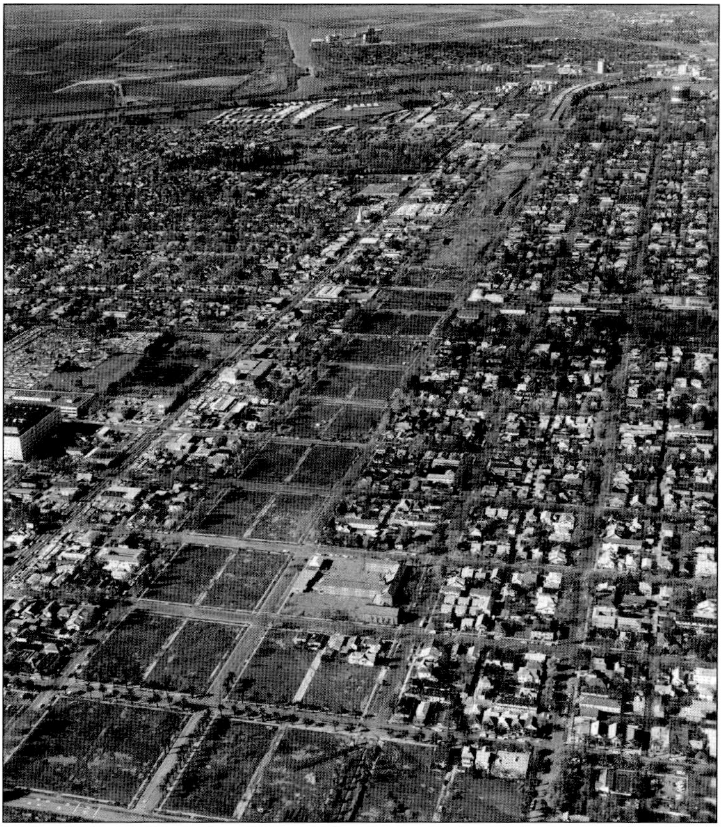

This 1965 aerial view looking southwest shows the W-X Street freeway interchanges and how the entire swath of W Street, bounded by nearly every numerical block on the original city grid, was completely demolished to make way for the new motor vehicle transportation network. The Newton Booth School can be seen at bottom center. (Courtesy of Caltrans.)

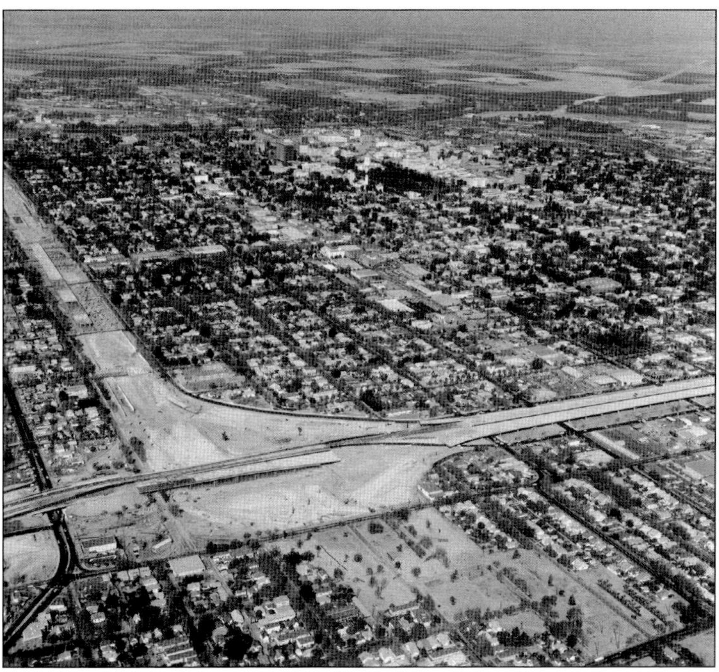

This 1966 aerial photograph of construction of the W-X Street freeway interchanges shows how the freeway project impacted the Newton Booth and Poverty Ridge neighborhoods. Notice the Newton Booth School campus at bottom center left. (Courtesy of Caltrans.)

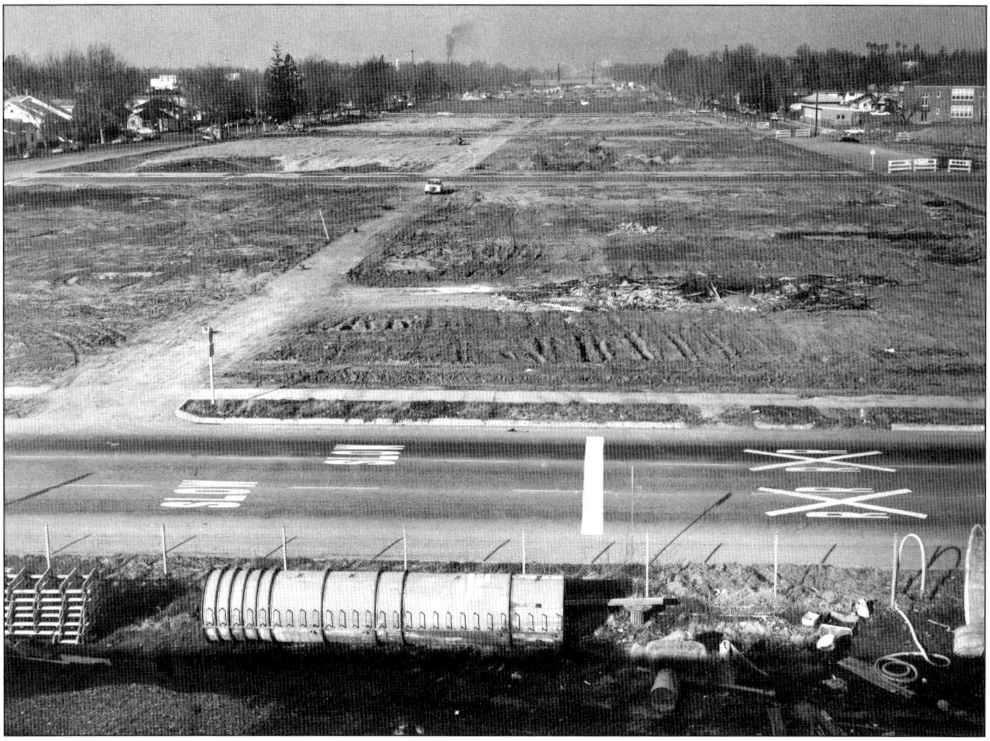

These c. 1966 images provide a western view of the W-X Street freeway project from Thirtieth Street, illustrating the dramatic change brought upon the neighborhoods by the construction. In both photographs, the Newton Booth School can be seen at top right. (Both, courtesy of Caltrans.)

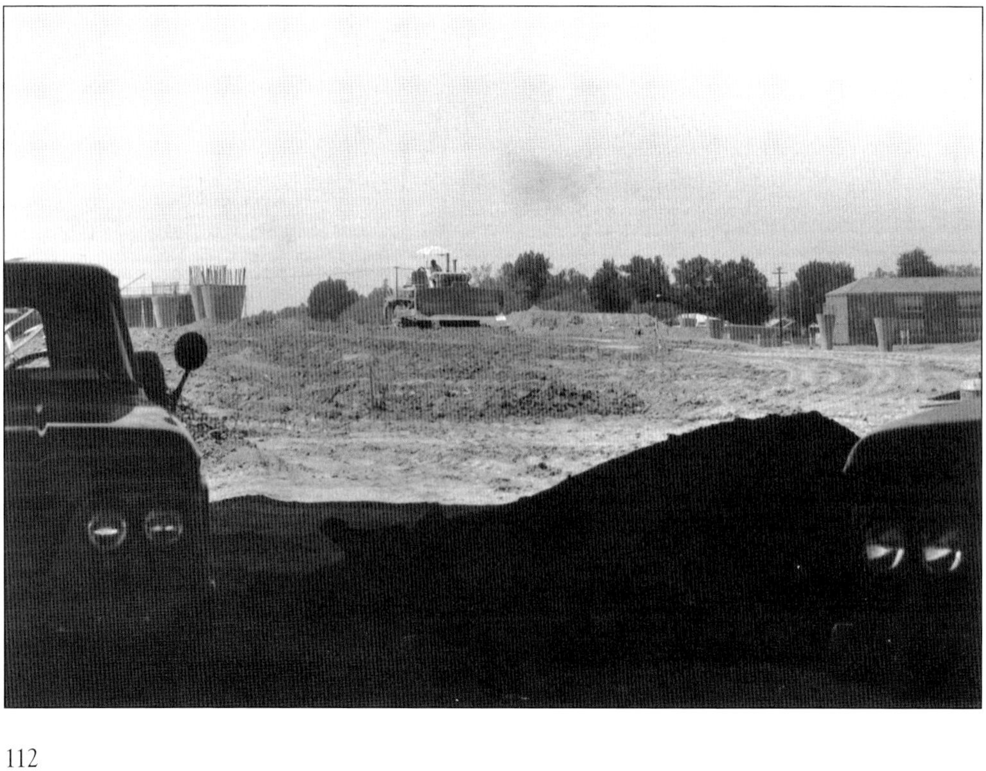

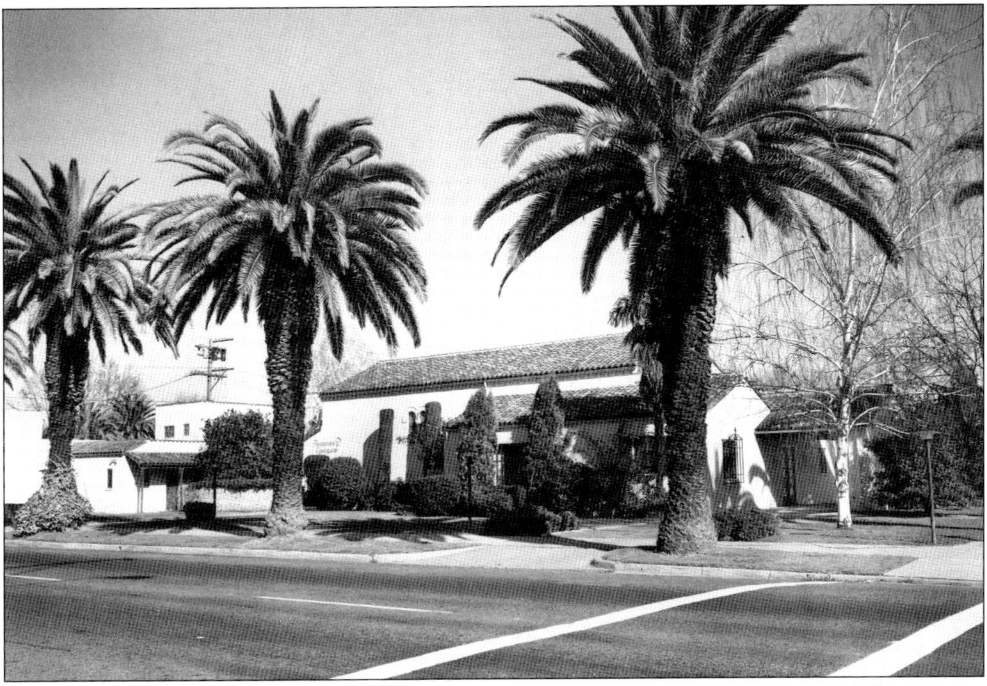

The Andrews and Greilich Mortuary Chapel was built in 1933 at 2221 Twenty-Eighth Street in Newton Booth. The mortuary and funeral chapel was designed in the Spanish Revival style, much in keeping with other civic, commercial, and religious neighborhood buildings such as the Newton Booth School and the First Church of the Nazarene. After construction of the W-X Street freeway, the mortuary home at Twenty-Eighth and W Street was demolished.

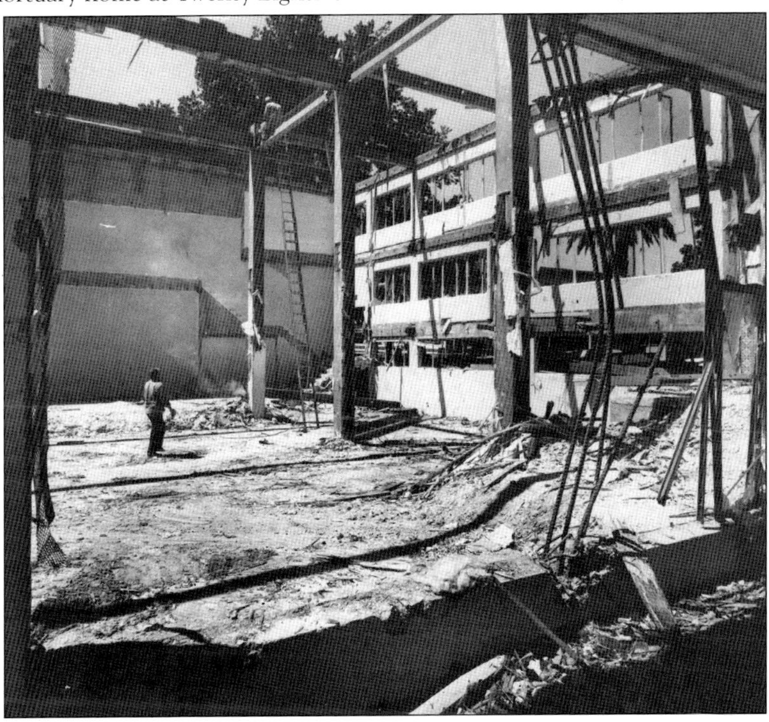

The Bethel Temple church was built around 1940 at Twentieth and W Streets in Poverty Ridge. This 1964 image shows the temple's annex demolished in order to make room for the new W-X Street freeway.

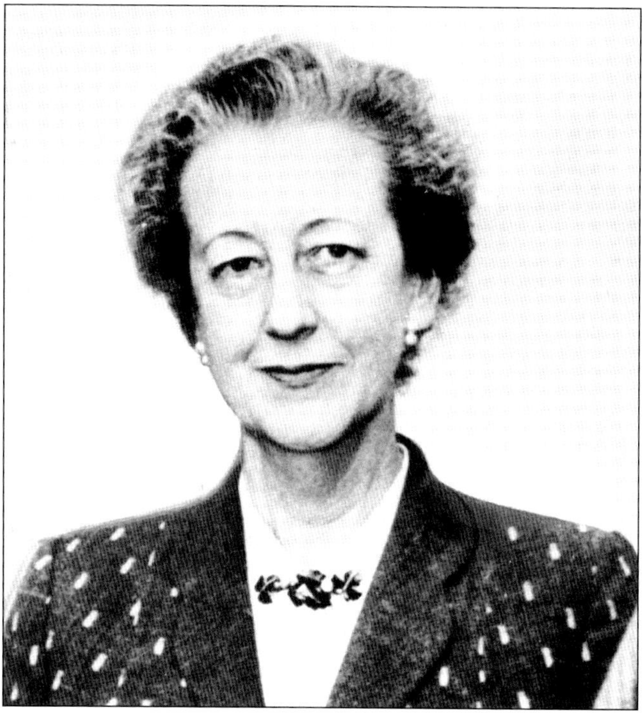

Even as many original homes were lost to the new economic, transportation, and demographic evolution of the city (of which freeway construction, land speculation, and even owner neglect were arguably only side effects), some historic properties were rescued by preservation-minded citizens. For example, Poverty Ridge resident Eleanor McClatchy protected several homes in the neighborhood, including the Herold home (2100 Twenty-Second Street) and the John Stevens home (2110 U Street).

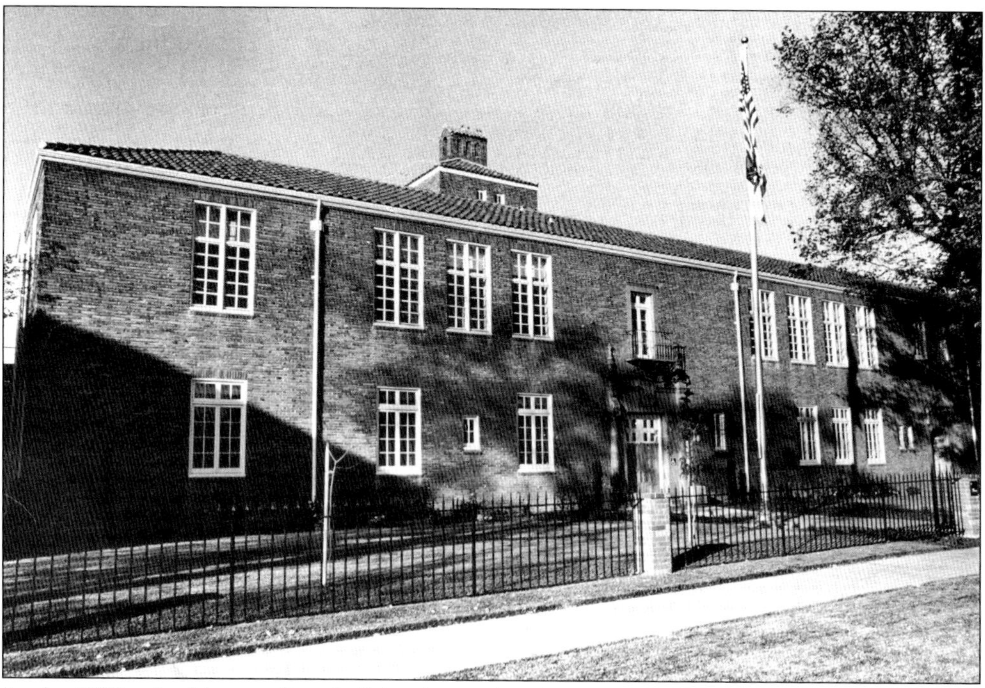

In the 1970s, the Newton Booth School was closed—as were other campuses from the early 20th century—due to the high costs of retrofitting buildings to modern safety standards. The school district sold the old school in the years following its closure. New corporate ownership retrofitted the building and leased it as office space. This c. 1985 photograph shows the former school repurposed as the headquarters for the Americare Health Corporation.

Seven

PRESERVATION AND URBAN RENEWAL

In 1927, the legendary Alhambra Theatre was opened, and it quickly became one of Sacramento's premier movie houses. Built by longtime Poverty Ridge resident George Peltier, the theater was a great source of community pride. Many current residents feel nostalgic toward the movie house and share fond memories of attending films and wandering its beautiful gardens as children. Years later, when a 1973 bond measure failed to permit the city to buy and protect the old theater, the property was sold to a developer. Not long after, the structure was torn down and a grocery store erected. The public outcry following the demolition was overwhelming and catalyzed a passionate preservation movement that continues to this day.

Preservation advocacy groups such as the Sacramento Old City Association (known today as Preservation Sacramento) were founded to help ensure that the city's vintage homes and buildings would not be avoidably lost in the name of progress. By the early 1980s, various preservation-minded families began moving into the vintage homes of the Poverty Ridge and Newton Booth neighborhoods and restoring them to their former glory.

In the early 1990s, when the city library system considered shuttering the Ella K. McClatchy Library in response to budget pressure, local residents formed a nonprofit organization to ensure the branch's continued survival. Thanks to their efforts, the McClatchy Library has been completely rehabbed and continues to receive much needed aid for library programs.

Similarly, the Newton Booth Neighborhoods Association (NBNA) was founded to advocate on behalf of neighborhood residents, promote the preservation of historic resources, and create a better sense of community among neighbors.

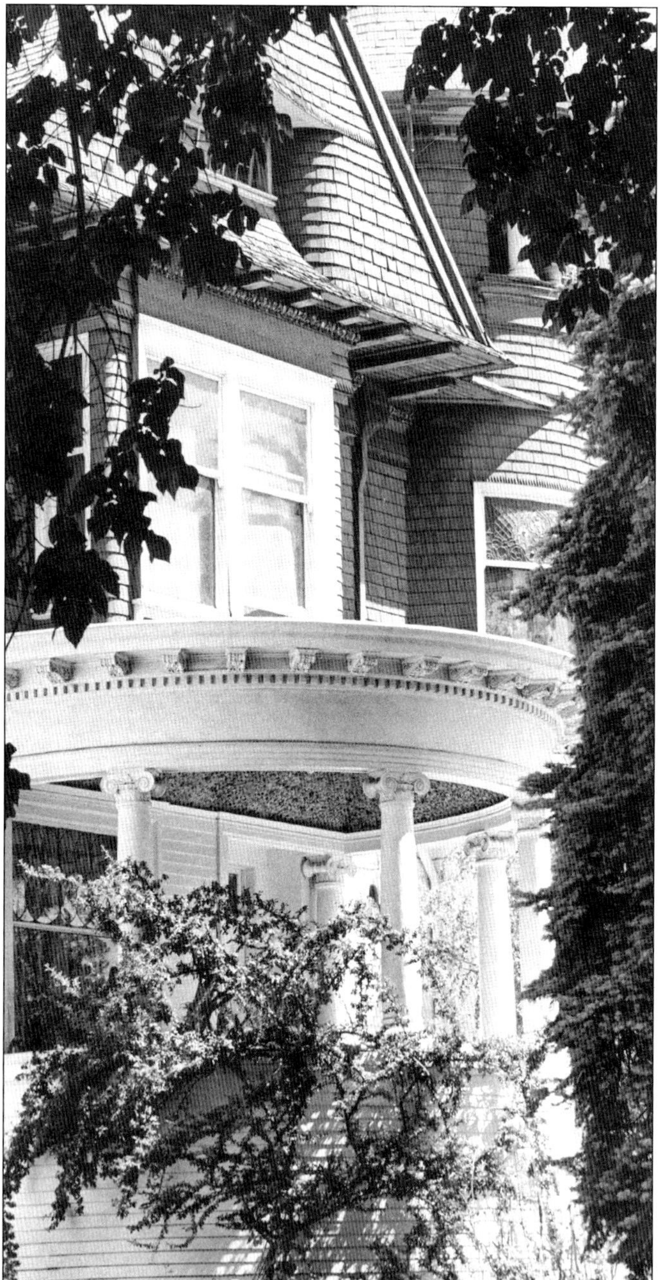

In the decades following Caroline Mason's death, the home she built with her husband at 1931 Twenty-First Street fell into disrepair and was at risk of being condemned. In 1969, Bill and Alice Smith, proprietors of a local photography studio, saved the property. The Smiths spent 14 years renovating and furnishing the home, including the installation of a new roof and adding steel beam supports to stabilize the structure. Even though the Smiths took pains to preserve the home, in the years following their deaths, the property once again needed major repairs. In 2017, a new family purchased the stately residence and performed a comprehensive and historically respectful restoration of this beautiful home.

In the late 1980s and early 1990s, Karen Jacques and Ken Wilcox purchased several historic Newton Booth homes in dire need of restoration. The couple quickly got to work rehabilitating the properties and performed most of the labor themselves. Over the following decade, they acquired and restored a total of four historic homes along the 26th block of S Street in addition to several other properties throughout the city. Pictured at right is the home at 1819–1821 Twenty-Sixth Street, a former drug house the city had condemned, being lifted in preparation for a new foundation. The picture below shows the property well into its restoration, with Karen painting the front trim of the c. 1890 home from an extension ladder. (Both, courtesy of Ken Wilcox and Karen Jacques.)

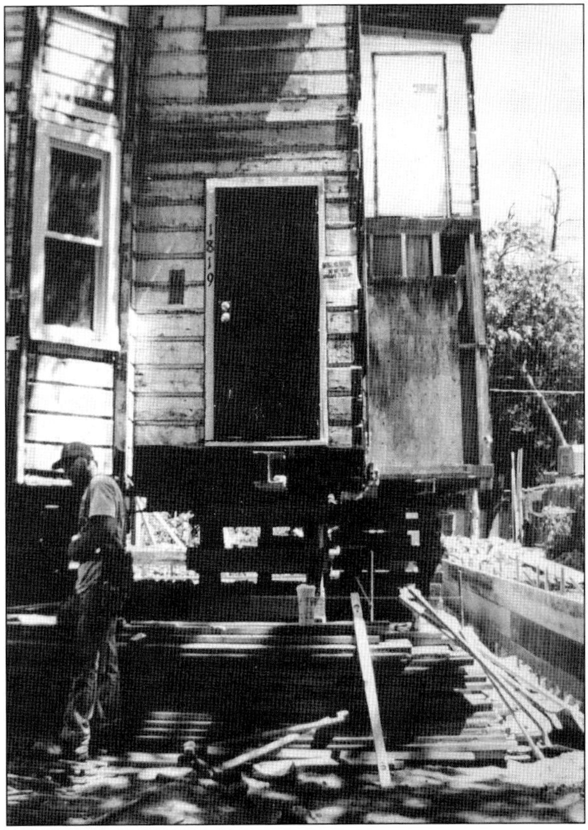

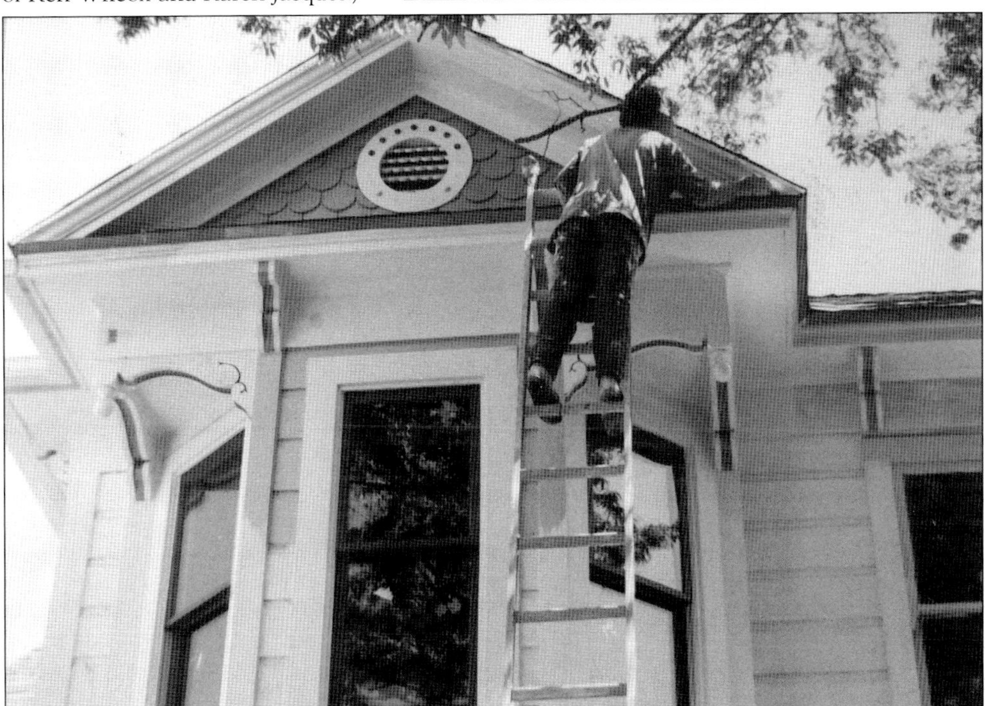

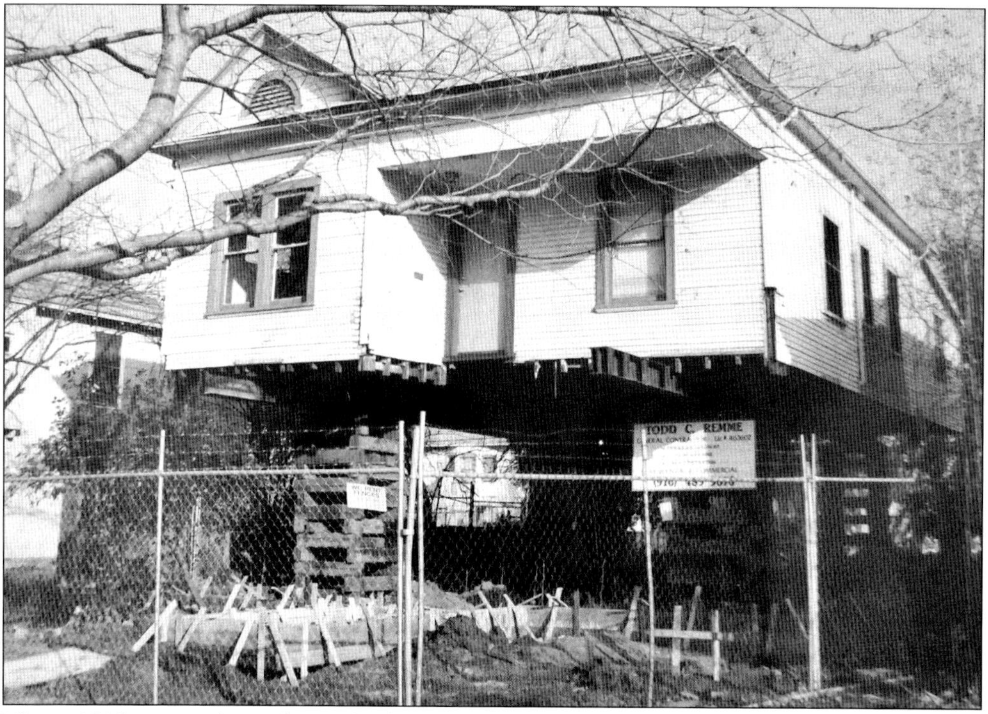

The c. 1990 image above shows the historic home at 2615–2617 S Street being raised while a new foundation is laid and a ground-floor unit is added by local preservationists Ken Wilcox and Karen Jacques. The property is shown below after its restoration. The couple also restored the home next door at 2619 S Street. Throughout the last two decades of the 20th century, many preservationists moved into the Poverty Ridge and Newton Booth neighborhoods and breathed new life into the community. (Both, courtesy of Ken Wilcox and Karen Jacques.)

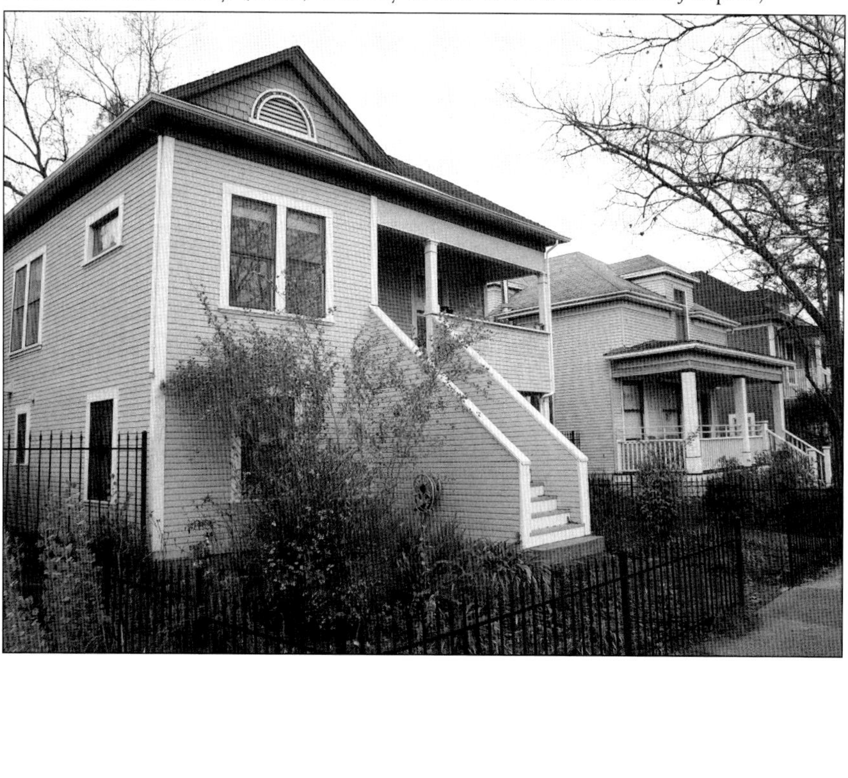

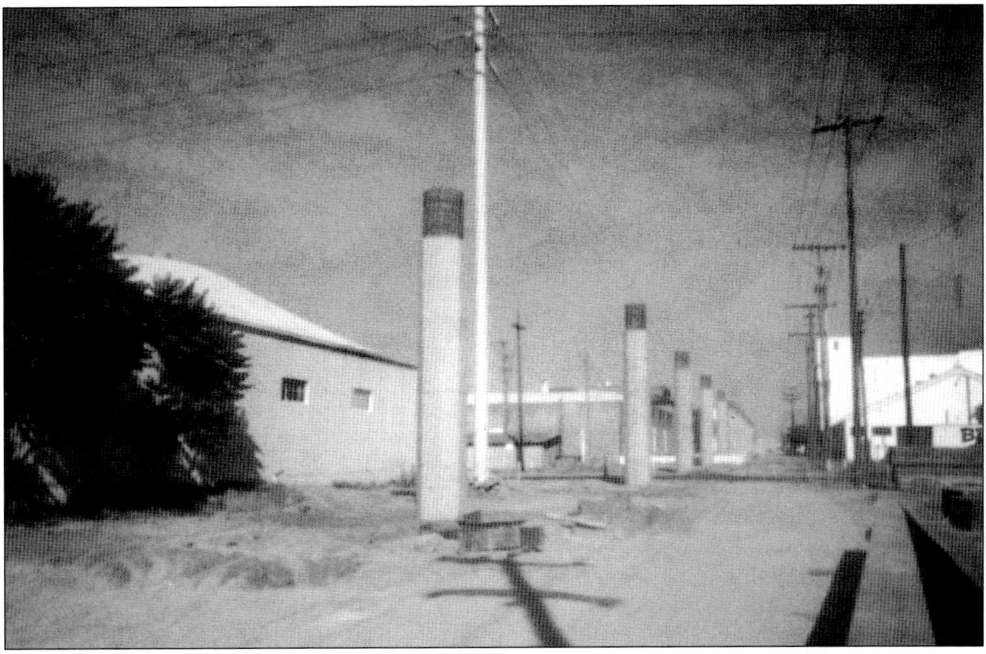

Pictured above are the pilings for the elevated Sacramento light-rail line looking east up R Street from Nineteenth Street while under construction in the 1980s. Just as in the early days of the neighborhoods, when streetcars enticed new residents with the promise of improved mobility, people working downtown in the 1980s and 1990s began to purchase homes in the Newton Booth and Poverty Ridge neighborhoods due to their close proximity to the light-rail stations at Twenty-Fourth and Twenty-Eighth Streets. Below is the elevated portion of the light-rail line at Nineteenth and R Streets. The light rail was raised in this particular section of the line to avoid interference with the *Bee*'s shipping and delivery network along the north side of R Street.

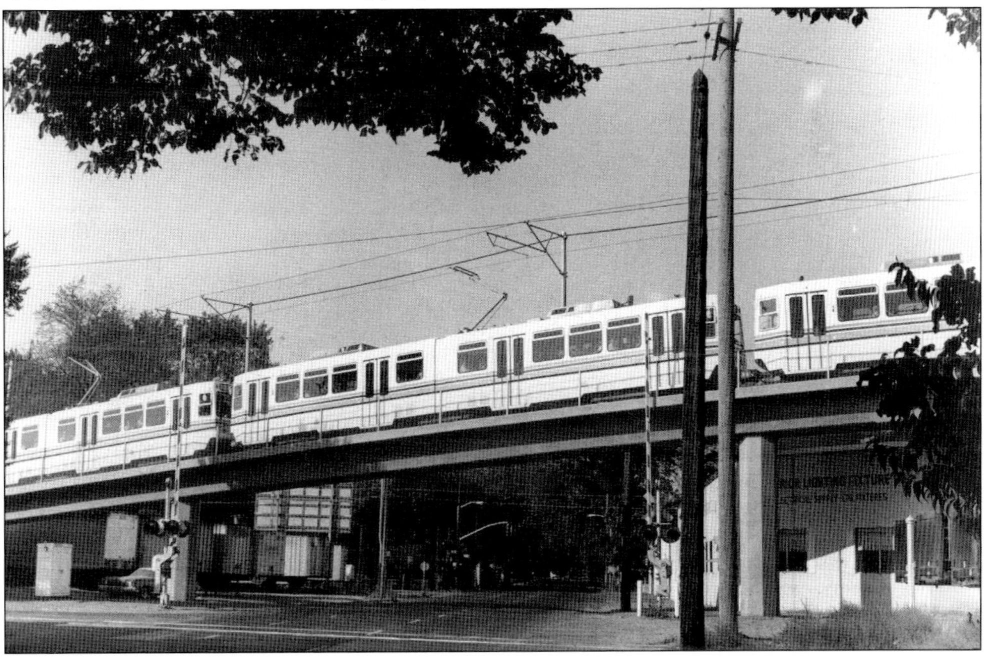

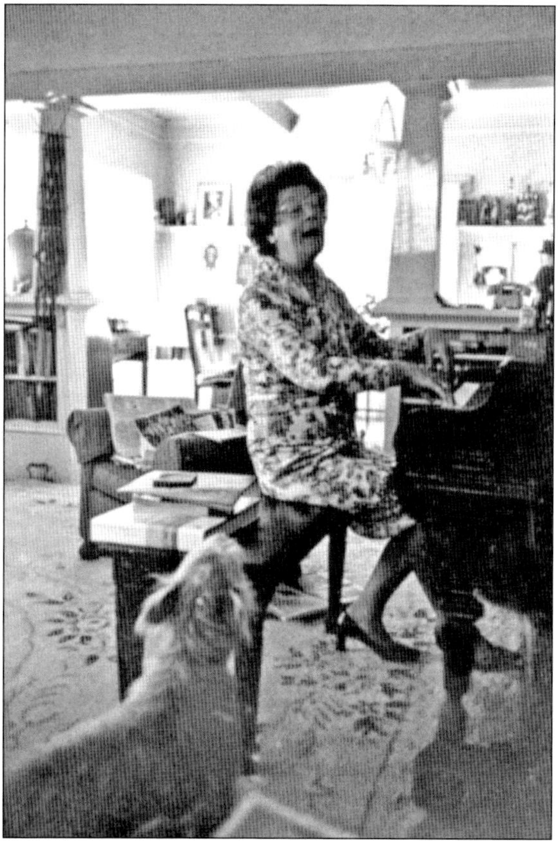

Lifetime neighborhood resident Birdie Boyles was the proud keeper of the home she was born in at 2523 U Street. She is pictured around 1970 playing the piano in her living room while accompanied by her dog George in a duet. Ever involved in the effort to improve herself and the community she lived in, Birdie was a historic preservationist and a founding member of the Artists Cooperative Gallery. Her woodblock art prints were featured at the Crocker Art Museum for many years. (Courtesy of Chris Boyles David.)

This c. 1980s photograph shows the Boyles family home covered in scaffolding as Birdie made repairs to the exterior, including the roof. (Courtesy of Chris Boyles David.)

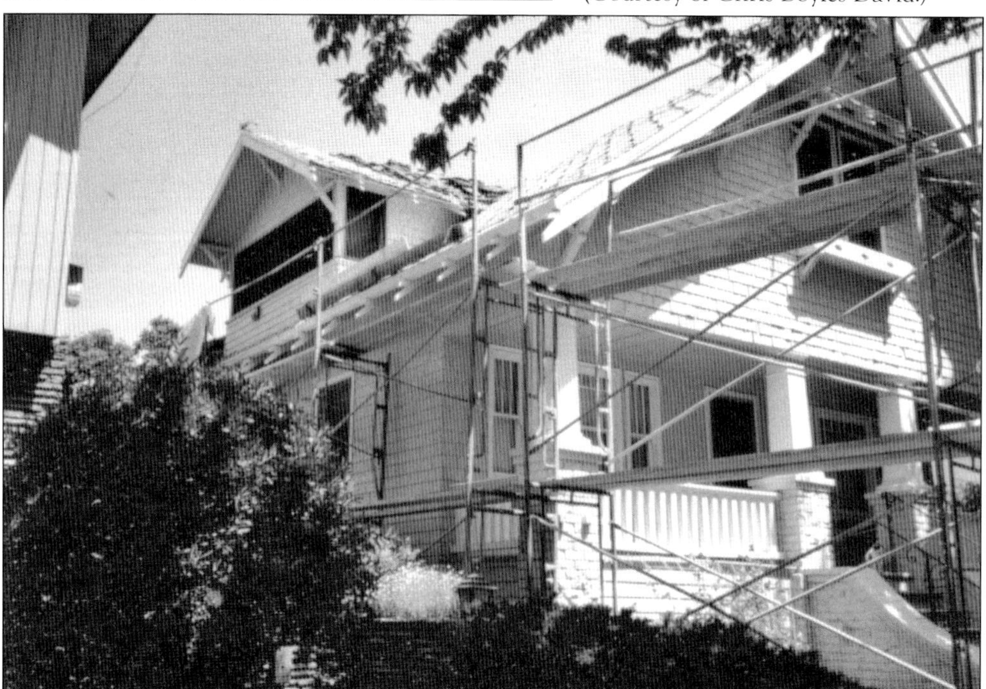

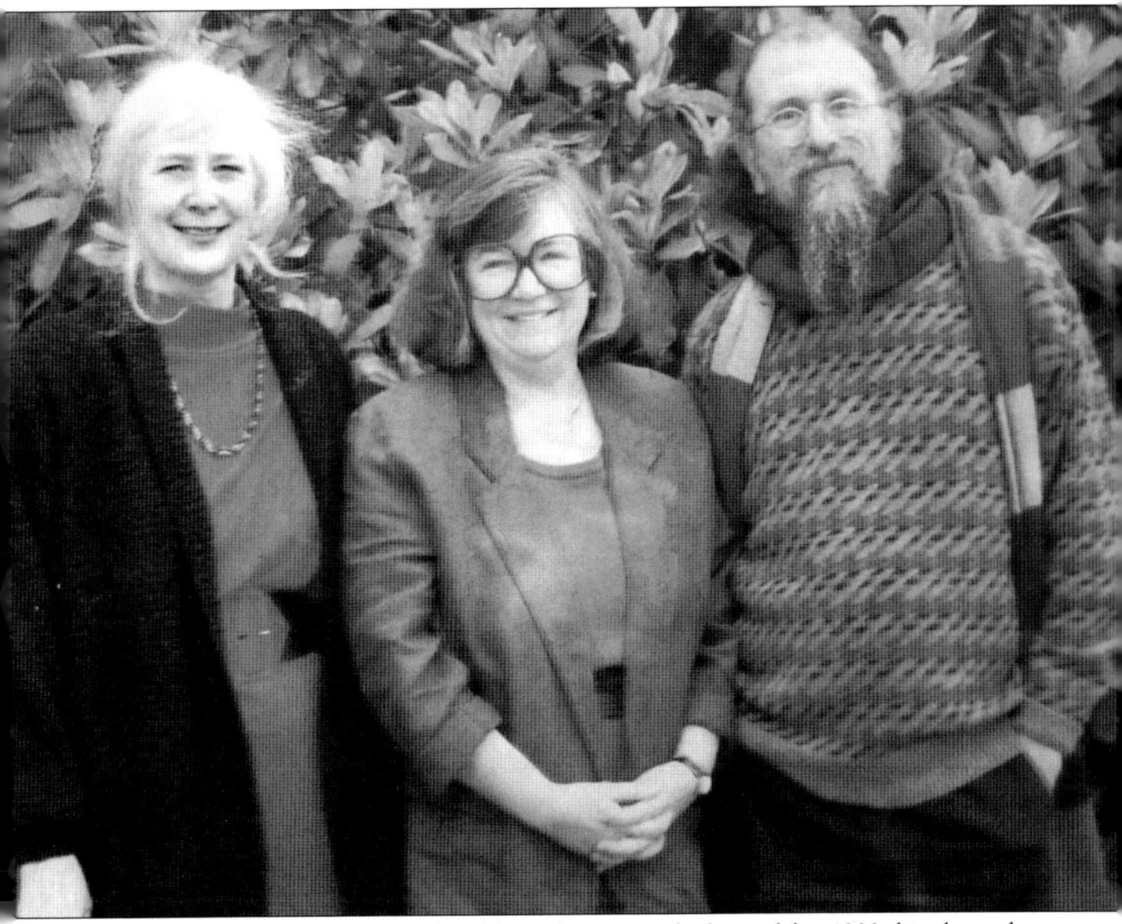

Stanley and Sharon Lunetta purchased and lovingly preserved a beautiful c. 1900 shingle- and Colonial-style home at Twenty-Second and U Streets in the years leading up to Sacramento's preservation movement. Stanley, a UC Davis professor of music and a renowned percussionist, was active in early neighborhood advocacy groups, fighting for street parking enforcement and leading neighborhood graffiti abatement outings. Stanley (right) is pictured with fellow early Poverty Ridge Neighborhood Association members Dagmar Brennar-Wicks (left) and Kathy Felch. The Poverty Ridge Neighborhood Association was an early predecessor of today's NBNA.

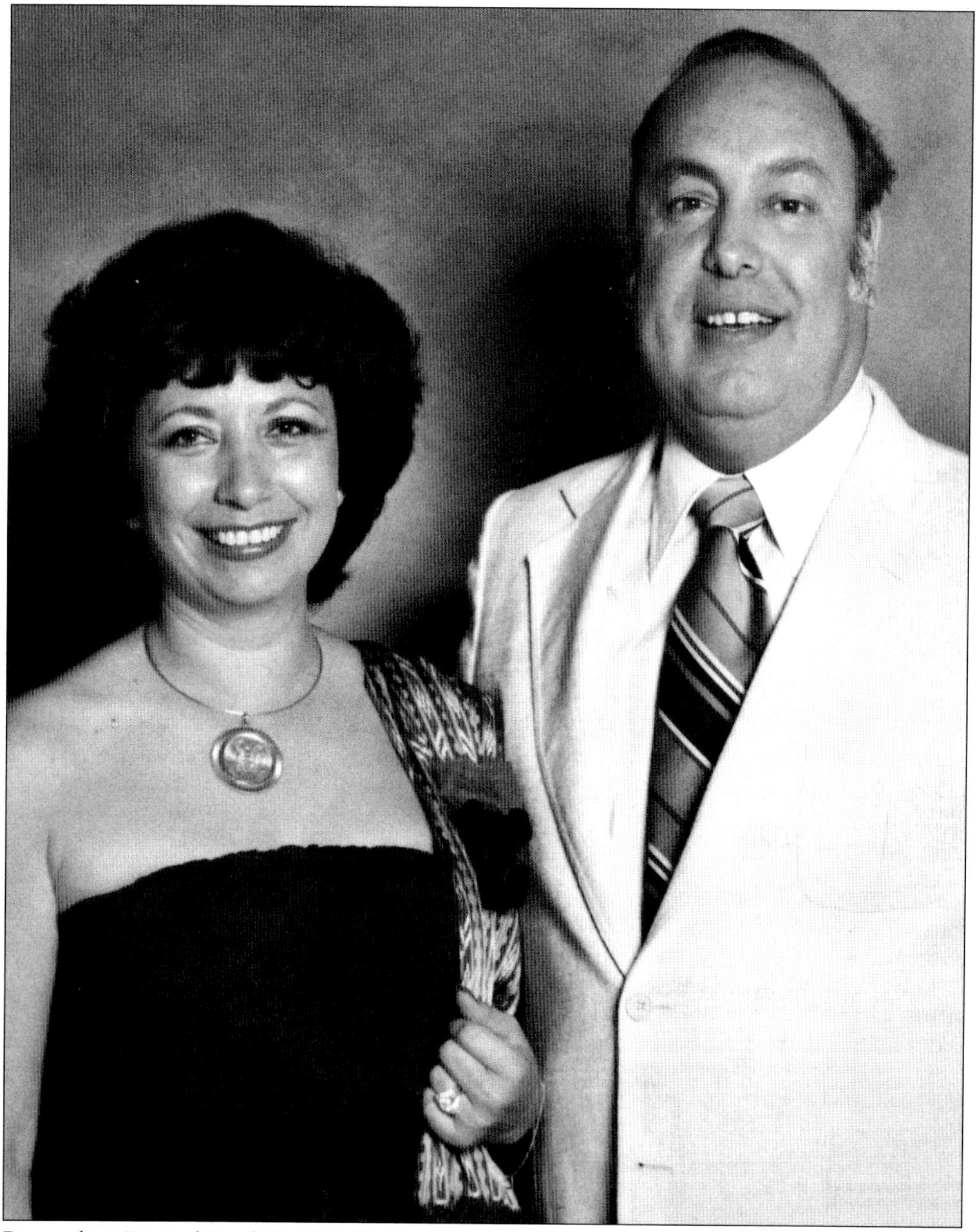

Pictured are Eva and Frank Garcia, who started a successful real estate brokerage firm in Sacramento in 1967. During the 1980s, the Garcias opened a new office in a mid-century commercial building at 2014 Twenty-First Street in Newton Booth, and later moved to 2100 Twenty-Eighth Street. Eva was the first Latina to become a broker in Sacramento, served as the first Mexican American on the Sacramento City School Board, and was a representative on the Sacramento City Council. She later served on the state board of education. Throughout the 1980s, 1990s, and 2000s, the Garcias continued to invest in and rehabilitate income properties in the Newton Booth and Poverty Ridge neighborhoods. Today, their children continue to run the family real estate business, Garcia Realty, at 2100 Twenty-Eighth Street and live in restored historic homes in the Newton Booth and Poverty Ridge neighborhoods. (Courtesy of the Garcia family.)

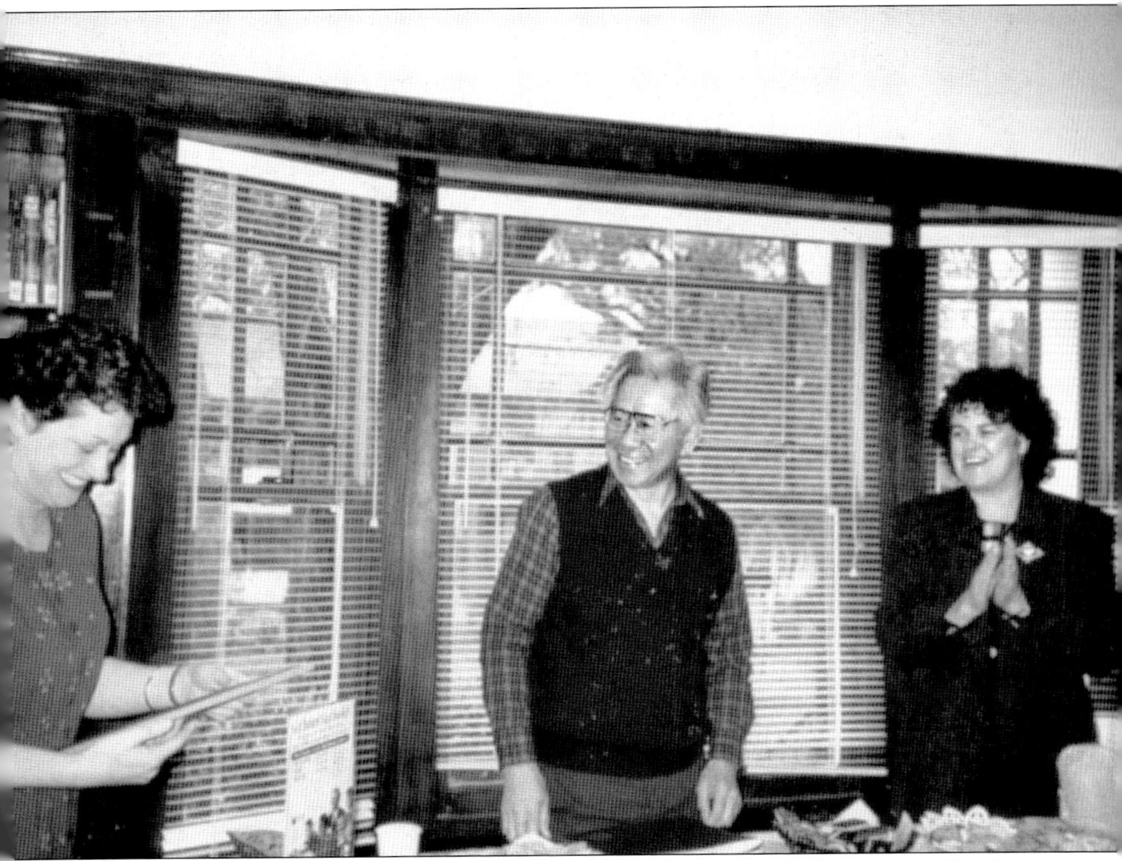

In 1995, plans were announced to close the Ella K. McClatchy Library. The historic McClatchy home–cum–neighborhood library was in need of serious upgrades and maintenance to ensure safety and accessibility. Upon receiving word of the city's plans to close the building, new Poverty Ridge resident Alice Levine worked with neighbors and many others to create the nonprofit Friends of the Ella K. McClatchy Library. Thanks to their years of advocacy, fundraising, and public outreach, the McClatchy Library has remained open, undergone extensive renovations, and launched countless successful community programs. The branch also now serves as a neighborhood polling place for local, state, and national elections. From left to right, librarian Shari Nichelini, city councilman Jimmie Yee, and Friends organizer and president Alice Levine are pictured shortly after saving the library from closure. (Courtesy of the Friends of the Ella K. McClatchy Library.)

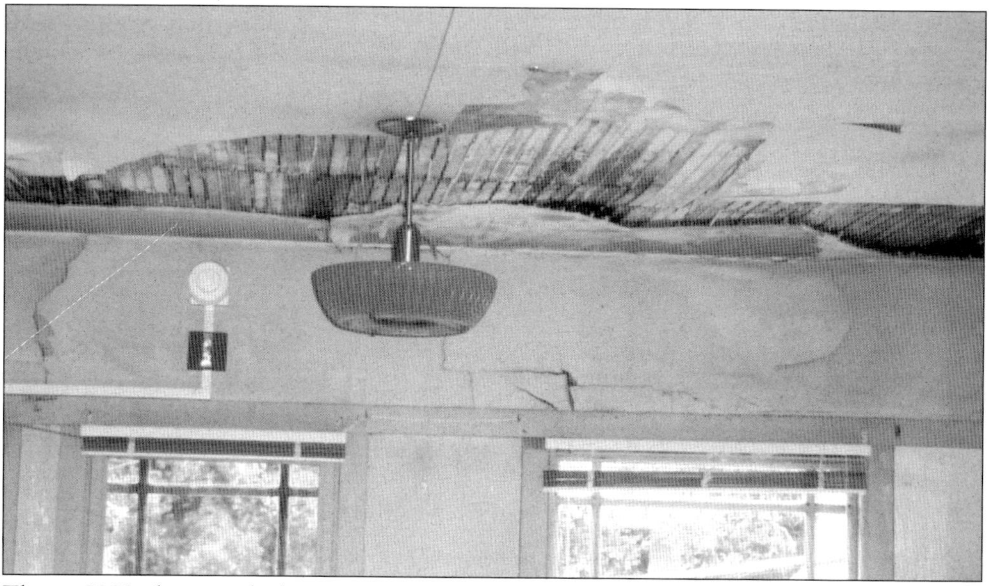

This c. 2008 photograph demonstrates the damage and disrepair found in one of the upstairs meeting rooms of the McClatchy Library. Due to lack of funds for crucial repairs, the second floor of the branch had remained closed to the public since 1969. A very generous private donation from a member of the Friends of the Ella K. McClatchy Library allowed for the second floor to be completely rehabilitated and reopened to the public. (Courtesy of the Friends of the Ella K. McClatchy Library.)

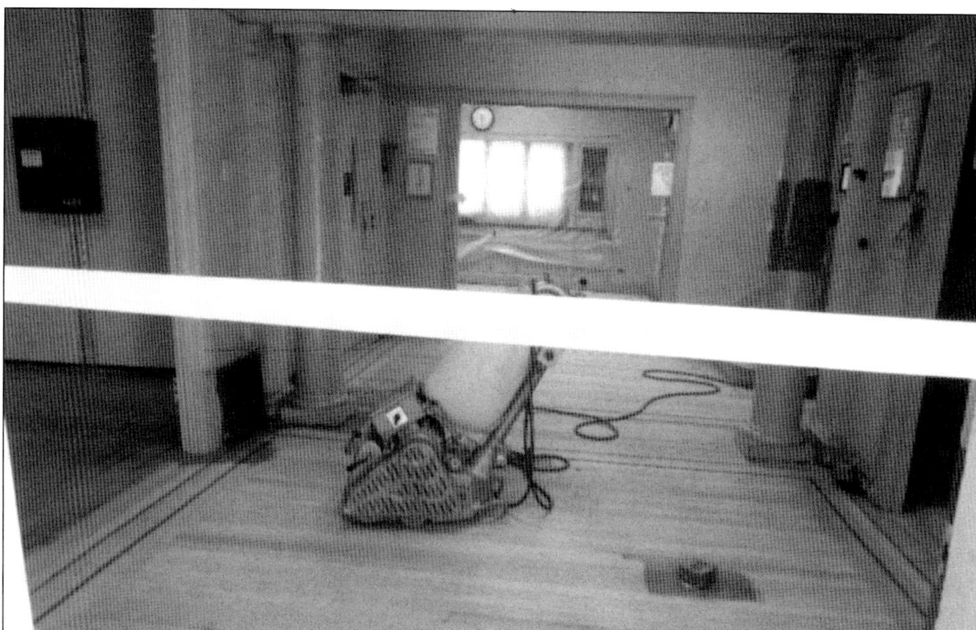

The Friends of the Ella K. McClatchy Library helped to raise funds for upgrades and repairs to the building. Pictured are the old hardwood floors of the library being stripped, restained, and sealed. The Friends also helped to raise funds for a Sacramento Heritage plaque identifying the Ella K. McClatchy Library and former McClatchy family home as a city historic landmark. (Courtesy of the Friends of the Ella K. McClatchy Library.)

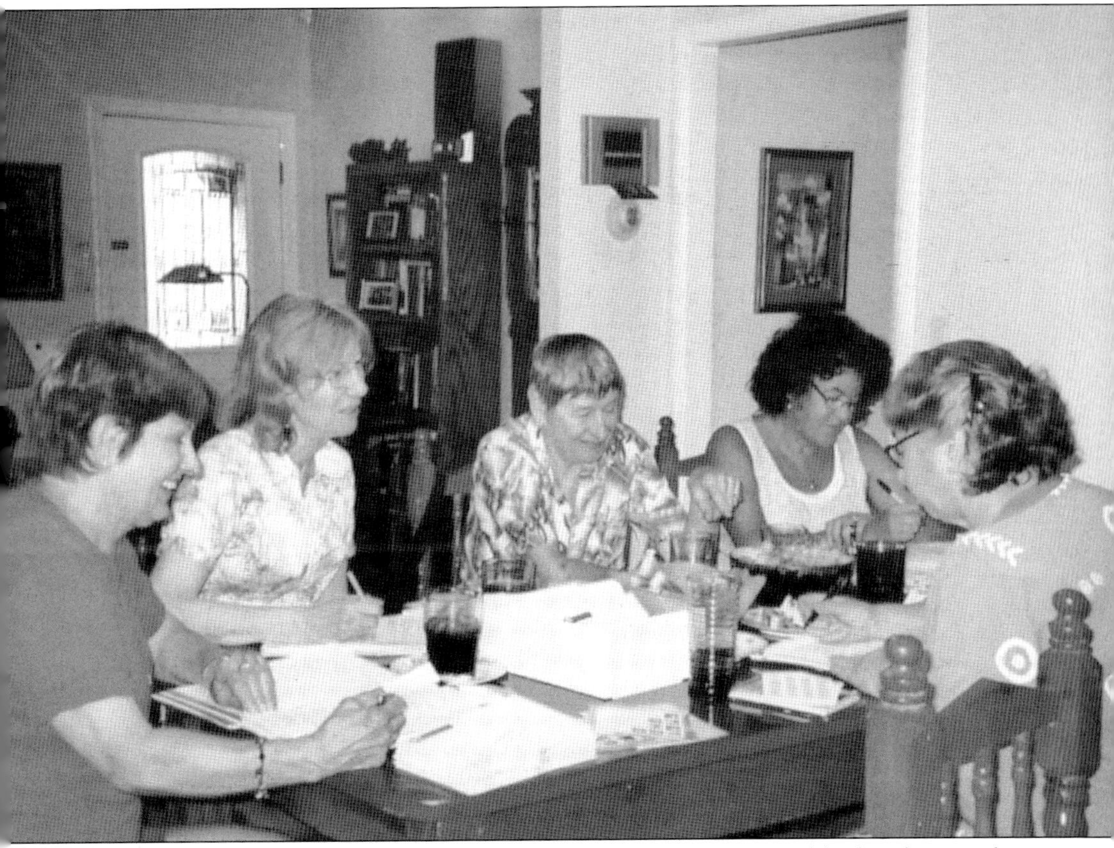

This c. 2012 image shows a group of volunteers and board members from neighborhood nonprofit Friends of the Ella K. McClatchy Library working to edit and prepare a book that celebrated and raised funds for the library. *Memories of the McClatchy Library* was published in 2013. The book contained 62 stories written by 44 authors regarding patron and staff experiences at the library through the years. The proceeds from the book were used to help support the library branch. From left to right are Virginia Kidd, Lynn Eder, Nancy Gotthard, Alice Levine, and Lenore Lesher. (Courtesy of the Friends of the Ella K. McClatchy Library.)

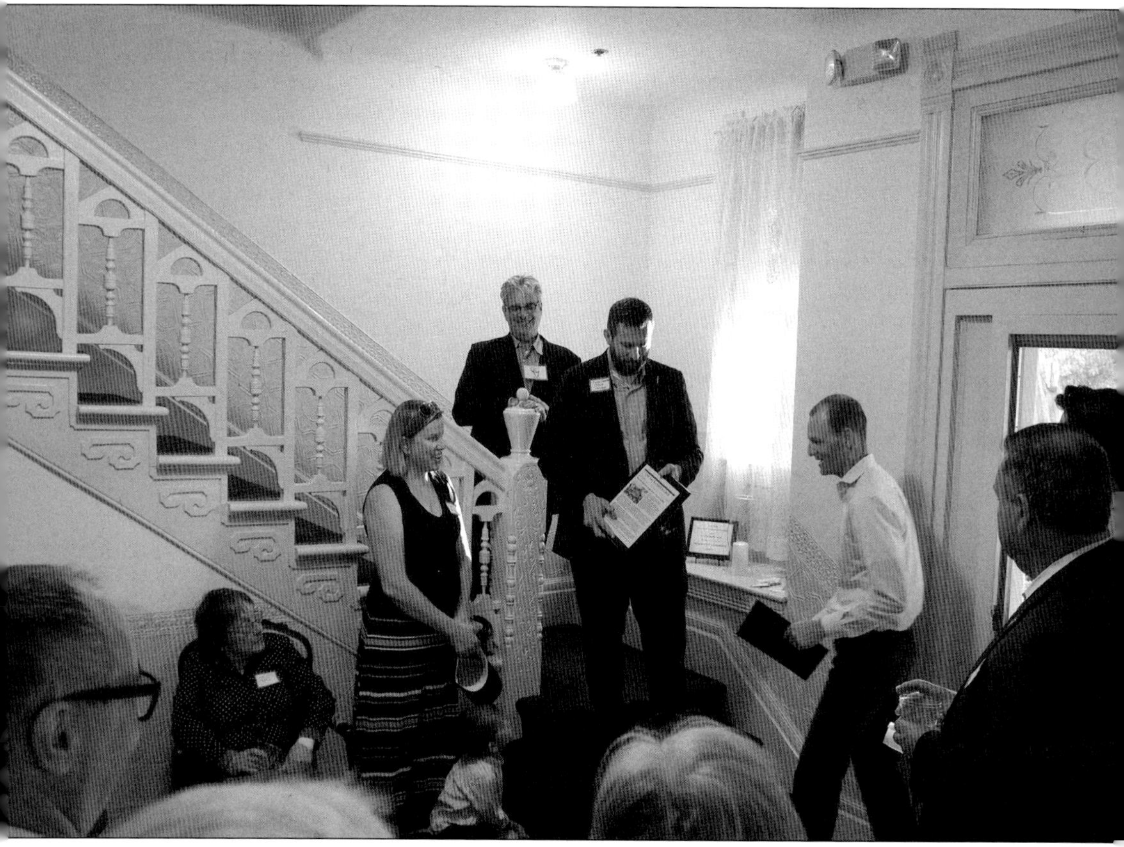

In 2003, after several early neighborhood groups from the 1990s, such as the Poverty Ridge Neighborhood Association, went dormant or inactive, the Newton Booth Neighborhoods Association was founded. Representing the southeastern neighborhoods of Newton Booth, Alhambra Triangle, and Poverty Ridge, the group seeks to protect and preserve the quality of life in the neighborhoods. The NBNA also advocates for policies and actions that will benefit the neighborhoods, including the preservation of historic neighborhood resources. Pictured here is a scene from the NBNA's annual Growing Together Awards event in 2017, which was held in the reception area of the historic Daniel W. Carmichael home at 1903 Twenty-First Street. The event honored a neighborhood family for restoring the A.A. Merkley home in Poverty Ridge as well as the local historic preservation nonprofit Preservation Sacramento for its efforts in helping to create the Newton Booth Historic District. From top left to right, NBNA president Jeff Slodowitz, city councilman Steve Hansen, and state assembly member Kevin McCarty prepare to present plaques to the evening's honorees. (Courtesy of the NBNA.)

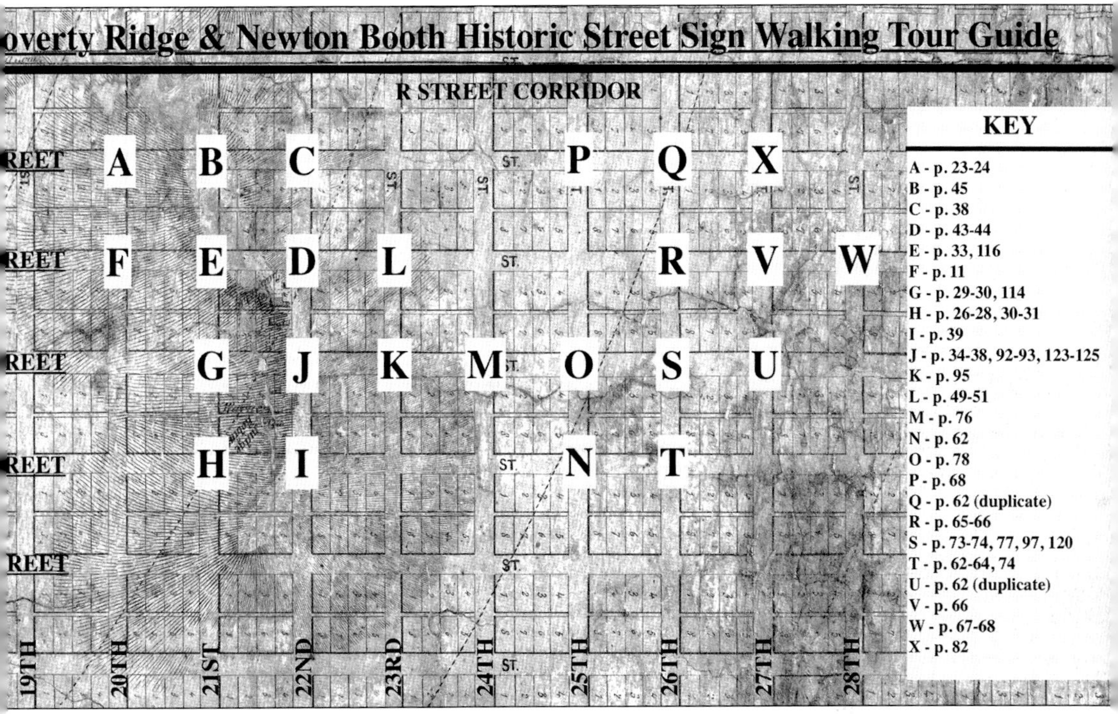

In 2019, the NBNA solicited sponsorship, raised funds, and worked closely with the City of Sacramento to design historic street markers for the Newton Booth and Poverty Ridge Historic Districts. Each sign features a noteworthy historic building or a historic figure linked to the neighborhood's past. Pictured is a walking tour map and guide to the different historic district street sign markers in the Newton Booth and Poverty Ridge Historic Districts. Not every historic building or person could be honored with individual markers; however, many more can be found in this book. Additional information on these people and places may be found on the pages listed in the key on the right side of the map:

A: Manuel Silva Nevis
B: Daniel W. Carmichael
C: Senator Grove Johnson
D: Joan Didion
E: Mason Home
F: Col. J.C. Zabriskie
G: John Stevens
H: Howe family
I: Rudolph Herold
J: McClatchy Library
K: Henry and Sally Taketa
L: Judge Peter Shields
M: Julius Asher
N: Gov. Newton Booth
O: Adolph Teichert Jr.
P: Pacific Bell Yard
Q: Governor Booth
R: Uhl family home
S: Birdie Boyles
T: Newton Booth School
U: Governor Booth
V: L. Huber Market
W: PG&E streetcar
X: First Church of the Nazarene

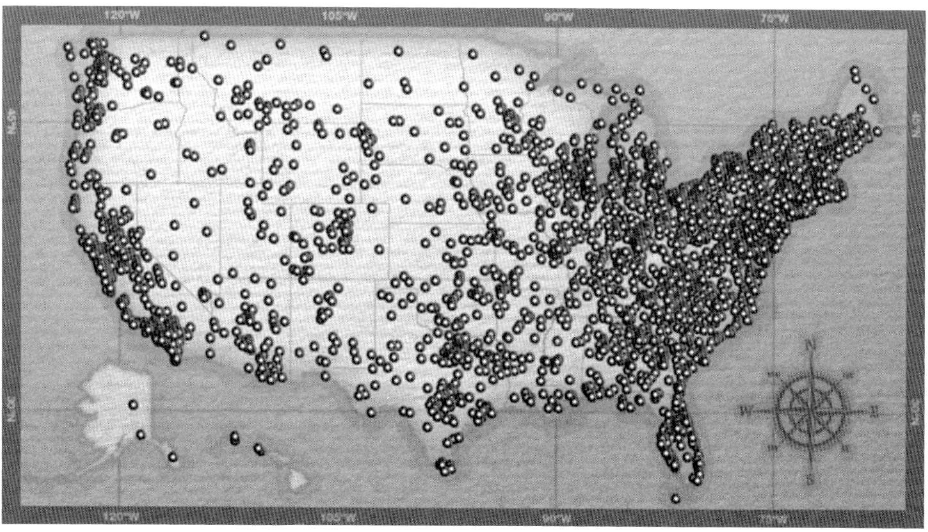